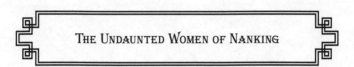

THE UNDAUNTED WOMEN OF NANKING

THE
UNDAUNTED WOMEN OF
NANKING

THE WARTIME DIARIES OF
MINNIE VAUTRIN AND
TSEN SHUI-FANG

Edited and Translated by
Hua-ling Hu and Zhang Lian-hong

Southern Illinois University Press
Carbondale

Southern Illinois University Press
siupress.com

22 21 20 19   4 3 2 1

Cover illustrations: Portraits of Minnie Vautrin and Tsen Shui-fang and photo of refugee students courtesy of Mrs. Emma Lyon; photo of Tsen's handwriting by China's Second Historical Archives of Nanjing, China; photo of Vautrin's handwriting by Dr. Chia-lun Hu, courtesy Mrs. Emma Lyon.

ISBN (paperback): 978-0-8093-3746-0

The Library of Congress has cataloged the hardcover edition as follows:
Vautrin, Minnie, 1886–1941.
The undaunted women of Nanking : the wartime diaries of Minnie Vautrin and Tsen Shui-fang / edited and translated by Hua-ling Hu, Zhang Lian-hong.
   p. cm.
ISBN-13: 978-0-8093-2963-2 (alk. paper)
ISBN-10: 0-8093-2963-8 (alk. paper)
ISBN-13: 978-0-8093-8561-4 (e-book)
ISBN-10: 0-8093-8561-9 (e-book)
1. Vautrin, Minnie, 1886–1941—Diaries. 2. Tsen, Shui-fang, 1875–1969—Diaries. 3. Nanking Massacre, Nanjing, Jiangsu Sheng, China, 1937—Personal narratives. 4. Sino-Japanese War, 1937–1945—China—Nanjing (Jiangsu Sheng). 5. Women missionaries—China—Diaries. 6. Ginling College (Nanjing, Jiangsu Sheng, China)—Officials and employees—Biography. 7. Sino-Japanese War, 1937–1945—Personal narratives. 8. Sino-Japanese War, 1937–1945—Atrocities. 9. Nanjing (Jiangsu Sheng, China)—Biography. 10. Nanjing (Jiangsu Sheng, China)—History, Military—20th century. I. Tsen, shui-fang, 1875–1969. II. Hu, Hualing. III. Shang, Lian-hong. IV. Title.
DS797.56.N365V38 2010
951.04'2—dc22   2009037023

Contents

CONTENTS

Illustrations

Maps
following page x

Japan's Invasion of China, 1931–37

China, 1937–38

Nanking, 1937–38

Nanking Safety Zone, 1937–38

Ginling College, 1937–38

Plates
following page 62

Central Building and 500 Dormitory of Ginling College in 1930s

Arts Building

Interior of the College Library Building

The three-member Emergency Committee of Ginling's refugee camp

Minnie Vautrin in junior high school

Vautrin's last portrait

Tsen Shui-fang in her early fifties

Tsen in her eighties

Two leaves from Tsen's handwritten Chinese diary

Pages from one of Vautrin's handwritten family letters

Vautrin and workers at the Red Cross rice kitchen serving refugees

Staff, volunteers, and visitors at Ginling's refugee camp

Vautrin, Rev. James McCallum, and Dr. Lewis Smythe

Refugee students at Ginling's camp

Vautrin with China missionaries, St. Louis, May 1941

The Order of the Jade bestowed on Vautrin in July 1938

Vautrin's grave in Shepherd, Michigan

Hua-ling Hu and Zhang Lian-hong visit Vautrin's bronze bust
on the campus of Ginling College, December 2003

ACKNOWLEDGMENTS

Zhang Lian-hong and I, Hua-ling Hu, are indebted to China's Second Historical Archives of Nanjing, the Center for Studies on the Nanjing Massacre of Nanjing Normal University, and the Disciples of Christ Historical Society of Nashville, Tennessee, for providing valuable source materials, photographs, and maps. We are also in debt to Dr. Wen-husan Chang, Cindy Chan, and other members of the Association for Preserving the History of World War II in Asia (AOHWA), based in Pittsburgh, Pennsylvania, for their generous donation to the subvention fund for the publication of our book

I would like to express my deep gratitude to Minnie Vautrin's niece, Emma Lyon, and grandniece, Mary Lou Kniffen, for their valuable gifts of Vautrin's artifacts, papers, and photos and for their friendship for all these years. During the compilation of this book, I have incurred many debts. Dr. Terry Mathis patiently worked with me, paragraph by paragraph, while I was translating Tsen Shui-fang's diary into English. Bonnie Smith kindly spent numerous hours in critiquing and editing the manuscript. McGarvey Ice repeatedly furnished sources and photos of Vautrin deposited at the Disciple of Christ Historical Society. Martha Smalley swiftly responded to bibliographical queries on Vautrin's papers archived at Yale Divinity School Library. Charlotte Hamilton of the United Board for Christian Higher Education in Asia of New York cordially answered a request for permission to use a copyrighted reference published by the United Board for Christian College in China more than a half-century ago. Cindy Chan offered Vautrin's pictures from her collection and contributed many fine ideas toward the publication of the manuscript. Walter Ko supplied a vital, out-of-print reference book on Ginling College and other publishing information on the Rape of Nanking. Dr. T. C. Peng bestowed insightful suggestions and encouragement. To all of them, I am immensely grateful. Meanwhile, I am equally grateful to two noted historians, Dr. Richard Chu and Dr. Joyce Lebra, for their generous help and scholarly advice. Finally, I should like to thank my husband, Dr. Chia-lun Hu, for guiding me through the intricacies of computers and procuring books from various libraries for me.

Zhang Lian-hong would like to express his sincere gratitude to Ginling College of Nanjing Normal University, to Ma Zhen-du and Guo Bi-qiang of China's Second Historical Archives, as well as to Liu Fa-quan and Ma Xiao-yan of Nanjing Normal University for their assistance.

Last but not least, we must thank our publisher, Southern Illinois University Press, and its devoted staff members Barb Martin and Kathleen Kageff. We especially thank Dr. Karl Kageff, editor-in-chief of the Press, for his profound interest in our project and generous help. We are grateful to John Wilson for superbly copyediting our manuscript. It is a privilege to work with them.

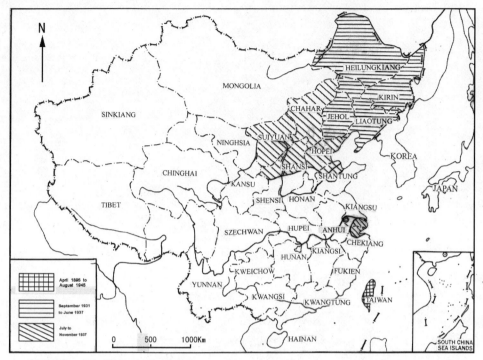

N

MONGOLIA

SINKIANG

HEILUNGKIANG

CHAHAR

KIRIN

JEHOL

LIAOTUNG

NINGHSIA

SUIYUAN

HOPEI

KOREA

SHANSI

CHINGHAI

KANSU

SHANTUNG

JAPAN

TIBET

SHENSI

HONAN

KIANGSU

SZECHWAN

HUPEI

ANHUI

CHEKIANG

KIANGSI

HUNAN

FUKIEN

KWEICHOW

YUNNAN

KWANGSI

KWANGTUNG

TAIWAN

HAINAN

SOUTH CHINA
SEA ISLANDS

April 1895 to
August 1945

September 1931
to June 1937

July to
November 1937

0   500   1000Km

Japan's Invasion of China, 1931–37. Drawn by the Center for Studies on the Nanjing Massacre of Nanjing Normal University.

China, 1937-38. Drawn by the Center for Studies on the Nanjing Massacre.

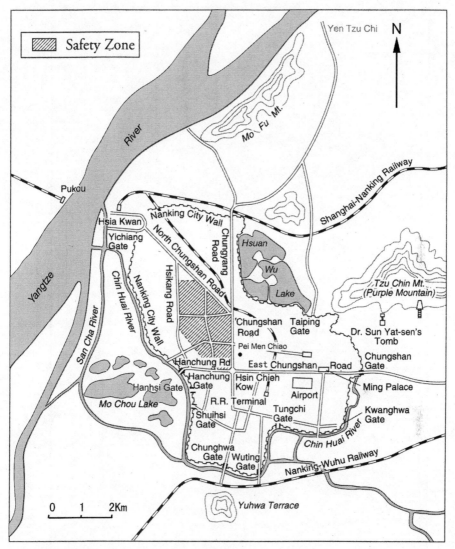

Nanking, 1937–38. Reproduced from *American Goddess at the Rape of Nanking*, by Hua-ling Hu (Carbondale: Southern Illinois University Press, 2000).

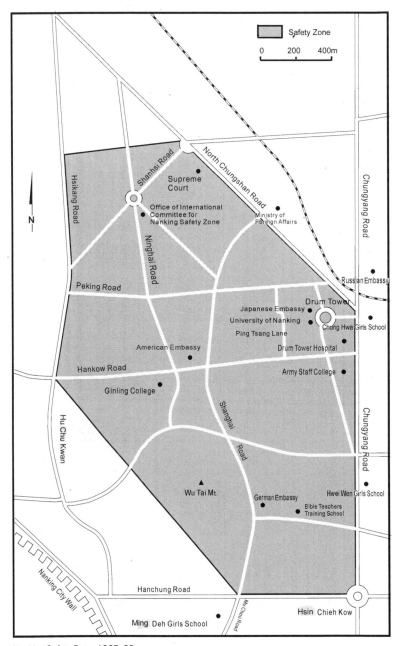

Safety Zone

0   200   400m

N

Hsikang Road

Shanhsi Road

North Chungshan Road

Chungyang Road

Supreme
Court

Office of International
Committee for
Nanking Safety Zone

Ministry of
Foreign Affairs

Ninghai Road

Peking Road

Russian Embassy

Drum Tower

Japanese Embassy
University of Nanking
Ping Tsang Lane

Chung Hwa Girls School

Chungyang Road

Drum Tower Hospital

American Embassy

Hankow Road

Army Staff College

Ginling College

Hu Chu Kwan

Shanghai Road

Wu Tai Mt.

Hwei Wen Girls School

German Embassy

Bible Teachers
Training School

Nanking City Wall

Hanchung Road

Mu Chou Road

Hsin Chieh Kow

Ming Deh Girls School

Nanking Safety Zone, 1937–38. Redrawn by the Center for Studies on the Nanjing Massacre from
American Goddess at the Rape of Nanking.

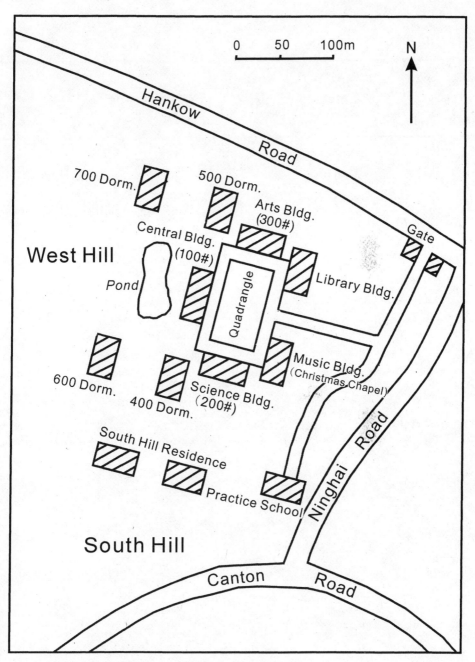

Ginling College, 1937–38. Drawn by the Center for Studies on the Nanjing Massacre.

THE UNDAUNTED WOMEN OF NANKING

INTRODUCTION

World War II broke out in Europe on September 1, 1939, when Hitler's troops assaulted Poland. Three years later, the United States declared war on the Japanese empire following the attack on Pearl Harbor on December 7, 1941. Prior to America's entrance into the war, however, the Chinese had been fighting the Japanese for ten years on Chinese soil, ever since the Imperial Army invaded Manchuria in September 1931.[1]

On December 13, 1937, Japanese soldiers occupied Nanking, the capital city of the Chinese Nationalists. As soon as Nanking fell, Japanese soldiers went on a rampage of killing, burning, looting, and raping. Within a few days, Nanking was reduced to a "hell on earth."[2] Gunshots and human wailing filled the air, corpses were piled on roads and in ditches, fires lit the sky at night, and smoke blackened the horizon during the day. Over half of the city was set ablaze. Homes and shops were broken into and looted, if not burned. Girls as young as twelve and women as old as eighty were raped, and some were tortured to death.[3] According to the verdict of the Tokyo War Crimes Trial of 1946, during the first six weeks of Japanese occupation, an estimated 200,000 Chinese were slaughtered, and in the first month at least 20,000 women were raped.[4] And the atrocities committed by the Japanese did not subside for several more weeks, until late February of 1938. And as the verdict of the court clearly stated, that estimate of 200,000 deaths did not include those bodies burned or thrown into the Yangtze River or otherwise disposed of by the Japanese army. Historians and other specialists on the Rape of Nanking still dispute the number of Chinese who lost their lives and the number of women who were raped.[5] Some estimates of the number of deaths and rape victims run in excess of 300,000 and 80,000, respectively.[6] On the other hand, some ultraconservative Japanese authors deny the existence of the Rape altogether.[7] Iris Chang in her best-selling book, *The Rape of Nanking: The Forgotten Holocaust of World War II*, puts the number of deaths in Nanking between 260,000 and 350,000 and the number of rape victims between 20,000 and 80,000.[8] However, Chang's book has been critically challenged by Japanese revisionists and some of the more recent works published in English.[9]

During those dark and tragic days, however, the besieged Chinese people of Nanking fortunately had some twenty Europeans and Americans stay with them to protect them. These Westerners, who had refused to evacuate Nanking, organized the International Committee for the Nanking Safety Zone and established a safety zone in the city to shelter refugees. They insisted that Japanese authorities recognize the zone's neutrality by keeping it off-limits to the soldiers. The safety zone comprised an area of 3.8-square kilometers, including Nanking University, the American embassy, Ginling College, and other missionary schools and institutes.[10]

At the zenith of the Japanese terror, an estimated 200,000 Chinese poured into the so-called safety zone for refuge, though it was by no means safe. Japanese soldiers ignored the zone's neutrality and went inside to commit atrocities as they pleased. Nevertheless, the undaunted efforts made by these few Europeans and Americans and their fearless protests lodged to the Japanese authorities saved the lives of thousands of Chinese and spared many women from rape. Among these humanitarian Westerners, Minnie Vautrin was the one most devoted to protecting Chinese women and children.

Vautrin, acting president of Ginling College, assisted by Tsen Shui-fang and a small Chinese staff, turned the women's college into a refugee camp specifically for women and children. At the height of Japanese atrocities, despite their lives being threatened by the intruding soldiers, the two women courageously protected over 10,000 refugees in the small campus designed originally for 2,750. In addition, they exhausted every possible means to care for the well-being of the refugees. As a trained nurse, Tsen also performed medical services for the sick. Both women labored without rest to save the people in their care.

No matter how exhausted and terrified both Vautrin and Tsen were during the darkest days of the Rape of Nanking, each woman recorded faithfully what she saw, heard, and experienced day by day. The two women's diaries detail the Japanese soldiers' atrocities committed on Ginling campus and reveal the suffering of the Chinese women and children. Vautrin and Tsen were under constant fear that if the Japanese intruders discovered the two diaries, they would be confiscated and the women's lives--and therefore the lives of everyone in their care--would be endangered. Whenever the soldiers barged into the campus, the two women would quickly hide their diaries in various secret places.

Vautrin's diary (1937–40) is a vital eyewitness account on the Rape of Nanking and its aftermath. It not only supports and supplements other recently unearthed primary sources, such as the diary of John Rabe[11] and memoirs by some Japanese soldiers on Japan's campaign of terror,[12] but also describes life in the desecrated Nanking after the Rape. While Rabe's diary and others have generally focused on the safety zone and the city, Vautrin's diary focuses on Ginling's refugee camp and the suffering endured by the women and children. It reveals a woman's voice on war in a foreign land as well as the humanity and courage of a female missionary in a time of terror. Before Tsen Shui-fang's diary was discovered, Vautrin's diary stood alone as the primary source on Japanese crimes committed inside a women's camp as well as the pain and fear imposed on the women by the soldiers.

Tsen's diary (1937–38) is the first known daily diary recorded by a Chinese on the Rape of Nanking; other accounts were recorded retrospectively. Penned in Chinese, this wartime diary by an ordinary Chinese woman focuses on what happened inside Ginling's camp and on the women and children's hardships as seen through a fellow countrywoman's eyes. It not only complements Vautrin's diary but also reveals a Chinese national's anger and deep sorrow as she witnessed the atrocities committed by the Japanese, humiliation over the inhumane plight of refugees, compassion for her war-torn country, as well as her pain and humanity in a time of crisis.

Selections of Vautrin's diary have been previously published in works such as *American Goddess at the Rape of Nanking* (by Hua-ling Hu, 2000), *Eyewitness to Massacre* (edited by Zhang Kai-yuan, 2001), and *Terror in Minnie Vautrin's Nanjing* (edited by Suping Lu, 2008). However, none of them utilize Tsen's diary, and it has never before been translated and published in English. For this book, we decided to present selections from Vautrin's diary on the Rape of Nanking juxtaposed with Tsen's diary, day by day, from December 8, 1937, to March 1, 1938, with annotations from a variety of primary and secondary sources. These sources include: the proceedings of the Tokyo War Crimes Trial of 1946; the diary of John Rabe, the German chairman of the International Committee for the Nanking Safety Zone; Minnie Vautrin's correspondence archived at Yale's Divinity School Library; *Ginling College*, by its first president, Mrs. Lawrence Thurston, and the dean of studies, Ruth Chester; a collection of biographies of Disciples of Christ missionaries titled *They Went to China*; as well as the afore-mentioned *American Goddess at the Rape of Nanking* by Hua-ling Hu. In addition, we have included biographical sketches of the two women; a note on the two diaries; a closing chapter on the aftermath of the Rape; an appendix containing two detailed reports by Vautrin on conditions inside Ginling College and Nanking during the Rape; a selected bibliography; photographs of the two women and their colleagues at Ginling College; and a series of maps to help orient readers. Finally, for academic accuracy, we correct discrepancies on Vautrin's life in Iris Chang's *The Rape of Nanking* and other publications. (For the discrepancies and corrections, please see notes 4, 5, 9, and 22 in the "Biographical Sketches" section of this study).

In this book, we generally employ the long-used Wade-Giles romanization system for Chinese names. However, a number of spellings of Chinese names in Vautrin's diary are different from those of the Wade-Giles and the Pinyin systems. In order to maintain the integrity of Vautrin's diary, we keep its original spellings and insert the Wade-Giles spellings parenthetically, like this: Giyung [Chuyung] . For the translated text of Tsen's diary, we adopt the Wade-Giles system to minimize confusion. The Pinyin system is occasionally used by individual writers and publishers cited in this book.

Finally, we believe that juxtaposing the diaries of Vautrin and Tsen will enrich primary sources on World War II, Sino-American relations, and Sino-Japanese relations, especially regarding the Rape of Nanking. It will equally add vital eyewitness accounts to women's studies regarding the impact of war on women and the history of missionary activities. This juxtaposition vividly reconstructs what transpired during the terrible months in Nanking, portraying an inside view of a women's refugee camp. It depicts the degradation of war, the suffering and devastation of women and families, as well as the spirit of humanity in that trying time. Further, it highlights the wartime experience of two courageous women, one American missionary-educator and one Chinese nurse. It also introduces a Chinese woman's real voice on the Rape, generally absent in the English-language works.

With the revival of militarism in Japan and steadfast denial of the existence of the Rape of Nanking by Japanese right-wing revisionists, we hope that these two women's eyewitness accounts will refute all doubters and provide further evidence of Japanese war crimes in Nanking in 1937–38. We have no intention to demean Japan. We sincerely hope that such human tragedy, especially the suffering and devastation of the Chinese women and their families, will never be repeated again in any corner of this world.

Biographical Sketches

Minnie Vautrin (1886–1941)

On her tombstone at Shepherd, Michigan, four Chinese characters, *Gin Ling Yung Shen* (Ginling Forever), are engraved on the top. On the lower section, the inscription reads:

Minnie Vautrin
Goddess of Mercy
Missionary to China
28 years
1886–1941[1]

Minnie Vautrin was born on September 27, 1886, in Secor, a small town in central Illinois. Her father, Edmund L. Vautrin, was a blacksmith who worked a small farm to supplement the family income. When Minnie was six years old, her mother, Pauline Lehr, died in childbirth. The little girl learned hard work as a child. She was a born student who dreamed of being a teacher and traveling around the world when she grew up. However, her father could not financially support her schooling. Vautrin realized that if she wanted to be educated, she must earn her own way—and she did. In the meantime, she often did volunteer work at the local churches in Secor. Her first teacher commended Vautrin, saying, "She could excel in most anything she tried, and was a genuinely Christian girl."[2]

After graduating in 1907 from Illinois State Normal College (today's Illinois State University), which was then a two-year teachers' college, Vautrin taught at a high school in LeRoy, Illinois, for several years. She then enrolled at the University of Illinois at Champaign-Urbana to pursue a bachelor of science degree, paying her own way through school.

While at the University of Illinois, Vautrin became interested in foreign missions. At the time, the missionary movement in the United States had become a crusade and was generating unprecedented enthusiasm on college campuses across the country for student volunteers to serve in foreign missions. Many young men and women went to foreign countries as missionaries, over one-third of them to China.[3] At the time, China had become more receptive to Western missionary activities. After the Boxer debacle of 1900, even the de facto ruler, the Empress Dowager of the Manchu court, was convinced that China must reform according to Western ways. The country wholeheartedly sought missionary help for its modernization, especially for overhauling its educational system. In 1911 the success of the Chinese revolution led by American-educated Dr. Sun Yat-sen generated even greater American zest for missions to China.

In 1912, after graduating from the University of Illinois with honors, Vautrin joined the Foreign Christian Missionary Society[4] and was sent to Hofei, China. At the time, she was twenty-six years old. In Hofei, Vautrin was moved by the pervasive illiteracy she found among Chinese women and by their extremely inferior status compared to men. She determined to devote her life to promoting women's education and to helping the poor in the community.

In the summer of 1918, after establishing San Yu Girls Middle School in Hofei and serving in China for six years, Vautrin returned to the United States for furlough and enrolled at Columbia University for a master of arts degree in education. One year later, she graduated from the university and was scheduled to proceed to Nantung Chow to establish a new girls' school. However, Ginling College in Nanking invited her to be its acting president while its current president returned to the States for furlough. Vautrin was very excited by the Ginling offer and wanted to accept it. At the time, she and her fiancé, who was also a missionary to China, were planning to be married soon. Further, the Foreign Christian Missionary Society had already assigned her to Nantung Chow. After continuous negotiations, the missionary society agreed to loan Vautrin to Ginling College. To everyone's surprise, Vautrin postponed her wedding to devote all her time to Ginling. Before long, she broke the engagement.

In the fall of 1919, Vautrin became the acting president of Ginling College and chairwoman of the education department.[5] At Ginling, she devoted herself to promoting women's education and improving the college's curriculum. Also, she launched a "good neighbor" policy to serve the poor in the vicinity of the college. She guided her students to open an elementary school and establish a free clinic for the poor of the neighborhood.

In July 1937, at the outbreak of the second Sino-Japanese war, Vautrin was very worried that the spreading conflict would bring devastation to the Chinese people and property. She decided that she should not leave China when it was in such a grave crisis, so she immediately cancelled her scheduled furlough to the United States. On August 12, one day before the Japanese military started air raids on Nanking, Vautrin began to keep a diary. which she continued to do until April 14 of 1940.

Later, under the intensified Japanese air raids of Nanking, Vautrin repeatedly defied the American embassy's order to evacuate the city. She joined the Nanking International Red Cross and made time to care for wounded Chinese soldiers. At the time, a large number of the wounded had retreated to Nanking only to find little or no medical care available because most of the doctors and nurses had already left the city. One night Vautrin saw two badly injured soldiers lying on the ground in agonizing pain with wounds that had not been dressed in days. She felt heartsick and tried her best to comfort them with words. She could never forget the heartbreaking scene.[6]

Vautrin was reappointed the acting president of Ginling, shortly before its current president, Dr. Wu Yi-fang,[7] departed from Nanking on December 2, 1937. In order to oversee the college's management during this extraordinary time, she organized a three-member Emergency Committee, including herself, Tsen Shui-fang, and Francis Chen, who was Ginling's business manager. At about the same time, a group of Westerners in Nanking organized the International Committee for the Nanking Safety Zone and established a safety zone with some twenty refugee camps in the city. Ginling College was specifically designated to be the camp for women and children refugees. Vautrin immediately held a long meeting of the Emergency Committee to finalize the measures for receiving refugees. Chen was in charge of training the janitors to be security guards and organizing the teenagers on campus, including Tsen's teenage grandson, into a service corps as guides. Vautrin and Tsen led a small staff to prepare eight buildings on the campus to house 2,750 refugees.[8]

For the protection of Ginling, eight American flags were flown on the outskirts of the campus and a newly made, thirty-foot American flag, replacing the original nine-foot one, was fastened to stakes in the main quadrangle.[9] Proclamations from the American embassy were fastened to strategically located buildings. These measures were taken to show the Japanese military that Ginling was American property and therefore neutral in order to avoid Japanese aerial bombardment and to deter soldiers from entering the campus.

As soon as Nanking fell, on December 13, 1937, the Japanese soldiers went on a rampage of killing, raping, burning, and looting. Among the most heinous crimes they committed, the Japanese soldiers raped and gang-raped Chinese women and tortured some victims to death. According to the estimates of Chairman John Rabe and Rev. James M. McCallum[10] of the International Committee for the Nanking Safety Zone, between December 16 and December

19, at lease one thousand women and girls were raped each night. McCallum wrote in his diary on December 19: "Never have I heard or read of such brutality. Rape! Rape! Rape! . . . People are hysterical."[11]

As the number and ferocity of these crimes intensified, thousands of women poured into Ginling day and night, tearfully begging for permission to enter the campus for protection. Before long, over 10,000 women and children were crowded into the campus. Everywhere the grounds were packed with refugees. Although the number of refugees at Ginling was four times its designed capacity of 2,750, under the management of Vautrin and Tsen, everything from food to medical service was handled in good order except for disposing of the waste of more than 10,000 people, which continued to haunt Vautrin.[12]

During the first four to five weeks of the occupation of Nanking, Japanese soldiers repeatedly forced their way into Ginling to look for Chinese soldiers, rape women, and loot property.[13] Vautrin realized that neither the American flags flown around the campus nor the proclamations from the American embassy fastened to the buildings could deter the soldiers. The security guards trained by Chen proved useless. Vautrin herself had to spend each day and night rushing to wherever the soldiers intruded into the campus to keep them from committing crimes.[14]

Vautrin not only shielded the refugees at Ginling, she also tried her best to help them locate their male kin whom Japanese soldiers had taken away. With the help of Tsen and others, Vautrin arranged services to comfort the refugees' spirits. At the time, many people in Nanking regarded Ginling as the safest among all the refugee camps in the safety zone. The International Committee's inspection team rated Ginling's leadership as "outstanding."[15]

Under pressure from the Japanese army, on February 18, 1938, the International Committee for the Nanking Safety Zone changed its name to Nanking International Relief Committee. It became purely a relief organization, and the safety zone ceased to exist. All but six of the refugee camps were closed. Ginling was one of the six remaining camps, and Vautrin and Tsen immediately made arrangements to provide better services to the refugees.[16]

At the end of May, the International Relief Committee decided to close the remaining six refugee camps. After seeing that the Japanese soldiers still engaged in rape, looting, and murder, Vautrin decided that Ginling would continue to protect 800 young women and their children. Later, in September, with Tsen's help, she started two projects, a homecraft-industrial program and an experimental secondary education program. The former was designed for the destitute women who had no skills to make a living, the latter for the high school girls in Nanking. Vautrin raised all the funding for the two projects.[17] (For details of the two projects, please see "Aftermath" in this book.)

By late 1938, Vautrin was extremely exhausted and looked "haggard." Her colleagues and friends all advised her to take her long-overdue furlough and return to the United States to rest for one year. She refused to do so. In fact, both the United Christian Missionary Society and Ginling's Executive Committee in New York offered Vautrin high paying positions in the States. She declined both. She instead remained in Nanking facing shortages of basic necessities and miserable living conditions, even though they were detrimental to her health, especially during menopause. She was determined to help as many women suffering under the harsh Japanese rule as possible.[18]

During the dark days of the Rape of Nanking, many refugees and their families whom Vautrin protected revered her as a "Living Goddess" or "Goddess of Mercy." They thanked her and respected her. An eighty-year-old widow kowtowed ten times daily at her home, asking heaven to bless Vautrin so she could continue to protect young women from the Japanese soldiers.[19] The Chinese Nationalist government, at its temporary seat in the southwest of China, awarded Vautrin the Order of the Jade, the highest honor bestowed to foreigners, to thank her for protecting women refugees.[20]

Nevertheless, the terrible strain of dealing with the Japanese soldiers taxed Vautrin's health and sapped her strength. She suffered terrible mental anguish from the daily exposure to Japanese atrocities committed against Chinese, and in May 1940, she experienced a nervous breakdown and had to return to the States for medical treatment. She first entered the Psychopathic Hospital of the State University of Iowa in Iowa City and then recuperated in Marfa, Texas, and in Indianapolis.[21] One year after her breakdown—and just seven months before the attack on Pearl Harbor that brought the United States to declare war on Japan—on May 14, 1941, Minnie Vautrin ended her own life.[22] She left a note, stating that she felt certain she would never recover and that she would rather die than go insane. She concluded that her life had been a "failure."[23] She was fifty-five years old. In her lifetime, she devoted twenty-eight years to serving the Chinese people. During her last days in Indianapolis, she repeatedly told her friends how much she missed China. She longed to return. China was her real "home."

Fifty-four years later, on May 26, 1995, I, Hua-ling Hu, stood in front of Vautrin's tombstone. While reading the inscriptions—"Goddess of Mercy, Missionary to China, 28 years . . ."—on the stone, I was moved to tears. I made a promise that I would surely write a detailed account of Vautrin's heroine's story, which had been buried under dust during the chaotic wartime.[24] Six years later, on May 12, 2001, a memorial service was held at Shepherd, Michigan, by a group of Chinese Americans to commemorate the sixtieth anniversary of Vautrin's passing. At the service, I revisited Vautrin's gravesite.

It was adorned with one thousand fresh red roses donated for the occasion by a grateful Chinese American from Chicago. Surrounded by over eighty participants of the memorial, I stood in front of the tombstone again to dedicate my book *American Goddess at the Rape of Nanking: The Courage of Minnie Vautrin* and its two Chinese language versions (published in Taipei and Beijing, respectively). In December of 2002, Vautrin's bronze bust was erected on the campus of Ginling College of the Nanjing Normal University in Nanjing. She was eventually able to "return" to her beloved home—China.

Tsen Shui-fang (1875–1969)

Tsen Shui-fang was born at Wuchang, Hupei Province, in 1875. After graduating from the Wuchang Nursing School, she served at the women's hospital of the local Methodist church, the first three years as its nurse and then as the administrator. From 1910 to 1922 Tsen became the director of the dormitory of St. Hilda's Girls High School in Wuchang. She then was named the principal of the high school's affiliated elementary school. In September 1924, Tsen was hired as the director of dormitories of Ginling College of Nanking, in charge of students' room and board.

According to Mrs. Yen Ling-yun, a Ginling alumna, Tsen was an exceptionally kind and responsible person. She made special efforts to keep the dormitories spotlessly clean and personally helped to sanitize the kitchen and utensils. She also served as the college's nurse. Most of the students liked Tsen very much and maintained close relationships with her.[25]

In November 1937, when the invading Japanese troops were marching toward Nanking, stories about their brutalities toward Chinese people in the conquered areas filled the air. Most of Ginling's personnel fled the city. Tsen, at age sixty-two, courageously decided not to leave Nanking. She wanted to remain at Ginling to help Minnie Vautrin, who had been reappointed acting president of the college, to protect the campus. Vautrin named Tsen to her three-member Emergency Committee.

Before long, as the Japanese launched air raids over Nanking, Tsen assisted Vautrin to pack and ship Ginling's valuable equipment and books to other, safer places. They sorted through all the college's papers and destroyed those that might later arouse Japanese suspicion. Tsen successfully procured rice and other necessities for Ginling's staff in case there were shortages. Despite her heavy workload, she, too, found time to go to Hsia Kwan, a waterfront district of Nanking outside the city wall, to attend to wounded Chinese soldiers. She also went with Vautrin to the press conferences given by the Chinese Nationalist civil officials and the representatives of the garrison commander to learn the newest developments of the war. Vautrin appreciated Tsen's companionship and wrote in her diary, November 29, 1937, "At 6 P.M. Mrs. Tsen went with me to attend the 'Press' conference. It is much better to have a companion although men are very cordial."[26] Tsen was worried about Vautrin's safety once Japanese troops entered the city and specifically made a Chinese dress for her in case of need. Vautrin said in her diary of December 6, "My good friend, Mrs. Tsen, has a Chinese garment made for me. . . . I may need it in some phase of the turn over, so it is well to be prepared."[27]

Vautrin fully trusted Tsen. For instance, she taught Tsen the combination of Ginling's vault, which contained the college's funds and valuables, so that only the two of them knew it.[28] Several days later, they together emptied the safe and vault to hide valuables in a safer place.[29]

In early December 1937, as soon as Ginling was designated as a special refugee camp, the Emergency Committee held a long meeting to plan for receiving the refugees. Vautrin and Tsen immediately led a small staff to clean and clear eight buildings on the campus to house refugees. They labeled all the rooms with numbers. According to their plan, when refugees came to Ginling, they were issued a room number at the front gate by the security guards and escorted to their assigned room by a teenage guide of the Service Corps. The Corps consisted of Tsen's teenage grandson Kuo-hsiang[30] and five other teenagers on the campus.

Immediately after the fall of Nanking, when the Japanese soldiers went on a rampage of committing crimes day and night, Vautrin herself guarded the front gate, while Tsen and another friend, Mary Twinem,[31] pitched in trying to keep them off campus. After several days, when the incidence of rape intensified, more than 10,000 women refugees poured into Ginling. Tsen assisted Vautrin in managing the overcrowded refugee camp. She also served as the only nurse in Ginling and provided first aid to the refugees. She delivered babies and attended to the dying and was especially sympathetic to the miseries of the "big belly"(pregnant) women in the stifling conditions of the campus. On Christmas Day, 1937, despite the severe shortage of baking ingredients in the city, she managed to make cookies for the party given for the children and staff of Ginling. On February 16, 1938, Tsen helped Vautrin host a farewell party for John Rabe, the chairman of the International Committee for the Nanking Safety Zone, before his return home to Germany. She regarded the German chairman as "very capable and courageous" and even asked him to stay longer in Nanking, but he felt obligated to go.[32] Later, when Vautrin got some milk powder and cod liver oil from the International Committee, Tsen instructed mothers how to mix milk powder and give the cod-liver oil to feed undernourished babies. She also helped Vautrin offer classes for school-age girls and for destitute widows who had no job skills.

Like Vautrin, Tsen worked tirelessly. But no matter how exhausted and terrified she was, she too kept a diary to record what she saw, heard, and personally felt and experienced day by day during this tragic time. For instance, one night, when she heard twelve young women being dragged out of Ginling by Japanese soldiers, she sadly entered in her diary, "I want to cry."[33] Another day, when she saw some of the middle-aged refugees shouting and fighting for the rotten apples and a small amount of candy given away by three visiting Japanese women, Tsen became "angry to death." She indignantly wrote in her diary that night, "Those [refugee] women simply have no shame. . . . They are low-bred. . . . Even if they starve to death, they should not eat food from the Japanese."[34]

Tsen started her diary on December 8, 1937, and ended it on March 1, 1938 (please see "A Note on the Two Diaries" section of this book). Like Vautrin, she hid her diary in secret places when the Japanese soldiers barged into the campus. Tsen's diary is regarded as the only known eyewitness account on the Rape of Nanking recorded daily by a Chinese national; other accounts were recorded retrospectively. In May 1940, when Vautrin had to return to the United States for medical treatment, Tsen stayed at Ginling and remained there until June 19, 1942, when the Japanese army took over the campus to use as the headquarters of Nanking's garrison. She and other Ginling staff were forced to move out of the campus, but she stayed in Nanking. On August 8, 1945, Japan surrendered unconditionally. At the end of September, Tsen represented Ginling in an effort to reclaim the campus from the Japanese authorities and participated in Ginling's rehabilitation, at which she "worked heroically" for months.[35] On April 8, 1946, Tsen submitted written statements to the International Military Tribunal for the Far East, which conducted the Tokyo War Crimes Trial.[36]

(It was from Tsen's statements recorded on the proceedings of the Tokyo War Crimes Trial that I, Hua-ling Hu, first learned Minnie Vautrin's name in 1991. I subsequently began my long quest for source materials on Vautrin's life story and eventually completed three versions of my biography of the American heroine.)

In 1952, under the reign of the People's Republic of China, Ginling College became a branch of Nanjing Normal University and ceased to be an independent college. Tsen retired to her native Wuchang. She received no pension. Seeing Tsen live nearly in poverty, Ginling's former president, Dr. Wu Yi-fang, arranged a monthly subsidy for her. At end of 1964, Dr. Wu and Ginling alumnae invited Tsen to visit Shanghai and Nanking. They took turns holding parties to celebrate her ninetieth birthday, invited her to stay with them, and accompanied her to see various places out of the past. Tsen was very excited to be able to revisit her beloved Ginling campus.[37] Four years later, in 1969, at age ninety-four,[38] this feisty woman of great humanity and courage passed away in her native Wuchang of Hupei Province.

A Note on the Two Diaries

Minnie Vautrin's Diary (1937–40)

Minnie Vautrin's wartime diary (1937–40), in its entirety, is archived at the Yale Divinity School Library in New Haven, Connecticut. A photocopy of a portion of the diary is deposited at the Disciples of Christ Historical Society of Nashville, Tennessee. And I, Hua-ling Hu, own an original onionskin paper carbon copy of part of the diary.

The diary at Yale is cataloged under the title "Wilhelmina Vautrin, Diary and Misc., 1937–1940, Archives of the United Board for Christian Higher Education in Asia, Record Group No. 11, Special Collection." According to Martha Smalley, special collection librarian/curator of the Day Mission Collection of the Divinity School Library, the diary was donated with other Ginling College records to the library by the United Board in "approximately 1981."[1] As to why the diary is labeled with the name "Wilhelmina," no one knows the reason the United Board employed this name instead of "Minnie." Vautrin's niece, Emma Lyon, repeatedly stated that her aunt had only one given name, "Minnie," and that she had never heard anyone in the family called her "Wilhelmina."[2] Also, after combing through the entire diary and all her correspondence (1919–41), which is also archived at the Divinity School Library, I concur with Mrs. Lyon that Vautrin used only the name "Minnie" during her lifetime. Further, it is the name recorded on her transcripts at Illinois State University and the University of Illinois at Champaign-Urbana[3] as well as engraved on her tombstone at Shepherd, Michigan.

The diary at Disciples of Christ is listed under the title Minnie Vautrin Papers. It covers the period from August 12, 1937, to July 1, 1938. According the chief archivist, Sarah Harwell, the diary was donated to the historical society by a gentleman named Joseph Smith on November 12, 1984. She had no information about the donor's background.[4] The original onionskin paper carbon copy in my possession covers the period from November 1, 1937, to July 30, 1938. The copy was given to me by Mrs. Lyon on May 26, 1995, when I paid my respects at her aunt's grave. The text of Vautrin's diary in all three copies is the same, but only Yale holds the complete diary.

Vautrin started her diary on August 12, 1937, when Ginling College began to make preparations for the forthcoming war. On the next day, August 13, the Japanese army attacked Shanghai and began air raids on Nanking two days later. Vautrin wrote, "Leaves from my diary started on August 12, 1937," prior to starting her first diary entry of the day. Yet, a journal of her activities from June 20 to August 11, 1937, enclosed in her letter to "Dear Friends" of August 12, was attached at the beginning of the diary.

The diary ended on April 14, 1940, when Vautrin was on the verge of a nervous breakdown. In the last diary entry, she wrote, "I'm about at the end of my energy. Can no longer forge ahead and make plans for the work, for on every hand there seems to be obstacles of some kind." Below the entry, someone at Ginling handwrote: "In May 1940, Miss Vautrin's health broke, necessitating her return to the United States."[5]

The original motive for Vautrin to start the diary was that the forthcoming war and all the extra tasks involved in preparing for it made it increasingly difficult for her to keep her friends informed by writing letters. In the letter to "Dear Friends" of August 12, she wrote: "I'll resort to the diary form again because my mind seems to work that way—probably a result of increasing age." Nevertheless, from the contents of the diary, especially the portion on the Rape of Nanking and its aftermath, it is evident that Vautrin intended to leave an eyewitness account of the crimes committed by the Japanese soldiers and the suffering of the innocent Chinese, especially women. She wanted to tell the world what really happened in desecrated Nanking. For instance, she entered in her diary on the night of December 16, 1937, "From a military point of view, the taking of Nanking may be considered a victory for the Japanese army but judging it from the moral law it is a defeat and national disgrace." On February 2, 1938, she recorded, "Several women came in to tell me their tragedies. . . . Some day I would like the women of Japan to know some of these sad, sad, stories."

It is also interesting to note that, in 1938, Vautrin tried to sell the already written portion of her diary to publishers in order to finance the courses she planned to offer for the destitute women refugees in the Ginling camp. It appears she also wanted more people to know about the atrocities committed by the Japanese soldiers from an eyewitness. Her friends in the States submitted the diary to Houghton, Mifflin, *Harper's Magazine*, and the *Atlantic Monthly*. All three declined. Only the *Classmate* of Cincinnati, Ohio, accepted, and it published the portion through September 26, 1937, under the title "Notes from a Nanking Diary" in its issues of April 30 and May 17, 1938.[6]

Vautrin's diary contains 526 typewritten pages (with three missing pages, 394–96), some of which are doubled-spaced and some single-spaced. Vautrin typed her diary on an old typewriter. During wintry months and in her unheated, icy cold room, she complained about the difficulty of hitting the keys on the machine. In her letter to Mrs. T. D. Macmillan of January 10, 1940, Vautrin wrote, "Yesterday and today it has turned suddenly cold and now my hands are stiff that it is with difficulty that I hit the right keys on this old typewriter. Some of my mistakes just blamed to this fact."[7] As she typed her diary, she made onionskin paper carbon copies—another indication that she intended it to reach a wider audience.[8]

Vautrin recorded her diary mostly at night and sometimes during daylight, whenever she could squeeze in some spare time or even between intrusions into the campus by the Japanese soldiers. Repetitions, misspellings, and typographic errors were unavoidable. Occasionally, she inserted some illegible Chinese phrases in the diary which have puzzled even native Chinese speakers. During the Rape, Vautrin was in constant fear that her diary would be confiscated by the Japanese soldiers if they discovered it. So whenever the soldiers barged into the campus, she always hid her diary in one or another secret place.

At first, no matter how tired, terrified, or sick she was, Vautrin faithfully kept a detailed account of what she saw, experienced, and heard in her diary day by day until spring of 1939 when her diary began to skip days. As early as October of the previous year, she often confessed in her diary how "dead tired," "much depressed," and "exhausted" she was.[9] On March 22, 1940, she wrote, "Almost three weeks have passed since I have written one line in diary. Why? The reasons have been not just one but many. Physical exhaustion the main one." Less than three and a half weeks later, she made the last entry in her diary.

Although the Yale Divinity School Library received Vautrin's diary, along with other Ginling papers, from the United Board in 1981, few people knew of its existence until the 1990s. In 1991, Chinese historian Zhang Kai-yuan "discovered" the massive collection of American missionary papers at the library while he was searching for materials on his former history professor, Miner Searle Bates of Nanking University. Later, historians and specialists on the Rape of Nanking began to study Vautrin's diary. For instance, in 1995 Zhang along with Nancy Tong edited and published a collection of documents, interviews, and papers on the Rape of Nanking under the title *Nan Jing: Yi jyou san chi nien shr yi yueh tsz ji jyou san pa nien wu yueh* [Nanking: November 1937 to May 1938] that contains fifteen pages of selections from Vautrin's diary. In 1994, I used a portion of the diary as the primary source in my first article on Vautrin, "Miss Minnie Vautrin—The Living Goddess of the Suffering Chinese People."[10] Later, I employed both Vautrin's diary and correspondence (1919–41) as vital source materials and quoted extensively from them in *American Goddess at the Rape of Nanking: The Courage of Minnie Vautrin* as well as its two Chinese-language versions (published in Taipei, 1997 and Beijing, 2000, respectively). Iris Chang, in her book, *The Rape of Nanking: The Forgotten Holocaust of World War II*, devoted twelve pages (129–39, 186–87) to Vautrin's story, including quotes from the diary. In 2001, Zhang Kai-yuan edited and published *Eyewitness to Massacre*, with thirty-five pages (355–90) of excerpts on the Rape of Nanking from Vautrin's diary and two reports by Vautrin from her correspondence, with four annotations. Seven years later, in 2008, Suping Lu edited *Terror in Minnie Vautrin's Nanjing: Diaries and Correspondence, 1937–38*. The book covers selections of Vautrin's diary entries from August 13, 1937, to June 12, 1938, as well as some excerpts from her correspondence and diplomatic papers with annotations. The annotations are in-depth, detailed, and many of them scholarly. Although Lu generally lists the major references he consulted in the introduction of the book and provides sources for the annotations of that section, he fails to cite individual sources for the annotations in Vautrin's diary itself. Readers have no way to check the origins of the sources or to pursue further study. Nor is there a bibliography attached. Meantime, some of the Lu's statements in the introduction are questionable.[11]

Vautrin's diary was translated into Japanese by Okada Ryonosuke and Ihava Yoko with annotations by Kasahara Tokushi and titled *Nankin jiken no hibi: Minibotorin no nikki* [Every day of the Nanking Massacre: Minnie Vautrin's diary]. It was translated into Chinese by the Center for Studies of the Nanjing Massacre of the Nanjing Normal University and titled *Wei te lin ri ji* [Vautrin's Diary].

Tsen Shui-fang's Diary (1937–38)

Tsen Shui-fang's diary is archived at China's Second Historical Archives in Nanjing. The Historical Archives, established in 1950, house all kinds of documents for the Chinese central government and its affiliate institutes. After 1949, Ginling College was taken over by the People's Republic of China and all of its documents were handed over to the Historical Archives.

Approximately 200 volumes of Ginling's documents cataloged under the title "Ginling Arts and Science College for Women" are deposited at the Historical Archives. In addition, there are some miscellaneous papers and documents that are difficult to categorize. At the turn of this century, researchers began to sort out the miscellaneous files. In 2001, they discovered a handwritten diary titled "A Segment of the Diary by a Colleague Remaining in Ginling at the Fallen Capital." Yellow watermarked paper was used for the cover sheet, and stationery, manufactured by Shanghai Stationery Company in the 1930s, for the text. It was handwritten in Chinese with a fountain pen in the traditional fashion, from right to left, top to bottom.

The diary, consisting of some thirty thousand Chinese characters, covers eighty-four days, from December 8, 1937, to March 1, 1938, detailing the ruthless atrocities committed by the Japanese soldiers in Ginling College and the Nanking Safety Zone as well as the suffering of the Chinese people. It also depicts its author's emotional trauma as a Chinese national during this tragic time.

The name "Chen Pin-chi" was written on the cover of the diary as its author. Chen was a graduate of Ginling who, after receiving her doctorate from the University of Michigan, returned to Ginling as a professor of biology. However, on the eve of the Rape of Nanking, she was asked by President Wu Yi-fang to escort some of the Ginling students from Nanking to Wuhan.[12] Among the names on the list of Ginling's personnel remaining in Nanking, there was no one identified as "Chen Pin-chi." But the diary is written in first-person and describes, among other things, the activities of its author's teenage grandson in the Ginling refuge camp. Chen Pin-chi was born in 1901 and only thirty-six years old at the time. She could not possibly have had a teenage grandson. After conducting meticulous research on the subject,[13] the researchers at the Historical Archives concluded that the real author of the diary was Tsen Shui-fang.[14] Tsen was the director of the Ginling dormitory and remained at Ginling with Minnie Vautrin to protect over 10,000 women and children and care for them. Because of her nurse training, she was named the head of the fourth district of the safety zone in charge of medical service, especially at Ginling. At the time, Tsen was sixty-two years old and did have a teenage grandson staying with her during the Rape.[15] Minnie Vautrin mentioned Tsen's grandson several times in her own diary, especially about the teenager's serving as a guide and scout in the refugee camp.[16]

After the discovery of the diary, it was publicized in the media in Nanjing. The researchers at the Historical Archives located the grandson, Tsen Kuo-hsiang, whom Tsen mentioned repeatedly in her diary. Tsen Kuo-hsiang now is in his eighties and resides in Hsian Tao of Hupei Province. He recalled that during the Rape he saw his grandmother write with a fountain pen every night in her room, but he had no idea that she had been recording a diary. He verified that the handwriting in the diary was his grandmother's. In 2004 and 2005, Tsen's diary was published in Chinese with the title "Tsen Shui-fang ri ji," by *Min kuo dan an* (Archives of the Republic) in three installments.[17]

Like Vautrin, Tsen was afraid that if the Japanese soldiers discovered her diary, it would endanger her life and jeopardize her colleagues' safety. When the soldiers barged into Ginling, she always hid the diary in one of various secret places. At the time the diary was recorded, Tsen was under high stress, constant fear, persistent danger, physical exhaustion, and insurmountable anger. The wording of the diary is often obscure, sentences incoherent and awkward, and the narrative lacks fluency. In translating it into English, we have striven to provide a faithful interpretation that reflects Tsen's own voice and the diary's contemporaneous nature.

JUXTAPOSITION—EXCERPTS FROM THE TWO DIARIES,
DECEMBER 8, 1937, TO
MARCH 1, 1938

1

―――✦―――

RECEIVING REFUGEES AT GINLING COLLEGE
UNDER INTENSIFYING BOMBARDMENT

―――✦―――

Historical Background: On July 7, 1937, the Japanese military launched a full-scale war against China. It swiftly occupied Peking and its seaport, Tientsin, and on August 13, attacked China's largest city, Shanghai. Two days later, the Japanese began air raids on their next target, the capital city of the Chinese Nationalists, Nanking. The Japanese proclaimed that they would take Shanghai in a couple of days and subjugate the entirety of China within three months. Yet, to the surprise of the Japanese, the Chinese military put up a stiff resistance and defended the city with exceptional bravery. It was only after Japan's deployment of 190,000 soldiers and a bloody battle lasting three months that, on November 15, Shanghai fell into the invaders' hands.[1]

The Japanese troops immediately regrouped and marched from three directions toward Nanking with the support of two hundred tanks, hundreds of warplanes, and a naval fleet. The Chinese Nationalist government moved its seat to Chungking in southwest China and left over 100,000 soldiers to defend the capital city. Among these soldiers were many who had just retreated from Shanghai, exhausted after a long bloody battle there, and many more who were ill-trained new recruits. Only some 35,000 men were well-trained and combat-ready. The Chinese defense consisted of only two battalions of artillery and ten tanks but with no aerial or naval support.[2]

As the situation in Nanking became very grave, the American embassy and other embassies made a last call to evacuate their remaining nationals. Minnie Vautrin and some twenty Americans and Europeans were determined to stay in the city to protect innocent citizens in time of need. They established a safety zone with some twenty refugee camps and designated Ginling College as the specific camp for women. By December 8, the Japanese troops had reached the outskirts of Nanking. The city was under thundering artillery and aerial bombing throughout day and night.

Wednesday, December 8, 1937

From Minnie Vautrin's Diary

At 9 A.M. this morning we practiced receiving refugees and have our method well in hand. Pupils of our neighborhood school, "Big" Wang's[3] three children and Mrs. Tsen's grandson are five ushers and they look quite important with their special sleeve bands. Six of the servants have also been assigned to help. Mr. Francis Chen[4] and Yang Szi-fu[5] are to stand outside the gate and try to get people in order according to families. We are to put local people in dormitories and refugees from cities like Wusih[6] [Wuhsi] into the Central Building. We are permitting local families to live in Neighborhood House and it is pretty well filled already.

We can hear distant cannonading today which seems to be at the south. How long it will be before the Japanese are in the city we do not know. I am fearful that Chinese army will be bottled up here.

This evening we are receiving our first refugees—and what heartbreaking stories they have to tell. They are ordered by Chinese military to leave their homes immediately[;] if they do not they will be considered traitors and shot. In some cases their houses are burned, if they interfere with the military plans. Most of the people come from near South Gate and the southeast part of city.

"Safety Zone" flags were put up today—the red cross in a red circle.

Tonight I look 60 and feel 80. Did not go to the Press Conference because I wanted to help receive refugees.

It is quite cold these days but fortunately we have sunshine and there is neither rain or snow.

Miss Lo[7] moved in to Practice School[8] today and will help us look after refugees.

She will supervise those in Practice School.

A notice from the Embassy reads—"Simultaneously with the departure of other foreign diplomatic officers, the remaining officers of the American Embassy will this evening board the U.S.S. Panay and establish temporary Embassy offices there. It is expected that officers of the Embassy will return to the premises on shore during daytime tomorrow. When information is received that the Hsia Gwan [Hsia Kwan][9] Gate is closed the Panay will move from its present anchorage off San Chia Ho [San Chia River]. Ropes for assistance in evacuating over the city walls are being given into the custory [custody] of Dr. M. S. Bates."[10]

From Tsen Shui-fang's Diary

Tonight [we] went to the meeting held by the International Committee for the [Nanking] Safety Zone. None of the government officials were there. Probably, they all have left. The Safety Zone was established two months ago. Because Japan denied the need for establishing a safety zone [in Nanking], it delayed its response to the request submitted [by the International Committee] quite a while ago. Later, Japan replied that it might or might not recognize [the neutrality of] the Safety Zone. Two months ago, the International Committee decided to establish the Safety Zone with or without Japan's recognition but did not raise its flags at the boundaries of the zone until today.

Tonight, when coming back from the International Committee, on the way, we saw many people have moved from the city's south to the Safety Zone. Some of them could not find quarters to stay, so they slept on the roads. According to the International Committee's regulations, all the private residences [in the zone] should be available for borrowing or renting. The public buildings have yet to be opened [to receive refugees]. The city's south and Hsia Kwan are all on fire. Some fires were set by our army for the sake of strategy; some started by the Japanese troops from outside of the city. They have already reached Liu Shou Hill.[11] We cannot help but open [Ginling campus]. We have decided only to receive women and children, but not men. Currently, we plan to receive 2,700 people, [12] all told, only opening #500, 600, and 700 three dormitories in addition to #300, 200, and 100 Buildings.[13] This is our plan. However, we have no idea how many will eventually come.

Thursday, December 9

From Vautrin's Diary

Tonight the flames are lighting the sky above the whole south west corner of the city and during much of the afternoon we have seen clouds of smoke rising from every direction save northwest. The aim of the Chinese military is to get all obstructions out of their way—obstructions for their guns and possible ambush or protection for Japanese troops. McDaniel[14] of Associated Press says he watched the fires being started with kerosene. The owners of these houses are the refugees who have been coming into the city in great crowds during the last two days. If this method delays the Japanese 12–24 hours in entering the city, I wonder if it is worth what it costs in human misery.

It is almost impossible to get mail out now—the post office is not receiving any more. This morning I wrote four letters, and tried, first, a man at the Metropolitan Hotel, then the British Embassy, and finally the American Embassy.

As we were at the press conference this evening a huge shell landed at Sin Giai Kow [Hsin Chieh Kow][15] which made us all start from our seats and I fear some turned pale. This was [the] first artillery fire we have had. There was not an hour today when we did not hear aeroplanes. The conference for a time tonight consisted of two press men, two Chinese and the rest were missionaries. It looks as if press conferences will be no more.

I found when I reached my room that the concussion was so great that it knocked a pot of flowers from my window.

We probably have 300 refugees on the campus tonight. Some have come from Wusih [Wuhsi], others from outside the city, and still others from our neighborhood. About 1500 are already at Bible Teachers' Training School.[16]

The one o'clock radio [broadcast] spoke of signs of peace after Nanking has been taken. I dread to learn the demands that will be made.

The stories of the refugees are heart-breaking. Today a woman came in weeping bitterly, saying she had come into the city on an errand, but her twelve-year old daughter could not get through the city gate, nor could she get out to her.

The little girl is at the Gwang Kwa men [Kwanghwa Gate] where the fighting is worst.

Another woman came from San Chia Ho [San Chia River] and was frantically looking for her mother. When she could not find her in our campus we sent her over to Bible Teachers' Training School.

Tomorrow will probably be a day of severe fighting, when [the] Japanese will try their best to get into [the] city. (Later found out from Fukuda[17] that an advance guard actually did reach Gwang Hwa Gate on December 10 but were repulsed.)

From Tsen's Diary

Today, all day, the artilleries are shelling continuously. Siren warnings from Liu Shou Hill have ceased to come. Da Shiao Chang[18] is captured. Quite a few people come inside the city. The thundering sound of the enemy's airplanes and artilleries filled the outside; inside the crying of women and children. Most of these people originally resided on the fighting fronts. Some came from outside of the city, and all were driven into the city by our army. There are 4,000 refugees in Hsia Kwan. Most came from Wuhsi and Chuyung.[19] The Japanese troops have already occupied Chuyung. Originally, these refugees planned to enter the Safety Zone. Today, after being dispersed, they crossed the [Yangtze] river and proceeded upward via railroad. Those who were unable to escape in time came to the refugee zone. They do not have bedding with them, but fortunately we have some. #500 and 100 Buildings are fully occupied. Looting began in the city's south side and is in total chaos. Nothing is for sale on the streets. There are nine sections in the Safety Zone. We belong to the fourth section with Chen Fei-rung[20] as the section head. I'm in charge of its medical group. Chi Chao-kao [Chi Chao-chang][21] and Pastor Shen[22] are the head of the third section and the leader of the medical groups for all nine sections, respectively.

Friday, December 10

From Vautrin's Diary

7:30 A.M. I had thought the night might be one of continued bombardment, but it was strangely quiet and peaceful save for the occasional sounds of people wandering on the street. At seven this morning the warning siren sounded but no planes have yet come. I can now hear the sound of machine guns off to [the] south. The weather is still warm and clear—an immeasurable blessing to the wanderers on the streets.

(The above paragraph I shall have to rescind. When I went to breakfast all the others spoke of the continual sound of guns during the night until about four this morning. Evidently I was so dead tired that I heard nothing.)

Refugees continue to come in this morning. The old Faculty House is about full, and Central Building is filling. Mr. Steele,[23] Chicago Daily News reporter, came over this morning to look around. Outside of our front gate the refugees are taking bricks intended for a new house and are fast building them into tiny houses—no brick-layers are needed. They cover with a piece or two of matting and there they have a room all their own in which they can be happy and independent. It is not a very safe place but they do not realize that. With considerable pride I was invited to inspect several.

The streets crowded with refugees and their belongings reminds me of the villages when the "big market" day is on.

This afternoon F. Chen and I went to our west boundary to help put up Safety Zone flags. The hope is that all military will be out by tomorrow and that telegrams to that effect can be sent to both parties. While we were out, there was a severe air raid and several bombs were dropped west of Seminary. For the first time I heard the whirr of a dropping bomb, and saw the flash from the anti-aircraft guns. We hid among the grave mounds while the planes were overhead.

There has been heavy shooting most of the day. The Japanese are said to be very near Gwang Hwa Gate. Fires have been seen around the city a good part of day, and tonight the sky to the west is aflame—the destruction of the houses of the poor just outside [the] city wall. John Magee[24] says his compound looks like an island in a sea of smoldering ruins.

At the press conference tonight the question was raised of the poor when the city is turned over. Who will take care of them during coming months?

The mother whose little twelve-year old girl was shut outside the city has stood outside our gate most of the day scanning crowds for some sign of her little daughter.

From Tsen's Diary

Today, #700 Building is fully occupied. People on the streets continuously move to the Safety Zone. The same has happened in the schools. No vehicles are available, so men, women, young and old have to carry and peddle their own belongings. They can not help but ignore as much as possible the thundering sound of airplanes and artillery. It is really tragic. All the new residential buildings are full with refugees. Some of them rent the housing; some simply move into the buildings.

Several buildings and the new library of the University of Nanking are occupied with refugees. Many tents are pitched on the campus ground too. They have more refugees than us because they receive both sexes while we only accept women and children.

We do not allow cooking on our campus, so some refugees have food delivered to them by their families. For the few who have no food to eat, we feed them. In the morning, we provide water for them to wash their faces and drinking water three times daily. There are more than 1,000 refugees on the campus, so we are extremely busy with providing water and boiling water, delivered twice a day. Now we are prepared to set up a rice porridge kitchen directly outside the front gate. In two more days, it will begin to feed refugees with rice porridge. To feed refugees is a much easier task than the difficult problem of disposing of their waste. Some refugees, when fleeing from their homes, did not carry their portable johns with them. Although outside the yard there are waste pits at four sides, which are for children's use, they release themselves before they reach there. Therefore, urine and waste are everywhere. [Our] palace-style buildings now have an additional color; ragged clothing and diapers are draped on the windows and trees. Mr. Wang's kids and Kuo-Hsiang[25] are led by Hsueh Yu-ling[26] to serve in the service corps. They guide the refugees to their assigned quarters when the latter come in. Many people come, so it makes them very busy. We also assign the refugee boys to cleaning squads, four per building, with two each upstairs and downstairs. Besides that, two workers serve as an inspection squad. The pond by #100 Building is becoming the place to wash portable johns and diapers. The pond on this side of the library becomes the place to wash laundry; some people wash dishes there too.

Saturday, December 11

From Vautrin's Diary

All night and all day there has been heavy artillery fire into the city as well as outside the city, especially to the southwest. In our little valley it has not seemed so loud and terrifying but in the city it has been pitiful. John Magee reported that many bodies were lying in front of the Fu Chang Hotel [27]and Capital Theater and in the Circle. In the night it sounded as if the heavy firing was over in the southeast part of the city. He also reported that [the] rest of Hsia Gwan [Hsia Kwan] is to be burned tonight. Such deep indignation at such destruction and suffering rises within me that I have difficulty in controlling myself. We no longer have signal planes, they just come.

Refugees continue to come in to our campus. By noon there were about 850. In addition three families are living at East Court and about 120 at Neighborhood House. We are building a mat shed between the two north dormitories and will let men we know sell food there. The rice kitchen, outside our front gate is not yet open in spite of all our pressure. Refugees have a naïve conception of the Safety Zone—seem to think it all right for them to stand out in [the] middle of [the] road when an air raid is on. At the press conference tonight we were all urged to ask people to stay inside of houses or behind walls.

Wrote a short article today for Chicago Daily News. Also sent names of thirty-eight college employees to American Embassy where they will write arm bands for them.

At four o'clock decided to go up to South Hill Residence[28] and put as many of the good things as possible into attics. A group of our faithful servants went with me and in less than two hours we had moved most of the best things up. Will try to get something to put in front of doors. In the living room I left Catherine's[29] piano. It was damaged in looting of 1927,[30] and may meet same fate again.

At press conference tonight there were 20 of us—all foreigners. Four press men were present and all the rest were missionaries excepting two German and one Russian lad. Searle gave a rather dismal report of breakdown in military authority. The lower officers disobeyed the Defense Commander's order—and the soldiers and artillery are not yet out of [the] Safety Zone. In fact this morning I discovered that trenches were still being dug within college boundaries.

As I write this there is heavy bombing and machine gun firing to southeast and southwest of city. People prophesy that the enemy army will be in in three days and in the interim there will be terrible destruction.

Tomorrow is Sunday, I believe. All days are alike now. Miss Wang,[31] Miss Hsueh and Miss Lo are giving us invaluable help. Mrs. Tsen is great in a time like this! Francis Chen who was afraid at first said today he is glad he is here and he has lost all fear. Our fellowship service this morning was real. Religion is made for times like these.

From Tsen's Diary

This morning two babies died; one was only a month old and suffocated, and the other, three months old, had been ill for some time. This afternoon, once again a baby was born. Now, there are births and deaths. Also five or six women are about to give birth. Today, the shelling of artilleries intensified. Tomorrow #300 Building will have to be opened for refugees' occupancy. Our original plan has failed. One cannot get into the rest room. Some people do not have portable johns and have to use others'; some simply release on the ground. So, [we] have to let them place their portable johns at their sides and every one takes care of her own needs. With so many people, it's easy to become chaotic and impossible to keep order. We must let people stay in the rest room.

There is no law and order on the streets. Our soldiers are about to flee shortly, nor are there any policemen. Some foot soldiers looted the North Gate Bridge areas and so did the civilians. A few military policemen who maintain order have shot several looters. Our army set fires in Hsia Kwan, and many places were burned down, including Chen Chun-liang's house. Probably, only the Episcopal Church is still standing. One section of the Ministry of Communication was hit [by explosives] too. People are jittery and nervous. The Japanese soldiers are about to enter the city.

Sunday, December 12

From Vautrin's Diary

As I write these notes at 8:30 this evening there is heavy artillery fire pounding away in the southwest sections of the city. The window panes are shaking, and I have taken the precaution of getting away from the window. All day there has been heavy bombardment. Some say the Japanese army has entered the city but we have not had the report confirmed. One soldier told our gateman that at Gwang Hwa Gate the Japanese troops entered four or five times and were driven back. Have also heard that the 88th Division are being replaced by the

87th. Sad to say troops have been going through [the] Safety Zone all day. At press conference tonight heard that Tang,[32] the Defense Commander, does not have much control over his troops, and in most places in the city—save in the Zone—there has been looting. (From the sound of that terrific bombardment I am afraid there is not much left of our fine old city wall.) Airplanes come freely now, and release their whole rack of bombs, and there is no interference from anti-aircraft guns or Chinese planes. I certainly think it was a terrible mistake to burn all the houses outside of the city wall, and many within, if the sacrifice has been of so little value. Who suffers by the destruction but the poor of China? Why not have turned city over undestroyed?

This morning at 10:30 went to Drum Tower Church. There were about sixty present. One member of the church emergency committee preached a good sermon. There are many refugees living in the church compound.

(The guns are practically quiet now. I wonder if it means that a breach has been made in [the] wall and Japanese are entering.)

Refugees continue to come in. We now have three buildings filled and are now beginning on the Arts Building. Unfortunately the rice kitchen to be managed by Red Cross has not yet opened up, so it has been most difficult for the people who brought no food with them. After repeated urgings we think we can get it open by nine in the morning—but if the city is turned over in the night even that may not be possible.

Funny things do happen in all this distress and terror. Gwoh, the tailor opposite our east gate, foolishly permitted the New Life Movement[33] to store some of their things in a room of his house before they left the city. He has begun to worry about them as [the] Japanese have drawn nearer. Today I called Mr. Fitch[34] in, and the two of us took responsibility for asking him to destroy all literature. All afternoon he and his wife and all their relatives have been carrying load after load to our incinerator, and there burning it. Drops of perspiration stood out on his forehead as he trudged along. They got rid of it just in time. (From sound of that shooting I would say the Japanese are in the city.)

Lin, the very efficient janitor in the Central Building[,] is hoarse tonight from his efforts to get the refugee women and children to be clean on his good floors. He was telling the gatemen this afternoon how difficult it was to keep children from wetting on his floors. The gatemen said, "Why don't you tell them not to?" "Tell them not to," said Lin, disgustedly, in his hoarse voice, "I do tell them but as soon as I turn my back they do it."

This afternoon at 5 P.M., as I went over to the English service, I saw a great ribbon of fire on Purple Mountain extending along [the] upper third of the mountain. How the fire started I have not heard, but it means that many pines are burned.

Between 9 and 10 tonight Mr. Chen and I made a tour of the campus. Hu, the laundry man, and Tsa, his farmer neighbor, were both up. They are fearful of retreating soldiers tonight, for they have young girls in their families. Few people will sleep in the city tonight. From the South Hill Residence we could see the South City still burning, and also Hsia Gwan.

Think I shall sleep with my clothes on tonight so I can get up if I am needed. Wish the night were over.

Just a year ago today General Chang [Chiang Kai-shek] was taken prisoner at Sian.[35]

From Tsen's Diary

Now, the artilleries are shelling continuously. Our soldiers are probably going to retreat. We heard they say that the Japanese army is approaching Wuhu and will probably surround our army. No one is on the street, nor are any goods for sale. Only refugees are fleeing for their lives. Today, [our] rice kitchen is open, providing food free of charge for the first day only. And tomorrow, it will begin to charge money. Those who have money pay three cooper coins for a bowl [of rice porridge]; those who are penniless pay nothing. [Rice porridge] is carried from outside [the gate] to the quadrangle [of the campus], and two stations are set up at the center to dispense food. There are too many refugees and very crowded. We have to be there to maintain order so we are so busy, so exhausted. For this and that, we could barely handle it. Today the [Japanese] airplanes are no longer bombing. These couple of weeks, the weather has been unusually warm. The warm weather is good for the refugees, but it helps the enemy's fighting too.

Monday, December 13

From Vautrin's Diary

(Have heard that Japanese entered Gwang Hswa [Hwa] Gate at 4 A.M.)

All night long the heavy artillery was pounding against the city gates. They say the south, but it sounded to me like the west. There was a good deal of shooting inside the city. I did not really go off soundly to sleep and in my half conscious state I thought the Japanese were chasing Chinese troops out of the city, and firing at them as they retreated. None of us took off our clothes for fear something might happen. Sometime after five I got up and went to the front gate. All was quiet there, but the gateman said retreating soldiers had been passing in large groups and some had been begging for ordinary civilian clothes. This morning many military garments were found inside our compound. Our neighbors have been wanting to come in but we have tried to help them to see that if they are in the Safety Zone they are as safe as we are and that all parts of the Safety Zone should be equally safe.

The soup or rice kitchen at our front gate served rice for the first time this morning. We fed the dormitories in order of their coming on campus. By 10:30 the meal had been finished. They are to have the second meal this afternoon.

Searle Bates came over about eleven and reported that the Ministry of Communications building has been destroyed (yesterday) according to Chinese orders, and that the next building was to be the Ministry of Railways. I am heart sick about it for I feel it is useless and wrong, and injures the Chinese far more than the Japanese. He also reported that $50,000 has been given to International Red Cross for use for the Military Hospitals. The first one will be established in the Ministry of Foreign Affairs. A committee of seventeen has been organized.

4 P.M. The report came to me that there were Japanese soldiers on the hill west of us. I went up to South Hill Residence to see, and sure enough our West Hill had a number [of them] on it. Soon I was called by another servant, who said that one had entered our Poultry Experiment Station and wanted chickens and geese. Immediately I went down and he soon left, after my efforts at sign language telling him the chickens were not for sale. He happened to be polite.

The city is strangely silent—after all the bombing and shelling. Three dangers are past—that of looting soldiers, bombing from aeroplanes and shelling from big guns, but the fourth is still before us—our fate at the hands of a victorious army. People are very anxious tonight and do not know what to expect. Plumer Mills[36] reported this evening that their contacts so far have been pleasant but, to be sure, they have been few.

7:30 P.M. The men managing the rice kitchen report that Japanese soldiers are occupying the house opposite our gate in which the rice is stored. Francis Chen and I tried to make contact with the head man of the group but got nowhere. The guard at the gate was as fierce as I care to meet. Later I went over to see the Director of Safety Zone about it and they will try to solve the problem tomorrow, but all agree it must be handled circumspectly.

Tonight Nanking has no lights, no water, no telephone, no telegraph, no city paper, no radio. We are indeed separated from all of you by an impenetrable zone. Tomorrow I shall try to get a radiogram through the U.S.S. Panay to Dr. Wu [Yi-fang] and also to N.Y. So far Ginling, people and buildings, has come through safely—but we are not sure of the coming days. We are all fearfully tired. On almost any occasion we give forth deep groans of weariness—a tiredness that permeates through and through. (There are many disarmed soldiers in the safety zone tonight. I have not heard if there were any trapped in the city.)

From Tsen's Diary

Last night, our troops retreated, and no anti-artillery sound could be heard this morning. This afternoon at 2:00 P.M., the Japanese soldiers entered the city from Shuihsi Gate. When our [campus] policeman Huang spotted Japanese soldiers on Canton Road from the South Hill, he ran, taking off his police uniform. After he reached #400 Building, he was so scared that he fell down, his face becoming pale. He was really a coward. We, at once, went to the South Hill to observe and saw more than ten soldiers standing behind Old Shao's[37] house. All the workers were frightened. Shortly, the Japanese soldiers came to the poultry place to ask for chickens. Workers went to find Miss Hwa.[38] She told the soldiers that the chickens are not edible and then they left. They came because of hearing geese cackling. Tonight, many refugees came to the college as the Japanese soldiers drove them out of their own homes, because the soldiers wanted to sleep there. Most of these refugees came empty-handed; the soldiers had taken their bedding. They were scared to death. This happened in the Safety Zone. People presumed that the Japanese soldiers would not enter into the Safety Zone.

I feel so sad. Nanking has not had peace since four months ago and fell only after three days' fighting. It is really pathetic. I have no idea what's going to happen tomorrow. Today, two more poor babies were born. Their mothers are suffering too and all sleep on the ground.

2

JAPANESE OCCUPATION OF NANKING—
SOLDIERS' RAMPAGE, RESIDENTS' TERROR

Tuesday, December 14, 1937

From Vautrin's Diary

7:30 A.M. The night was one of peace without, but within one's own conscious-
ness there was fear of unknown danger. Toward morning there seemed to be
heavy artillery pounding at the city wall again—perhaps at the remaining
barricades at the city gates that interfere with the entrance of the main army
today. There was also occasional rifle firing—probably by Japanese guards at
marauding of Chinese soldiers or looters.

I could also hear firing at Hsia Gwan [Hsia Kwan] and in my imagination it was at small sampans filled with soldiers, trying to cross the Yangtze
and get away to the north. Poor fellows, they had little chance to escape that
merciless firing. It came to me that, if war is to be equally borne, all should
volunteer who wish it declared. Women who want it could serve in military
hospitals and provide clothes and comforts for wounded soldiers; even middle
school girls could help tremendously in the thousand tasks that must be done
to equip and maintain an army; middle school and university boys who want
it could serve either in the army or in the Red Cross or Social Service Units.
And both of these groups would have a challenging task after the war is over
taking care of widows and children of the dead soldiers, not to mention the
great task of providing for the care of maimed soldiers.

Those of us who believe war is a national crime and a sin against the creative
spirit at the heart of the Universe, could give our strength toward rehabilitation

of innocent sufferers, those whose homes are burned and looted or who are injured by bombs and artillery.

This weather is a blessing to the poor. It is as warm and balmy as October, and to sleep out on the hills as some are forced to do does not mean great suffering.

Tales are coming in from people who were forced to leave their homes last night by Japanese soldiers; also, of some looting by them this morning. Mr. Miao's house,[1] which had an American flag and an Embassy Proclamation on it, was entered—what was taken I do not know. They slept outside Lao Shao's house, using his fuel for [a] mattress—he and his family have moved down. Stories of young girls who were mistreated are coming in, but I have not had a chance to check them.

At 4 o'clock went down to Headquarter of Safety Zone. Mr. Rabe,[2] the chairman [of the International Committee for the Nanking Safety Zone], and Lewis Smythe[3] have been trying all day to get in touch with commander of Japanese forces but were told he will not be in until tomorrow. Some of the officers whom they saw were extremely polite, and some extremely gruff and rude. John Magee who is organizing an International Red Cross Hospital has been out all day. He says the same thing—some men polite and courteous, others terrible. They have no mercy on Chinese soldiers and do not care much for Americans.

At 4:30 Plumer Mills wanted me to go with him down to Hausimen [Hanhsi Gate] to see the Presbyterian compounds there—I to act as keeper of his car. All are in good condition save for a few broken window panes. Japanese soldiers had been in but had not looted. I sat in the car while Plumer went in and talked to the gatemen. On our way back saw one dead body on road near Hillcrest.[4] Remarkably few bodies around, considering the terrible shelling city has been through. A little past Hillcrest saw Mr. Sone[5] on road and took him into the car. Said his car had just been taken—he had left it out in front of his house when he went in for a few minutes. There was an American flag on it and it was locked.

Many Japanese flags flying from houses of poor and some of better houses. The people had made them and put them up thinking they would receive better treatment.

When we got to Ginling the vacant space in front was filled with soldiers and about eight were just in front of our gate. I stood at the gate until they left and had a chance to bring Chen Szi-fu out of their clutches. Had I not been there they would have taken him along as a guide. Wei, the college messenger, was sent out this morning and is not yet back. We fear he has been taken. While I was standing at the gate a number of the soldiers looked at my International

Committee badge and one of them asked me the time. Compared with that fierce one of last night these were quite mild.

Tonight people are very much afraid, but I rather think things will be better than last night. It seems as if they are moving over to the section east of Safety Zone.

Durdin,[6] New York Times correspondent, who tried to get through to Shanghai, was turned back at Giyung [Chuyung]. Said there were thousands and thousands of soldiers on their way to Nanking.

Our refugees have had rice twice today for which we are grateful. We were afraid they would not get any today because soldiers are in building where rice is stored.

I had made up my mind to bury the Chinese soldiers' clothes, which had been thrown on to our campus by fleeing soldiers night before last, but when I got out to the carpenter shop found that our gardeners had been wiser—they had burned them, and the hand grenades they had thrown into a pond. Mr. Chen hid the discarded gun.

Let us hope tonight will be peaceful.

From Tsen's Diary

Many more refugees came [to the college] today. All fled to here from the Safety Zone because the Japanese soldiers came to their homes to demand money and to rape. Quite a few people were bayoneted to death on the streets. The situation in the Safety Zone is [terrible] like this and it is even worse outside the Zone. Nobody dares to go out of the Safety Zone. Most of the dead were young men. Today, the third floor of #500 Building was fully occupied by refugees. At noon, seven soldiers came [into the campus] by jumping over the fence behind # 300 Building. Miss Vautrin was not here to stop them so [we] had to let them wander around. It was during the time to sell rice porridge, and the soldiers wanted to see the refugees. It scared the refugees to death. Several brave workers escorted [the soldiers] to various places. Some went to #500 Building and some to #100 Building. I escorted one of them too. When he saw refugees, he did not react much. But, when he saw a frightened young man, he immediately called several soldiers to his side and pointed his bayonet toward the young man, ordering him to take off his clothing. I asked the man to do so, and he complied. Nothing happened and then the Japanese walked away. When he [the soldier] spotted the American flag on the ground of the quadrangle, he asked the servant not to roll it up and the servant had to nod. These soldiers belonged to a group. When someone called from outside, they all left. Fortunately, they did not go to #400 Building because when seeing nobody inside, they would rob money there. This morning, Old Wei[7] delivered mail to the Drum Tower Hospital and he has not returned yet at night. Probably he was taken away by the Japanese soldiers. Many people on the street were taken away. Alive or dead, unknown. Now, Ginling has four or five thousand refugees.

Wednesday, December 15

From Vautrin's Diary

This must be Wednesday, December 15. It is so difficult to keep track of the days—there is no rhythm in the weeks any more.

From 8:30 this morning until 6 this evening, excepting for the noon meal, I have stood at the front gate while the refugees poured in. There is terror in the face of many of the women—last night was a terrible night in the city and many young women were taken from their homes by the Japanese soldiers. Mr. Sane [Sone] came over this morning and told us about the condition in the Hausimen section, and from that time on we have allowed women and children to come in freely; but always imploring the older women to stay home, if possible, in order to leave a place for younger ones. Many begged for just a place to sit out on the lawn. I think there must be more than 3000 in tonight. Several groups of soldiers have come but they have not caused trouble, nor insisted on coming in. Tonight Searle and Mr. Riggs[8] are sleeping up in South Hill House [Residence] and Lewis is down at the gate house with Francis Chen. I am down at Practice School. We have a patrol of our two policemen—now in plain clothes, and the night watchman who will be up all night making the rounds.

At 7 o'clock I took a group of men and women refugees over to the University [of Nanking]. We do not take men, although we have filled the faculty dining room in Central Building with old men. One woman in the group said she was the only survivor of four in her family.

The Japanese have looted widely yesterday and today, have destroyed schools, have killed citizens, and raped women. One thousand disarmed Chinese soldiers, whom the International Committee hoped to save, were taken from them and by this time are probably shot or bayoneted. In our South Hill House Japanese broke the panel of the storeroom and took out some old fruit juice and a few other things. (Open door policy!)

Mr. Rabe and Lewis are in touch with the commander, who has arrived and who is not too bad. They think they may get conditions improved by tomorrow.

Our four reporters[9] went to Shanghai today on a Japanese destroyer. We get no word of outside world and can send none out. One still hears occasional shooting.

From Tsen's Diary

Last night, Vautrin and I did not go to bed until midnight. We were afraid that soldiers might come. Fortunately, none of them came. This morning, a large number of refugees poured in. Miss Vautrin spent most of the time guarding the front gate to deter soldiers from coming into the campus. Sometimes, when they read the proclamation [issued by the American Embassy at Vautrin's earlier request] posted on the front gate, they left. The soldiers even entered the residences in the Safety Zone to look for money, food, and girls. They threw the residents out but kept the girls. Thus, many of these people came here. None of them dare to do business. Today, soldiers came to [the campus] and left. Some went to the South Hill Residence, breaking the doors. Inside were Western foods, tomatoes, and other small items. At the time, Mr. Riggs came and was asked to chase the soldiers away. And he did. Soldiers not only took things from here but also even took tobacco and wine from the International Committee. It really made the Committee [members] loses face this time. Previously they were worried that our troops would rob them and believed that the Japanese soldiers had better discipline. Whenever they held meetings, they always expressed the same belief. Now, they feel differently. Seeing the Japanese soldiers did not even recognize the Safety Zone, the Committee realized the ruthlessness of the soldiers. They became a little scared. The Japanese troops are stationed inside the Safety Zone. Their foot soldiers also came into the zone. So did several groups of advancing forces. They [members of the International Committee] always made a fuss about it and asked which country's soldiers the intruders were. Not many soldiers came [into the Safety Zone] from the South Gate. Now, the refugees wear the Japanese flag. Miss Vautrin is a Westerner and she is too busy [to deter the Japanese soldiers] because there are always several groups of soldiers coming into the campus daily. The Western gentlemen outside the campus are very busy too. She is reluctant to ask for those gentlemen's help.

Thursday, December 16

From Vautrin's Diary

Tonight I asked George Fitch how the day went, and what progress they had made toward restoring peace in the city. His reply was "It was hell today, the blackest day of my life." Certainly it was that for me too.

Last night was quiet, and our three foreign men were undisturbed, but the day was any thing but peaceful.

About ten o'clock this morning an official inspection of Ginling took place—a thorough search for Chinese soldiers. More than a hundred Japanese came to the campus and began with the —— Building.[10] They wanted every room opened—and if the key was not forthcoming immediately they were most impatient and one of their party stood ready with an ax to open the door by force. My heart sank when I saw the thorough search start, for I knew that in the geography office upstairs were stored several hundred padded garments for wounded soldiers—work of the National Women's Relief Association,[11] which we had not yet gotten rid of—we have been loathe to burn them because we know that poor people this winter will be desperate for clothes. I took the soldiers to the room west of the fatal room and they wanted to get in through an adjoining door, but I did not have the key. Fortunately I took them up to the attic where there about 200 women and children and that diverted their attention. (Tonight after dark we buried those garments, Mr. Chen threw a rifle in the pond which he had.)

Twice they grabbed hold of one of our servants and started to take them off saying they were soldiers—but I was there to say "No soldier. Coolie," and they were released from the fate of being shot or stabbed. They went through all the buildings in which we had refugees. A small group of four with petty officer wanted a drink and we took them over to Mrs. Tsen's dormitory. Fortunately we did not know that there were probably as many as six machine guns trained on the campus, and many more soldiers on guard outside, ready to shoot had there been the slightest running. When the highest officer left, he wrote us a statement saying we had only women and children. This has helped us the rest of the day to keep out smaller groups.

Soon after noon a small group got in at the gate to the old infirmary and they would have taken Tung's[12] young brother, had I not been there. Later they went along the road and demanded entrance at the laundry gate, and I was there in time. Had they found any suspected person his fate would have been the same as that of the four men following them whom they roped together. They took them to our west hill, and there I heard the shots.

There probably is no crime that has not been committed in this city today. Thirty girls were taken from Language School last night, and today I have heard scores of heartbreaking stories of girls who were taken from their homes last night—one of the girls was but 12 years old. Food, bedding and money have been taken from people—Mr. Li[13] had $55 taken from him. I suspect every house in the city has been opened, again and yet again, and robbed. Tonight a truck passed, in which there were 8 or 10 girls, and as it passed they called out "Gin Ming"—save our lives. The occasional shots that we hear out on the hills or on the street, make us realize the sad fate of some man—very probably not a soldier.

Most of my day has been spent sitting at the front gate as guard excepting when I am called to run to some other part of the campus to escort a group of soldiers. This evening, Shen Szi-fu, the servant at the South Hill House came down saying all the lights were on in the residence. My heart sank for I thought it was occupied by soldiers. We went up to find that Searle and Mr. Riggs had not turned off their lights last night.

Djang [Chang] Szi-fu's son, Science Hall janitor, was taken this morning, and Wei has not yet returned. We would like to do something but do not know what we can do—for there is no order in the city, and I cannot leave the campus.

Mr. John Rabe told the Japanese commander that he could help them get lights, water and telephone service but he would do nothing until order was restored in the city. Nanking is but a pitiful broken shell tonight—the streets are deserted and all houses in darkness and fear.

I wonder how many innocent, hard-working farmers and coolies have been shot today. We have urged all women over forty to go to their homes to be with their husbands and sons and to leave only their daughters and daughters-in-law with us. We are responsible for about 4000 women and children tonight. We wonder how much longer we can stand this strain. It is terrible beyond words.

From a military point of view, the taking of Nanking may be considered a victory for the Japanese army but judging it from the moral law it is a defeat and a national disgrace—which will hinder cooperation and friendship with China for years to come, and forever lose her the respect of those living in Nanking today. If only the thoughtful people in Japan could know what is happening in Nanking.

Oh, God, control the cruel beastliness of the soldiers in Nanking tonight, comfort the heartbroken mothers and fathers whose innocent sons have been shot today, and guard the young women and girls through the long agonizing hours of this night. Speed the day when wars shall be no more, when Thy kingdom will come, Thy will be done on earth as it is in heaven.

From Tsen's Diary

This morning, no later than 8:30, several Japanese soldiers came to inspect, Miss Vautrin received them, and I was there too. We had no idea how they intended to inspect. They claimed that they wanted to find Chinese soldiers. We're not worried about it because there were no soldiers on the campus. Not simply looking for Chinese soldiers per se, they would insist that Chinese soldiers hid on the campus if they saw uniforms. When we were at #300 Building, Miss Vautrin and I were a little bit apprehensive, for many wounded soldiers' uniforms and vests, made by ourselves or shipped here from other places, were stored in the upstairs room of the Geography Department of the #300 Building. I stood at the door there, while Vautrin took [the Japanese soldiers] to see other rooms. At the time, many refugees were there. Later she took them to the third floor and then went downstairs, skipping the Geography Department room. Only then, I felt a little bit relaxed. They were very fierce. To them, all gray color clothing must be [Chinese] soldiers' uniforms. At the time, people were scared to death and threw their gray clothing into the pond as if they had encountered ghosts. Vautrin took the soldiers to #400 Building for tea. One of them walked with me to #100 Building, and I had no way out but to enter the building. At first, I did not even want to see them, but there were so many soldiers that Vautrin could not handle them all by herself. So, I pitched in. They wrote [Chinese] characters asking me if there were any soldiers here. I replied no, so did Vautrin. She not only served them tea, but also treated them with snacks. I was really mad at her for thinking that if we treat the soldiers better, they would behave. They wrote characters asking us to promise that no [Chinese] soldiers be allowed here.[14] They also wanted us to swear about it. She [Vautrin] did. They wrote characters to ask me if I understood what they meant. When they left the front gate, they gave Vautrin a notice to show the [other] Japanese soldiers and deter them from entering the campus. As a matter of fact, it was useless. In the afternoon, soldiers came again and took Little Tung's brother away and accused him [of being] a Chinese soldier. He looked a little bit like [a] soldier. Twice, he was released on Vautrin's vouching for him. The workers heard that the Japanese soldiers tended to take away males with long hair. So, some of them shaved their heads. They had no idea that the Japanese soldiers treated the shaved heads even more harshly. They thought that all [Chinese] deserters shaved their heads. It's too late for the workers to regret to have their hair shaved. One group of soldiers after another continued to come, which made Vautrin busy to death. This time, soldiers saw Mr. Li, searched his body, took fifty dollars cash from him, and slapped his face. He should not have so much cash with him. At noon, meal time, [I] had reminded him to be careful about money. This morning, Li Szi-fu[15] of #700 Building was robbed of ten dollars too; a Japanese soldier later returned one dollar to him. This soldier still had some conscience and left one dollar for Li to use.

Soldiers came again, asking for chickens. Vautrin had again to talk them out of it. She was so angry that she wanted to kill all the chickens and ducks to avoid their being taken by the soldiers for food. Today, the whole day, quite a few groups of soldiers came. Some again went to the South Hill to loot. Vautrin was exhausted from running back and forth to deter them from looting. I was very worried that the soldiers would hurt her, so I asked a worker to escort her. Although the worker would not be able to do much good, he would know what the soldiers could do. I cannot run there. It worries me to death. Now, there are seven or eight thousand refugees here.

Friday, December 17

From Vautrin's Diary

Went to gate at 7:30 to get message to Mr. Sone who slept down in house with F. Chen. Red Cross kitchen must have coal and rice. A stream of weary wild-eyed women were coming in. Said their night had been one of horror; that again and again their homes had been visited by soldiers. (Twelve-year-old girls up to sixty-year-old women raped. Husbands forced to leave bedroom and pregnant wife at point of bayonet. If only the thoughtful people of Japan knew facts of these days of horror.) Wish some one were here who had time to write the sad story of each person—especially that of the younger girls who had blackened their faces and cut their hair. The gateman said they had been coming in since daylight at 6:30.

The morning spent either at gate or running from South Hill to one of the dormitories or front gate, wherever a group of Japanese was reported to be. One or two such trips were made both during breakfast and dinner today. No meal for days without a servant coming [to say,] "Miss Vautrin, three soldiers now in Science Building or . . ."

The afternoon spent at gate—no easy task to control the traffic, to prevent fathers and brothers from coming in, or others from coming in with food or other conveniences. There are more than 4000 on campus and when 4000 more bring in food the task becomes complicated, especially when we have to be very careful about those who come in.

The crowd coming in all day we simply cannot take care of—if we had room we do not have strength enough to manage. Have arranged with University to open one of their dormitories and they will have a foreign man on duty all night. Between four and six I took over two large groups of women and children. What a heartbreaking sight; weary women, frightened girls, trudging with children and bedding and small packages of clothes. Was glad I went along for all along the way we met groups of Japanese soldiers going from house to house, carrying all kinds of loot. Fortunately, Mary T. [Twinem] was on the campus, so I felt I could leave. When I returned she said that at 5 P.M. two soldiers came in, and seeing the big American flag in [the] center of Quadrangle they tore it from the stakes and started off with it. It was too heavy and cumbersome to take on bicycles, so they threw it in a heap in front of Science Building. Mary was called from front gate and when the soldiers saw her they ran and hid. She found them out in a room at the powerhouse and when she spoke to them they flushed, for they knew they were wrong.

As we finished eating supper, the boy from Central Building came and said there were many soldiers on campus going to dormitories. I found two in front of Central Building pulling on door and insisting on its being opened. I said I had no key. One said, "Soldiers here. Enemy of Japan." I said, "No Chinese soldiers." Mr. Li, who was with me, said the same. He then slapped me on the face and slapped Mr. Li very severaly [severely] and insisted on opening of door. I pointed to side door and took them in. They went through both downstairs and up presumably looking for Chinese soldiers. When we came out, two more soldiers came leading three of our servants, whom they had bound. They said, "Chinese soldiers," but I said, "No soldier. Coolie, gardener"—for that is what they were. They took them to the front and I accompanied them. When I got to the front gate I found a large group of Chinese kneeling there beside the road—Mr. F. Chen, Mr. Hsia and a number of our servants. The sergeant of the group was there, and some of his men, and soon we were joined by Mrs. Tsen and Mary Twinem, also being escorted by soldiers. They asked who was master of the institution, and I said I was. Then they made me identify each person. Unfortunately there were some new people, taken on as extra help during these days, and one of them looked like a soldier. He was taken roughly over to right of road and carefully examined. Unfortunately when I was identifying the servants Mr. Chen spoke up and tried to help me; and for that he was slapped severely, and roughly taken to right side of road and made to kneel.

In the midst of this procedure, during which we prayed most earnestly for help, a car drove up in which was G. Fitch, L. Smythe and P. Mills—the latter to stay all night with us. They made all three of them come in, stand in a line, and remove hats, and examined them for pistols. Fortunately Fitch could speak some French with the sergeant. There were several conferences among [the] sergeant and his men again and again, and at one time they insisted that all foreigners, Mrs. Tsen and Mary must leave. They finally changed their minds when I insisted this was my home and I could not leave. They then made foreign men get into car and leave. As the rest of us were standing or kneeling there we heard screams and cries and saw people going out at the side gate. I thought they were taking off [a] large group of men helpers. We later realized their trick—to keep responsible people at front gate with three or four of their soldiers carrying on this mock trial and search for Chinese soldiers while the rest of the men were in the building selecting women. We learned later they selected twelve and took them out at side gate. When that was complete they went out front gate with F. Chen—and we were sure we would see him no more. When they went out we were not sure they had left but thought they might be on guard outside, ready to shoot any who moved. Never shall I forget that scene—the kneeling at [the] side of [the] road, Mary, Mrs. Tsen and I standing, the dried leaves rattling, the moaning of the wind, the cry of women being led out. While we were there in silence, "Big" Wang came, and said two women had been taken from East Court. We urged him to go back. We prayed most earnestly for Mr. Chen's release and for those who were carried off—those who had never prayed before I am sure prayed that night.

For what seemed an eternity we dared not move for fear of being shot; but by a quarter to eleven we decided we would leave. Du, the gateman looked stealthily out of the front gate—there was no one. He stole to the side gate—it seemed to be closed, and so we all got up and left. Mrs. Tsen, Mary, and I went to the Southeast dormitory. No one was there. Mrs. Tsen's daughter-in-law and all the grand children were gone—I was horrified, but Mrs. Tsen said calmly she was sure they were hiding with the refugees. In her room we found everything in confusion and realized that it had been looted. We then went to Central Building and there found Mrs. Tsen's family, Miss Hsueh, Miss Wang and Blanche Wu.[16] Then Mary and I went down to the Practice School. To my surprise there we found Mr. Chen and Miss Lo sitting silently in my sitting room. When Mr. Chen told us his story, I realized that surely his life had been saved by a miracle. We had a little meeting of thanksgiving. Never have I heard such prayers. Later, I went down to the gate and stayed in Mr. Chen's home all night—in room next to gate house. It must have been long after midnight when we went to bed—and I venture none of us slept.

From Tsen's Diary

Now it is midnight. I am sitting here to write this diary and cannot go to sleep because tonight I have experienced the taste of being a slave of a toppled country. During the day, [Japanese soldiers] came four times, twice to the South Hill, and once to where the chickens are raised. Unexpectedly, they would come at night. During daylight, they came to check upon directions [of the campus] and girls. Before we were about to finish supper and leave, servants came to report that many Japanese soldiers were coming. Vautrin at once went to #100 Building to meet them at the entrance. She told them there were no soldiers. One soldier slapped her face. After he left, I asked all young male workers to go to where the refugees stayed, as I was afraid that soldiers would come to #400 building. They all came to #100 Building. As soon as the soldiers reached [the building], some of them stood there. And some dared not enter the building. One stood at the stairway. Mrs. Twinem and I went to find Vautrin, asking everyone if they had seen her. They all said no. Seeing soldiers standing there, I felt uneasy to say more so I went with Twinem to find Vautrin. Upon coming out of #100 Building, I saw a soldier running toward #400 Building, and I immediately followed him. He went in through the south door, came out of the north door, and ran to the kitchen. As I was about to reach the entrance of the kitchen, he went to #600 Building and pounded on the center side door. I went over to tell him that the door could not be opened because refugees slept there. I then took him to the north door to enter the building. Twinem was with me. In addition, Mr. Yang[17] went inside of the building with him. Another soldier came out of #600 and went with us to #700 Building. I thought Vautrin might be there. I had no idea when we reached the place to turn that we would see Chen accompanying three soldiers, who pushed open the door of #700 and came out of it. When we gathered there, those soldiers asked us all to proceed to the front with them. I asked Chen if he had seen Vautrin. He said no. I presumed that she was at the front where the soldiers asked all of us to go. I realized it is bad news. Chen said we all [should] walk together. Unexpectedly, when getting there, we saw Vautrin alone and several soldiers standing there. Many people knelt on the ground. When Chen reached there, they made him kneel down. Only I, Vautrin, and Twinem were standing. Among the ones kneeling, some were workers, some were Mr. Hsia's family members. Mr. Chang[18] made all of us go out there and asked Vautrin who I was. Vautrin replied that I'm her assistant and also in charge of workers. He asked about Twinem; Vautrin said she was an English teacher. Then he asked about the people kneeling on the ground one by one. Upon the newly hired worker's turn, Chen was afraid that Vautrin might not know him, so, instead, he responded for her, "coolie." Chang immediately slapped and kicked Chen. He then dragged Chen to stand on the other side and then ordered him to kneel on the ground. If [Chen] had kept his mouth shut, he would not have been slapped. During a lunch time, Vautrin and I had asked him not to hire many young people in order to avoid having [Chinese] soldiers among them. If there are too many males [on the campus], it would arouse the Japanese soldiers' suspicion. And he should ask them [young male workers] to leave. The fewer new workers the better. Some of them Vautrin does not recognize nor can she identify them if she is asked to do so. Chen put the newcomers in #700 Building and did not inform [us] about them. This individual was the one being dragged out from #700 Building. Thus, [Chen] was afraid that Vautrin could not recognize him, so he could not wait to speak out. As a matter of fact, even if he did not say anything, Vautrin would say that he was a worker. After the inquiry, several Japanese soldiers talked randomly. Some of them were running back and forth, probably looting our belongings inside.

At eight o'clock, Rev. Mills came for the night to give a hand. Mr. Smythe and Mr. Fitch drove him here. As soon as they arrived at the front gate, the Japanese shouted to stop them, asking Smythe to come in. Fitch at first did not come out from the car. Japanese soldiers ordered him to come out, asked who they were, wanted to see their passports. And they asked Vautrin, Twinem, and me to leave with them [the three gentlemen]. Vautrin replied, "I cannot leave. I live here," [but said that] Twinem could leave [since] she lived outside [the campus].

Twinem had not come to the campus until this very day. I asked her for help because Vautrin could not handle [so many things] by herself. Further, [I thought] she shouldn't live outside by herself. I asked her to come [to the campus] for some time, but she declined, not willing to live under the protection of American flags. So, I had to ask her to help us.

Therefore, Vautrin said [to the Japanese soldiers] that Twinem could leave. The Japanese soldiers insisted on our leaving, so Fitch asked Vautrin to leave [with him] for the time being. Vautrin had no choice but to leave. When reaching the gate, only 4 or 5 steps away, she was ordered to return. They [the Japanese soldiers] again asked Fitch if he could speak French. Fitch could speak a little. After a while, again [they asked] the three [foreign gentlemen] to leave, but stopped them when they started their car. So, the three just sat in the car. After having looted inside and finding girls, [the Japanese soldiers] asked [the men in] the car to leave. Five of the soldiers left from the front gate and took Chen Fei-rung with them. They did not say anything to us. Then, after a short while, we heard wailing, "help," from the rear of the campus because some of the soldiers left from the back door. We had no idea and, instead, presumed there were more soldiers inside and did not come out. We thought that once Chen left, he would lose his life. We were standing there and praying for him, begging God to save him. Before [the Japanese soldiers] left, I was so provoked and wished that I had a knife to stab them to death. Yet, in my heart, I asked God to show them the righteous way.

After we stood there for quite a while, Mr. Wang, Vautrin's [Chinese language] tutor, came. They [Wang and his family] lived in the east courtyard. He came to say that his daughter and niece had been dragged away. At that time, Vautrin thought there were still soldiers inside and asked Mr. Wang to go back at once. Du Szi-fu[19] said that soldiers had left from the back door. I suggested we all go to the rear [of the campus]. Both Vautrin and Twinem were not willing to do so, preferring not to move. They feared that the soldiers would come back or the three [foreign] gentlemen[20] would return. I replied they would not come back because martial law is enforced on the street, and there is not much that can be done. After waiting for another while, no one came. I again said that gentleman [those three gentlemen] had returned home to sleep. It was already eleven o'clock. We had stood at the front for three hours. Besides, it was so cold at night.

We all returned to #400 Building and saw not even one soul there. Miss Vautrin thought my grandchildren and others all have been taken away by the soldiers. She was so frightened. I said it might not happen and probably they all went to #100 [Building] refugees' building. Then we went to #100 to find them. After all, they were all there. Miss Wang, Miss Hsueh, and Miss Wu were worried to death; they thought we were taken away by the Japanese soldiers, and none of the workers dared to come [to look for us]. Upon returning to our sleeping rooms, [we saw] things were tossed around and messy, but not many items were taken. Eighty dollars rent from Hsieh Wen-chou[21] was taken. During recent several days, I was too jittery to put the rent money away on the third floor. Kids' candies, fountain pens, and some small items were also taken. Several eggs were eaten. Yet, there were other things which I could not remember clearly.

[Loss] of material things is real minor compared to Chen's being taken away [by the Japanese soldiers] with an unknown fate, life or death. This kind of slavery life is very difficult to endure. If I were not struggling for the survival of our Chinese race, I would commit suicide.

Tonight, it was also very dangerous for Miss Wu. She ignored the situation and dressed too well to look like a refugee among the crowd. The Japanese soldiers saw her standing there and ordered her to sleep. She then had to pretend sleeping. Then, after collecting more information, [we] heard that eleven girls, all told, were dragged away tonight. [We] did not know where they would be dragged to and be molested. I wanted to cry. What kind of future would these girls have? Chen Fei-rung's house was also looted, and so was #300 Building, but not many things were taken. Now, someone came to tell me that Chen Fei-rung is back. Really thank God. He had already returned and came in from the rear door. [We] did not know about it until reaching the Practical School. Those soldiers took him to Canton Road, and he was forced to take off his clothing. At the time, he thought they would stab him to death, so he knelt down on the ground to beg them, saying that he had an old mother and wife at home. In fact, they did not want to stab, but, instead, they wanted to search his body to see if he had money. They took his wallet, which had only several coins, and then told him to go home. It does not matter what is lost; it's very, very fortunate for him to return.

These several days, I have been frustrated to death, having no idea what's going on with the war, no communication with the outside world. Embassies have no Westerners left. Not many Americans are here, and they are helpless. The refugees come here to seek shelter and insist upon coming in. It really made me angry to death. It's better not to let them in than see them being dragged from here; it is better not to see what happens to them outside. Each night, outside, every place is burning. A lot of people at Hsia Kwan died. Why must Chinese people suffer like this? Today, several times soldiers went to the South Hill. I do not want to write any more. When thinking about the Chinese people, I cannot help but feel heartbroken. Another boy was born today.

Saturday, December 18

From Vautrin's Diary

All days seem alike now—filled with stories of tragedies such as I have never heard before. From early morning crowds of women and girls and children come streaming in—with horror written on their faces. We can only let them in but we have no place for them to stay—they are told they must sleep out on the grass at night. Unfortunately it is much colder now and they will have one more bitterness to bear. We are more and more trying to persuade the older women and even married women with young children, to go home and leave the place to the young unmarried girls. It seems to me that my days are spent running from one place on the campus to another saying "American school. Sie Gakuin."[22] In most instances it is sufficient to enduse [induce] the soldiers to leave, but in some cases they are defiant and look at me with a dagger in their eyes, and some times a dagger in their hands. Today, when I went to the South Hill Residence to stop the looting, one of the men pointed a gun at me, and then at the night watchman who was with me.

Because of the terrible experience of last night I took "Big" Wang, who is now my personal secretary, as it were, with me, and we decided to go to the Japanese Embassy to see if we could get any help after reporting our case to them. When we came to the place where Hankow Road crosses Shanghai Road, I stopped, not knowing whether or not it was best to go to get Searle to go with me, to go alone, or to go the American Embassy to see what I could get there. Fortunately I went to the Embassy and there I found a very, very helpful Chinese secretary or clerk, Mr. T. C. Teng. He wrote me two special letters and sent me in the Embassy car, so I went in state. I reported our difficult experience and also the Friday night incident and then asked for a letter which I could carry with me in order to drive out the soldiers, and also for some proclamations for the gate. I received both, and came home grateful beyond words. Also Mr. Tanaka,[23] a very understanding and distressed person, said he would go and get two gendarmes to keep guard during the night. When I tried to tip the Embassy chauffeur at the end of the time he said, "The only thing that had saved the Chinese people from utter destruction was the fact that there were a handful of foreigners in Nanking." What would it be like if there were no check on this terrible devastation and cruelty. With Mr. Mills and two gendarmes at the gate last night I went to bed in peace and for the first time for days felt that all would be well.

I wish you could hear the roar and noise outside of my door as I sit here in my office and write this. I imagine that there are 600 people in this building alone and I suspect that there must be five thousand on the campus tonight. They are sleeping on the covered ways tonight for lack of other space and all the halls are full, and the verandahs. We no longer try to assign rooms—in our first idealism we tried to do that but now we just let them crowd in where they can.

Mary Twinem and Blanche Wu have moved into the Practice School.

From Tsen's Diary

All the girls, except one, who were taken away last night were released and came back. [I have] no idea where the missing girl is or if she feels too ashamed to come back. These couple of days, a large number of refugees came here; inside and outside, people slept everywhere. Again, soldiers came several times today. If [they] did not go to South Hill, they just came here or to the chicken coop. Mrs. Twinem did not go home last night; when she saw what happened, she dared not go. Outside, many homes were looted. [Soldiers] looted places regardless of nationalities. They took whatever automobiles [they] saw; even the American Embassy's car was taken away.

Miss Vautrin wrote to the Japanese consul, asking to see him. Yet, she did not get a chance to meet him. She wanted to tell him that their Japanese soldiers committed inhumane acts. Last night, after they took away eleven [girls], they came again, searching for people [girls] two more times at #100 Building. They wanted to find Miss Wu and [presumed] she slept at #100. Because she changed place, they could not find her and left. The Japanese consul dispatched two military police [to the campus] tonight, but not during daytime as they only have a few military police, 17 for all of Nanking. The soldiers ignored the proclamation issued by the consulate when [we] showed it to them. Instead, they just barged in. Rev. Mills wrote to Shanghai for help but had no way to deliver it. Nobody from the International [Committee] came [to help]. Really overwhelmed. These [Japanese soldiers] were extremely ruthless; they committed all kinds of crimes, killing and raping whomever they like, no matter young or old. One family has mother and daughter. The mother, over 60 years old, was raped by three soldiers consecutively, and daughter, 40-some years old, by two soldiers. Both of them are widows. It is simply inhumane!

Now, Ginling has over 9,000 refugees. Outside and inside, walkways and hallways, people slept everywhere as if sardines packed in boxes. I'm worried that soldiers will come again tonight. The military police slept at the front gate. It's useless because soldiers do not enter from the front gate. People can come into this place of ours [Ginling] from anywhere. Too many people are here and they would not follow orders, no matter how hard we and the workers shout until breaking our vocal cords. The Japanese soldiers wanted everything. The outside was looted to devastation. We had no idea to where they moved the valuable loot.

Today, three more babies were born. There are many big belly women. These women are really suffering to give birth and they sleep on the ground. Too many pregnant women need my care. I have no way to take care of them all. There are buildings not yet opened [to refugees] at the University of Nanking. We cannot accommodate so many so Vautrin has asked Mr. Chi to open a building there and she plans to send some refugees there.

Sunday, December 19

From Vautrin's Diary

Again this morning wild-eyed women and girls came streaming in at the gate—the night had been one of horror. Many kneeled and implored to be taken in—and we let them in but we do not know where they will sleep tonight.

At 8 o'clock a Japanese came in with Mr. Teso from the Embassy. Having been told we had not enough rice for the refugees, I asked him to take me over to headquarters of [the] Safety Zone; this he did, and from there a German car took me over to see Mr. Sone, who has charge of rice distribution. He promised to get us rice by nine o'clock. Later I had to go back with the car to Ninghai road; the presence of a foreigner is now the only protection for a car. Walking back to college, again and again mothers and fathers and brothers implored me to take their daughters back to Ginling. One mother, whose daughter was a Chung Hwa[24] student, said her home had been looted repeatedly the day before and she could no longer protect her daughter.

Later the morning was spent going from one end of the campus to the other trying to get one group of soldiers after another out. Went up to South Hill three times I think, then to the back campus and then was frantically called to the old faculty house where I was told two soldiers had gone upstairs. There, in room 538, I found one standing at the door, and one inside already raping a poor girl. My letter from the Embassy and my presence sent them running out in a hurry—in my wrath I wished I had the power to smite them in their dastardly work; how ashamed the women of Japan would be if they knew these tales of horror.

Then I was called to the northwest dormitory and found two in a room eating cookies—they too went out in a hurry.

Late in the afternoon two separate groups of Japanese officers have come and again I have had the chance to tell of the Friday night experience and this morning's doings.

Tonight we have four gendarmes on our campus and tomorrow we hope to have one. Great fires are burning in at least three sections of the city tonight.

From Tsen's Diary

Last night there were military police sleeping at the front [of the campus]. At night, soldiers still came in and went to the crowd in the living room of #500 Building to rape. Today, during daylight, two soldiers went to #500 Building: One stood at the door of a room and another inside. He wanted all the people out except one young girl and raped her. Miss Vautrin was at the chicken coop because soldiers demanded eggs there. If not for the sake of eggs, Miss Vautrin would have gotten there sooner so the girl would not have been molested. When Miss Vautrin reached there, it was already too late. Speaking to this point, I could not help but cry. You think it over: If this is not torture, then what is torture? Vautrin is deadly busy, tired, because every day [Japanese soldiers] come several times. Most times, not just one or two but five or six come together, with two at one place and two at another place. Mrs. Twinem is scared [of them]; Vautrin is not and is more courageous. Yet, the pitiful thing is that no one is fearless. [Should one] Neglect one's own [safety]? Previously, I followed them [the soldiers], but not now. On the one hand, [I am] too busy to do so; on the other, I cannot bear witnessing the Japanese soldiers' bad deeds. During daytime, [they] dare to come and engage in such deeds; at night even worse. Today, at noon, Riggs came. He intended to ask married women with husbands to go home so the Japanese soldiers would not come [to Ginling] to find [women] so often. Because they have all run into refugee camps, no women are left outside. What [Riggs] meant was that it is okay for women with husbands to return home, but not for the maidens. If a husband stays home alone, Japanese soldiers would accuse him of being a [Chinese] soldier because he has no family. Although there is nothing wrong with this reasoning, yet, as soon as I heard it, I cried. I thought that my own country is not strong, so it suffers this kind of humiliation. When can we shed the shame?

Today, [Japanese soldiers] came eight times; they ate food at South Hill four times. They broke down the doors because things were piled inside, each teacher having something there. Few belong to the Westerners. Things were tossed and littered on the floor: some were taken away, and some [of these things] got back by Miss Vautrin. She runs to so many places [to deter the Japanese soldiers], once to the chicken coop, thrice to the dormitories. If Vautrin is not available, Mrs. Twinem does likewise. Yesterday, [soldiers] asked for chickens from Miss Wu, and she was not willing [to comply]. Japanese soldiers asked [for chickens] like this, so I was afraid that they would just come to take them. I said to her, "Tomorrow, I want two geese and two chickens for the workers to eat. We have not eaten meat for ten days, and everybody is tired too." She did not approve. I was mad. The following morning, I sent a worker to the chicken coop, requesting her [Miss Wu's] worker to fetch two chickens and two geese and asking the worker to tell her. Later, when she knew what happened, she went to Vautrin, telling lies about me. And she alleged that I caught her experimental chickens. The chickens I got were cocks because, if [you are] asking her for eggs, she always claims that most of her birds are cocks. Besides, Vautrin has already said to kill these chickens. Otherwise, I would not have fetched the chickens. Vautrin advises her [Miss Wu] to only save the ones for experiment, but not others. She is not willing [to do so]. This situation is bad, but Miss Wu does not care. She writes things about the chickens behind the closed door of her room. Vautrin and Twinem are so busy, and there is no feed grain. I feel sorry for them too. If [the chickens] are taken by the Japanese soldiers, I would be very unwilling [to allow it to happen]. I heard that several of the University of Nanking's cows were taken [by the Japanese soldiers]. It is difficult enough to save human's lives; why should chickens be so important? There is nothing wrong with her [Miss Wu's] experimental efforts for science. On the one hand, it's valuable, [but] the remaining chickens can do the job. If Miss Vautrin had not gone to save the chickens, there would not be any left! In the future, she [Miss Wu] will be able to brag about her big achievement [saving the chickens] in front of President Wu. [She] also wants to hang in the chickens' coop one of the proclamations issued by the Japanese military police. It's laughable!

This afternoon, the Japanese consul came to see Vautrin. She took him to see the refugees sleeping on the ground leaving no place to walk through. Naturally, his mouth [said] their troops are not good. His heart must be elated.

Today, a number of rooms in #200 Building are opened [to refugees]. No way out. Too many people. A lot of people come everyday; we can no longer boil water because there are too many people to be served. Instead, Miss Vautrin asked two individuals from outside to boil water and sell it to the refugees. Also our old chief cook had nothing to do so [we] asked him to sell cooked rice and fried flour twists under the makeshift shed between #500 and #700. Nothing is for sale outside. Quite a few of the houses in city south were burnt down, more burning every night. These refugees are really pitiable. Some of their homes have been burnt down. Some have husbands who have been killed or taken away by the Japanese soldiers; we don't know whether they are alive or dead. Some cried; some wailed. It's tragic beyond words. Chang Szi-fu's[25] son of #200 was taken away by the Japanese soldiers on the 16th. He was in #100 to look after the building. Probably, on his way to come here, he was taken. Wei Szi-fu has not returned yet. Outside, buildings are either vacant or burning. Japanese soldiers set fire to buildings for fun. They are afraid of cold temperature too. At first they made fires with furniture inside to keep them warm. Whenever they want to leave, they just take off. If fire touches the building, it burns it down. Sometimes, they put corpses inside and then set fire to the building.

Monday, December 20

From Vautrin's Diary

The clear weather with sunshine continues seemingly the only blessing in these days of misery and suffering.

8–9:00 at the gate, trying to persuade the older women to return to homes and let Ginling be used to protect their daughters. They all agree in principle but are loathe [loath] to go home, for they say soldiers come to their homes again and again and again in the course of a day—looting everything.

From 10 to 12 tried to work in my office, writing an official report of acts of soldiers on our campus to present to Japanese Embassy—to no avail, for I am called from one end of the campus to drive out groups of soldiers. Found two in South Hall [South Hill] Residence again, looting Dr. Wu's chest of drawers and suitcases. During noon meal Mary and I went to three sections of campus to drive them out—they seem to love to come at meal time. We are trying to get a gendarme to stay on campus during the day.

At 3 high military officer came with several other men, and he wanted to inspect buildings and refugee work. I hoped most earnestly that while he was on campus some soldiers would come. Sure enough, as we had finished seeing refugees crowded in Central Building, a servant from the Northwest dormitory came saying two soldiers were there, in process of taking off five women. We rushed over, and when they saw us they ran—one woman ran back and kneeled before me asking to be saved. I went back in time to stop one soldier from escaping and played for time until the officer came. They reprimanded him, and let him go—not the severe treatment he needed in order to make this dastardly thing stop.

At 4 P.M. "Big" Wang and I went over to our Embassy, and from there were taken over to Japanese Embassy. Reported conditions again, and asked for return of two servants and for gendarme in day time. Mr. Atcheson's[26] cook reports his old father shot, but none dared to go home to bury him.

To our surprise, just after supper twenty-five gendarmes were sent to us as a guard for the night—the afternoon's incident was effective, evidently. By making a map I showed them the danger spots on the campus—especially pointing out the northwest corner.

We probably have more than 6000 refugees tonight, covered ways full. Eastern sky vivid tonight. Looting continues in city.

From Tsen's Diary

Today, again many refugees came. The third floor of #200 Building is fully occupied. They thought that this place is protected by military police. In fact, some military police dragged girls to the yard and raped them. They are not human beings, but animals no matter where. At noon, a soldier dragged two girls [out] and took their things. By chance, an officer came to visit, and Vautrin asked him to see what his soldier was engaging in. He was very embarrassed. In fact, it does not matter much to him, as Chinese are his enemies. Vautrin does not understand this logic. She is really busy; if not chasing the soldiers, then receiving the officers. Chen Fei-rung was frightened to death by the last incident so he dared not come out these two days. [I] have no idea where he is hiding. I'm almost tired to death. These refugees do not follow orders, urine everywhere, and no place to set foot. And at night, we simply dare not to walk. These several days, Vautrin and I went to bed extremely late because we feared something would happen. Tonight, that officer [who came to visit during the day] dispatched twenty-four soldiers and one sergeant to protect the campus. What good does it do to have so many here? Besides, we have to prepare sleeping quarters for them. Fortunately, there is enough bedding; otherwise, where can we find so much bedding? In addition, we have to make fires [to keep them warm] and ask servants to serve them with tea and tobacco. As a matter of fact, it is better to have military police [here]; two or three are adequate. Tonight, it is uncertain if they are reliable. Looking at their appearances, they are not good guys. Now, it is really suffering; no news from anywhere.

Yesterday, the Americans signed their names and petitioned the Japanese consul to telegram Shanghai for sending more people here to help out. When they [the Americans] went [to the Japanese consulate], the consul replied that he was too busy to send the telegram today but would do it tomorrow. It was his excuse, as I told Vautrin. He would not send the telegram. As it turned out, he did not. Seemingly, [the Japanese] want to imprison us to death. Outside, it is burning again. Thinking about it, it's better to die under artillery bombs than to live miserably like this.

Today, one baby died and three were born. In a week, three deaths and more than ten births, all told.

Tuesday December 21

From Vautrin's Diary

The days seem interminable and each morning you wonder how you can live through the day; twelve hours.

After breakfast we collected facts about the harm done by our guard of 25 last night (two women raped) but we realize that those facts must be handled with care and tact, or we will incur the hatred of soldiers and that may be worse for us than the trouble we have at present.

Mary and Mrs. Tsen are trying to teach the women to stand in line for rice, and perhaps they will teach them in time, if they are patient. We never have enough rice for them and some people take more than they need.

At 11 Mr. Wang and I went over to the Embassy to make arrangements for a car to take us to [the] Japanese Embassy in the afternoon.

At 1:30 I went with Mr. Atcheson's cook in Embassy car over to street west of us. He had heard that his old father of 75 was killed and was anxious to see. We found the man lying in the middle of the road. They took his body over to the bamboo grove and there covered it with matting. The old man had refused to go to Embassy for protection, saying he was sure nothing would harm him.

When we went to [the] Japanese Embassy at 2 P.M. the consul was not in, so we arranged to call again at 4 P.M. Fortunately, as we were going out of gate, we met the consul's car and went back for interview. We told him we were very sorry we could not furnish charcoal, tea, and "dien sin" (cakes) for such a large group, and wondered if we might have just two military police for night duty, and one for day. He was wise enough to understand that all was not well on our campus last night with 25 guards.

All foreigners in [the] city this afternoon sent in a petition pleading that peace be restored in Nanking—for [the] sake of the 200,000 Chinese here, as well as for the Japanese army's good. I did not go with the group, having just been there.

After leaving Japanese Embassy, again went with our Embassy servant to the home of Mr. Jenkin[s][27] at San Pai Lou.[28] Although his house had been protected by an American flag, Japanese proclamation and special telegram to Tokyo, it was thoroughly looted. In the garage, found his trusted servant dead—having been shot. He had refused to leave his master's house for the shelter of the Embassy.

Those of you who have lived in Nanking can never imagine how the streets look—the saddest sight I ever hope to see. Buses and cars upset in street, dead bodies here and there, with faces already black, discarded soldiers' clothing everywhere, every house and shop looted and smashed if not burned. In the Safety Zone the streets are crowded—outside you seldom see anyone but Japanese.

Because it is not safe for any car with any flag to go on the streets without a foreigner inside, I took the Embassy car back to the Embassy. Walking home with Mr. Wang and Lao Shao—I would hesitate to go out alone—a man came up to us in great distress asking us if we could do anything for him. His wife of 27 had just gone home from Ginling—only to have her home entered by three soldiers. Her husband was forced to leave and she was left in the hands of those three soldiers.

Tonight we must have 6 or 7000 (9 or 10,000?) refugees on our campus. The handful of us who are managing are worn out—how long we can stand the strain we do not know.

Great fires are now lighting the sky to the northeast, east and southeast, each night these fires light the sky and by day clouds of smoke make us know that the work of looting and destruction still continues. The fruits of war are death and desolation.

We have absolutely no contact with the outside world—know nothing of what is happening and can send out no messages. While watching at the gate tonight, the gateman said that each day seemed like a year, and life had lost all meaning—which is true. And the sad thing is we see no future. The once energetic, hopeful capital is now almost an empty shell—pitiful, heartrending.

Have not yet been able to send out radiogram that I worded days ago.

From Tsen's Diary

The [Japanese] soldiers dispatched here last night were for protection in name only. They came to change shift. Vautrin thought that the officer was so nice to send people to protect [us]. In fact, he is resentful of losing face because no matter how [we] receive girls from outside, the soldiers still come to take them away, day and night. I told Vautrin, "You should not forget that we are their enemies. You should not believe their sweet words." What they say is not what they really believe in their hearts. Now, they [the Westerners] all see every inhuman deed and empty sweet words which the Japanese engaged in. Sometimes, when Vautrin went to the Japanese consulate to report their troops' bad deeds, I said to her that the more you report, the more harm they would do. Fortunately, there are still two Germans[29] here. Not adequate to have only Americans. Now, the several Americans are also helpless, deadly tired too. But, on the other hand, if there were not several Americans here, the Chinese

57

would only face a death road. This morning, Vautrin went to South Hill to get some small things. I fear most that if Vautrin encounters bad soldiers and is stabbed to death, it would be disastrous. I said to Vautrin what President Wu had said—things are not important, but people are. One time, I did not say this for a couple of days. I saw her aging a lot. Every time, when going to the [South] Hill, although she claims that she is not scared, she is. At first, she dare not go inside. And then after slowly saying "hello" several times, she goes in. Yet, some of the soldiers are a little bit fearful of her; they leave when they see her. Some are not afraid and take her things away and pay no attention to her when Vautrin says, "You cannot take these things." Sometimes, she gets things back from their hands. Twice, when Vautrin went up [to South Hill], [Japanese soldiers] had already taken things away. Because sometimes Vautrin is at the front gate, and it is quite a distance for her to get to South Hill in time. Her days are simply unbearable; sometimes at mealtime, the Japanese soldiers came and everybody left, but Vautrin had to face them. They come several times a day. And we have no idea what they will do. It really makes people tremble. Last night again, two soldiers came and took [raped] two girls on the ground. It's really heart-rending. In the past, I heard people say that they [the Japanese soldiers] were inhuman. Now, it has indeed become a reality.

Wednesday, December 22

From Vautrin's Diary

There is a great deal of machine gun and rifle firing this morning. Is it merely practice or are more innocent people being shot?

My strength has suddenly come to an end and I feel utterly exhausted from the terrific strain and sadness of these days. Save for an interview this morning with a Japanese Embassy police official, and this afternoon with Mr. Fukudu, military attaché, and this evening with the head of our guard for the night, I've done nothing. Have tried to get as much rest as possible during the day. It is such a blessing to have Mary here to help and Big Wang. Mrs. Tsen is very wise in all her advice and is invaluable. She, too, is terribly tired.

Today we are serving rice to the refugees simply because it has become unmanageable. We are taking time to reorganize our system, sewing on each person too poor to buy, a red tag—and they will be served first, hereafter. Also have prepared tickets for those who do not get rice each day—it always runs out before we get around—so that they will come first on the next serving. I dare not estimate how many we have on the campus—some think about 10,000. The Science Building, which has only two rooms, the hall and attic open, has about

1000 in it—so the Arts Building must have 2000. They say the attic alone of that building has almost 1000. On the covered ways at night there must be 1000. Mr. Fitch came over tonight and asked us if we would like Hwei Wen[30] opened for our overflow, and we said we certainly would.

Mr. Forster[31] of the American Church Mission came in this afternoon and told this sad story. The Japanese Embassy wanted the electric light plant repaired so that lights could be turned on. Mr. Rabe therefore got fifty employees together and took them down to the plant. This afternoon forty-three were shot by soldiers saying they were the employees of the Chinese government. Mr. Forster also wanted to know if we could have an English Christmas service here on Saturday. Mary and I are inclined to think it is not wise for all foreigners to get together, for fear we might attract too much attention.

A guard of twenty- five soldiers has been furnished us each night. The first night we had them we had several unfortunate incidents, [but] last night all was well, and the night was peaceful. Tonight we tactfully suggested that the same method be used tonight as last night—they guard on the outside, we on the inside.

People say conditions are somewhat better in [the] city—certainly there are fewer fires, although there are still some. We still have no contact with the outside world.

From Tsen's Diary

These two days, at the front, there are soldiers to guard the gate. The number of soldiers coming in decreased a little. Last night, a soldier came in. [Seeing] the walkways inside #300 Building were fully occupied with sleeping people and no room for him to step in, he left. All the hallways in each building are filled with sleeping people, and it's a good thing that they are impassable. The Germans and the Americans asked [the Japanese authorities] to protect people. Now, it has been almost ten days. They promised to protect people the day after tomorrow, and then said the 37th Division would come, and so would Chi Hsieh-yuan.[32] They also demanded people register. I do not know what kind of tricks they are playing. More than 9,000 people live here [on campus]. Can you imagine how crowded it is? Luckily, it is winter. If it were spring, the stink would be unbearable. The Americans requested the Japanese consul to telegram Shanghai for more manpower to help here. They refused. They deliberately did so. The German consul at Hsia Kwan is not allowed to enter the city. Naturally he stays on the ship. He [the Japanese consul] wants neither the third country [Germany] to see their immoral deeds, nor people to see the corpses lying on the roads. Some of the roads, [people] can only see dead bodies, but not the road. [The Japanese] simply treat the Chinese people not as human beings. The Japanese troops have taken away a lot of good things. Those things which they do not want are grabbed by the civilians, who took doors, flooring to make fires. In some places, the Japanese asked them to take things and then took pictures, which were sent to other nationalities to view. It proves that not they but the civilians were looting. Our civilians have no idea about their [the Japanese] motives.

Mr. Bates talked about celebrating Christmas. I responded to celebrate the holiday in hell. He thought the same way. Really live in hell. Everyday, there are women giving birth. I just cannot handle it. And it makes my body and mind uneasy, so I ask them to seek midwives' care. Too many births. My spirit is frustrated and body exhausted, so I am in no mood to care for so many of them. I have not taken a bath for two weeks. First, I was too busy. Second, I dare not take a bath during the day time for fear that soldiers might enter into the bathroom. [They] go everywhere once they get inside. Third, there is no light at night. During the first several days, we had light at mealtime, and then we dare not have light. If seeing lights, they [the soldiers] would come, because there is no electric lights outside [the campus], all broken. Only here has electric lights. Several times, Japanese soldiers came to attack our electric light building, but they had no idea where our electric lights came from. Sometimes, we even dare not to light candles. It is pitch black.

Thursday, December 23

From Vautrin's Diary

Two days before Christmas! How different from the usual life on our campus at this time of year. Then all is so busy—preparation, anticipation and joy, now all is fear and sadness, not knowing what the next moment may bring forth. Our campus yesterday and today has been more peaceful—yesterday three groups of soldiers strayed in and today but one. The past two nights have also been peaceful. Our guard is changed every day—and with each new group Mr. Wang and I explain by every means possible that if they will guard outside the campus we will guard inside.

This afternoon at 2 o'clock a high military adviser came with three other officers. They wanted to inspect the buildings where refugees are living. Again and yet again we said that just as soon as city becomes peaceful we will urge them to go home. They say that things are better in the city and they think they can go home soon.

Our neighbor Swen from Hu Gi Gwan [Hu Chu Kwan],[33] who is living at East court, said that last night from sixty to hundred men, mostly young, were taken in trucks to the little valley south of the Ginling Temple, shot by machine gun fire, later put into a house and the whole set on fire. I have been suspecting that many of the fires we see at night are to cover up either looting or killing. Am fearing more and more that our messenger boy and the son of the biology servant have both been killed.

We have decided that it is not safe to have a Christmas service together for fear of what might happen on our campus while we are absent. Mary and I also afraid the gathering might create suspicion.

Food is getting more and more scarce. For several days now we have had no meat—it is impossible to buy anything on street now—even eggs and chickens are no longer available.

Lights go off at 8:30 tonight. We have been using only candles in Practice School for days for fear of attracting attention.

As soon as the way opens up, I am anxious for Francis Chen, Mr. Li and Mr. Chen to leave Nanking, for I do not feel that youth is very safe.

Mary Twinem's house was thoroughly looted today. Most residences have been looted unless a foreigner is present in them and that has been impossible when people are so busy.

It is raining today. All people who have been sleeping on verandahs will have to squeeze inside somehow. The good weather of past weeks has been a great blessing.

From Tsen's Diary

Last night, no soldiers came in. They went to other camps to find [girls]. Fewer soldiers came during daytime. Those soldiers guarding the gate want to make fires [to keep warm]. They need firewood, charcoal, and treats to eat. Where can we find treats for them? Not to say we have none. Even if [we] have, we would not give to them. Because, on the first day when they came, Vautrin took some peanuts and cookies that remained in the South Hill to treat them. Then, everyday they want some. It's a lot, which we do not have.

After consuming salted vegetables for two weeks, now we are able to purchase a little bit of green cabbage, three or four hundred dollars [Chinese currency] a pound, really expensive. There is also salted food for sale, all looted from elsewhere.

Wei Szi-fu has not yet come back. People say that he had several ten dollar bills with him. If it's true, his life may not be saved. His son has not yet returned to #800 Building. Soldiers looted Liao's and Chen's homes and several things were taken away. It is cold and raining today so those who have slept on the outside verandahs really can no longer sleep there. We wanted to open Hwei Wen [for refugees] but no Westerners are available to take care there. It won't work. We have not made fires in the stove and dare not. Only Vautrin's place has made a fire in the stove. Ten days under them [Japanese soldiers], people have suffered so much. Today, a girl was carried in and could not walk, being molested by several soldiers and [her] belly swollen. Now, we tried to find ways to treat her. Probably, we will send her to the hospital tomorrow. In the future, there will be quite a number of bastards to be born in Nanking. Hateful! Hateful!

Central Building (left) and 500 Dormitory (far right) on the campus of Ginling College, 1930s.
Courtesy of Mrs. Emma Lyon.

Arts Building on the campus of Ginling College, 1930s. Courtesy of Mrs. Emma Lyon.

The interior of the Ginling College Library Building. Courtesy of Mrs. Emma Lyon.

The three-member Emergency Committee with staff and volunteers at Ginling's refugee camp.
Minnie Vautrin (front row, center) is flanked on the left by Francis Chen and on the right by Tsen Shui-fang.
Courtesy of Mrs. Emma Lyon.

Minnie Vautrin in junior high school.
Courtesy of Mrs. Emma Lyon.

Vautrin's last portrait before her death.
Courtesy of Mrs. Emma Lyon.

Tsen Shui-fang in her early fifties.
Courtesy of Mrs. Emma Lyon.

Tsen Shui-fang in her eighties.
Courtesy of the Center for Studies on the Nanking Massacre.

Two leaves from Tsen Shui-fang's handwritten Chinese diary.
Photo by China's Second Historical Archives of Nanjing, China.

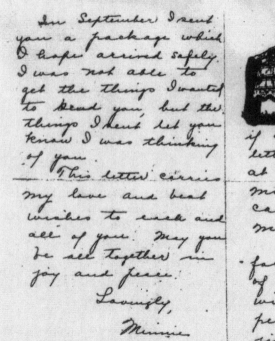
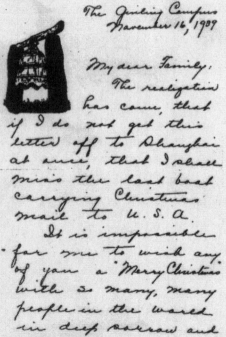

Pages from Vautrin's handwritten family letter of November 16, 1939, discovered in the attic of her niece Emma Lyon's home in May of 2006. Photo by Dr. Chia-lun Hu.

Vautrin (far left) and workers at the Red Cross rice kitchen serving the refugees. Courtesy of Mrs. Emma Lyon.

Staff, volunteers, and visitors at Ginling's refugee camp. Vautrin (center) is flanked on the left by Francis Chen, Blanche Wu, Miss Lo, and two unidentified ladies; and on the right by Tsen Shui-fang, Mary Twinem, and others. On the back row: behind Vautrin stands Ernest Forster; behind Twinem is "Big Wang"; and David Yang and Mr. Li are second and third from the right. Courtesy of Mrs. Emma Lyon.

Vautrin, Rev. James McCallum (second to the right of her), Dr. Lewis Smythe (far right) and others in Nanking, summer, 1938. Courtesy of Disciples of Christ Historical Society of Nashville, Tennessee.

Refugee students at Ginling's camp, September 24, 1939. First row, left to right: Blanche Wu, Vautrin, and Pastor David Yang. Courtesy of Mrs. Emma Lyon.

Vautrin (second from the left) with five China missionaries of the Disciples of Christ at a St. Louis convention, May 1941, shortly before her death. Courtesy of Disciples of Christ Historical Society of Nashville, Tennessee.

The Order of the Jade bestowed on Vautrin by the Chinese Nationalist Government in July of 1938. Photo by Dr. Chia-lun Hu.

Vautrin's grave in Shepherd, Michigan. Photo by Dr. Chia-lun Hu.

Hua-ling Hu and Zhang Lian-hong visit Vautrin's bronze bust on the campus of Ginling College of Nanjing Normal University, December 10, 2003. Photo by Ma Xiao-yan of Nanjing Normal University.

3

OBSERVING HOLIDAYS IN A TIME OF HORROR
AND THE REFUGEES' "GODDESS OF MERCY"

Friday, December 24, 1937

From Vautrin's Diary

The day before Christmas! About ten o'clock I was called to my office to interview the high military adviser for the ——— division. Fortunately he had an interpreter with him, an old Chinese interpreter for the Embassy. The request was that they be allowed to pick out the prostitute women from our ten thousand refugees. They said they wanted one hundred. They feel if they can start a regular licensed place for the soldiers then they will not molest innocent and decent women. After promising they would not take any of the latter, we permitted them to begin their search, the adviser sitting in my office during the search. After a long time they finally secured twenty-one. Some, they think, made off when they heard such a search was to be made and some are still hiding. Group after group of girls have asked me if they will select the other seventy-nine from the decent girls—and all I can answer is that they will not do so if it is in my power to prevent it.

This afternoon Mary has been decorating a Christmas tree and the room for our Christmas services. Have chosen a north facing room upstairs for which I have a heavy green curtain for the one window. The room is lovely now with its heavenly bamboo, its Christmas tree, its red Christmas schrolls [scrolls].

This evening at 6:30 we had a simple Christmas service there with only ourselves and Mrs. Tsen's daughter-in-law and four children. The little children enjoyed the simple gifts,—it was wrong not to have something for them, .

although the grandmother did not approve. Tomorrow we shall use the room four times for other groups.

At 4:30 went over to the University [of Nanking] to check the report that a number of weeping women brought to me. They were told that a number of men have been selected out from refugees and are to be killed unless they are identified at once.

Many women are faced with terrible dilemma—to stay with their husbands and be raped by soldiers when their husbands are turned out of house at point of bayonet; [or] to come to Ginling, and leave their husbands—the latter then runs risk of being carried off and killed.

Stray groups of soldiers have almost ceased to come to the campus since we have the guard and patrol at the gate. This lessens the strain for me a great deal.

Great fires still light up the southern and eastern sky. Evidently all shops are being thoroughly looted and then burned. I do not want to see Nanking for I am sure it is a desolate waste. People say conditions in city are somewhat better. Still no connection with outside world—I learned this from calling at American Embassy today.

From Tsen's Diary

Yesterday the soldiers guarding the gate were better. [The situation] on the streets is improving. Those bad soldiers left and went to Hsu Chow[1] [Hsuchow] to fight. The day before yesterday, [the Japanese authorities] said they would protect people. It's difficult to enforce. I don't think they will do it. Every day [the Japanese soldiers] loot outside and take everything, even searching for a few cents, including coins [they take] from women. They are extremely poor. Today, a certain Japanese staff officer came here with several Chinese to find prostitutes. If prostitutes would engage in their profession outside, the soldiers would not frequent the [refugee] camps to find nice girls to molest. This kind of talk has some merit. There are a number of prostitutes here, so [we] let them look, and several Chinese in the group could identify prostitutes. During two days recently, some Japanese prostitutes arrived. Under the circumstances, [the soldiers] can do whatever they like. [Chinese] people being humiliated is the government's fault. It is really sad.

Today, it's very cold. The soldiers guarding the gate were given two stoves [to keep warm]. No more charcoal. My room also had a fire in the stove. I can not stand [the cold]; my feet are frozen and it is difficult to walk. Everywhere is cold. It is even colder for people sleeping on the verandahs. It is really piti- ful. These people have no self-esteem, and it is despicable. No one lives in the high school dormitory or in #400 Building except for four blind girls. If we let them [the refugees] occupy these two buildings, we would not be able to sleep nor conduct business. They are not allowed to live in the library because of the wood flooring. The six buildings they are occupying will cost seven or eight thousand dollars to repair later on. All the walls need to be repaired, being entirely covered with snot. There are lice too. Several days ago, two men came with three sheep that belonged to the foreign gentlemen. Shortly, we are going to slaughter and eat them. Otherwise, the Japanese soldiers will take them. Very few groceries [are for sale] on the streets; quite a few items from Nanking. But, there is still not enough food for the future.

I have to hide the diary every time after I write, fearing it will be confiscated by the Japanese soldiers. So does Vautrin. Today, another child died after a long illness. Every day, there are births, deaths, and sicknesses. They are unavoidable among some ten thousand people.

Saturday, December 25

From Vautrin's Diary

At Christmas dinner today Searle Bates said he had been trying to write an article on "Christmas in Hell." It really has not been that for us here at Ginling; in fact we have had some bits of heaven on our campus,—although the day certainly has been different from any Christmas I have ever experienced at Ginling.

The night again was one of peace—with our guard of twenty-five at the gate patrolling both Hankow and Ninghai Roads. For the first time in weeks and weeks I slept soundly through the night.

In the south studio at 7:30 this morning we had a very wonderful prayer meeting led by F. Chen. Every hymn we sing has a meaning to us now and we eagerly accept the comfort and strength it gives. There were nine of us present including Big Wang. No one thinks of preparing a talk for a prayer meeting these days—we pray for the deep longings in our hearts.

Between 8:30 and 9:30 two groups of soldiers came, but they caused no trouble—were interested largely in the power plant.

At 12:30 Blanche and I went over to Buck[2] home for Christmas dinner. Grace Bauer[3] was also a guest. Searle and C. Riggs were called out again and again to go either to University or to a residence to rescue a truck, a group of men or some women—they spend their days doing such tasks now.

Going over I had an interesting experience. Just as we went out the gate a woman came imploring me to save her daughter who had just been taken from their home. I hurried along in the direction she showed me and went south on Shanghai Road only to be told they had turned north. Just as I started north I saw Mills in a car, halted him, and got in with the mother and Blanche. Soon we saw two soldiers going along with the girl following. As soon as she saw me she turned and appealed for help, and then when she saw her mother she rushed into the car. The soldier seeing what had happened was quite insistent that we had mistreated him, sat in Mills seat and refused to get out. An officer came along who understood some English and he tried, in what seemed to us an unnecessarily gentle way, to get the soldier out and let us go. It was not until Mills said he was sorry we had taken the girl that he let us go on.

At two this afternoon very successful Christmas was held for campus servants in the little Christmas chapel, Miss Wang in charge. At three Miss Lo had a Christmas service for the Christian neighborhood women and some refugee families on campus. At seven this evening, Miss Houch [Hsueh] had a Christmas service for the day school pupils and the other children who have helped her in the Service Corps. We could do nothing for the large group of refugees—impossible to handle.

Tonight we have no guard. One police has been sent to us from the Embassy. Soldiers are being moved out of the city. Some of our refugees going home, although S.M.B[4] says it had been a bad day at the University [of Nanking] so far as taking women is concerned.

From Tsen's Diary

Today is Christmas. All the teachers had a morning prayer. It used to be held at 7:30 daily, and today is a bit special. There were services for the servants at noon, Miss Lo's congregations in the afternoon and Hsueh Yu-ling's youth Service Corps at night. All were held in the high school. Vautrin and Twinem decorated a room [for the services]. Last night, there was a tea party for teachers, and the children of my family also attended. Vautrin was on guard outside of the room, nor did I attend the party in fear that soldiers would barge in. Mr. Bates and others invited four of us, Vautrin, Twinem, Wu, and me for dinner. Twinem and I did not go in order to watch home [the campus], fearing soldiers coming. Besides, I have no appetite. [I'm] really sad about this kind of situation whenever I think about it. During the past two days, although fewer soldiers came, the situation in people's homes was still the same. The soldiers guarding here have been transferred out; only one military police and one police remain. At night, Mr. Mills came here and slept in Chen Fei-rung's room because Chen was scared. When the guarding soldiers were here, Chang Szi-fu[5] let them use his room. Most of the things in the room belong to his relatives and friends and were all taken away by those soldiers, including military uniforms and other things. Vautrin heard that Chang Szi-fu had these things in his room. Fortunately, Mr. Shen's home is not looted because Mr. Hsia guards the doorway, which makes it impassable. The room had things that belonged to [Chinese] government personnel, though civilian officials.

Today, there are so many patients; most have diarrhea.

Sunday, December 26

From Vautrin's Diary

Another night of peace. Only one Embassy police at front, but his presence was a help in that it gave a feeling of safety. They say headquarters for military police is the American Embassy.

Several groups of soldiers came on the campus this morning but they are not obnoxious as they were. A group of military police came to inspect—certainly superior to ordinary soldiers.

At 7:30 this morning had our group prayer meeting, and at two this afternoon are having a Sunday service for Chinese on campus. Am sorry not to be able to go to Drum Tower Church. Wonder if they had any service yesterday and today. A great pity that the pastor evacuated.

Wei came back this morning—too tired and worn to tell about his experiences.

This afternoon again being at end of my strength, I rested.

All the refugees on University campus registered today. We shall probably go through the same process in a day or two, so tonight I started Mr. Chen making a list.

Weather still clear and warm during the day. We still have no news of outside world and, as far as we know, they have no news of us excepting that furnished by Domei.[6]

This will be a year without Christmas. Did not even have time to think of my friends.

From Tsen's Diary

It was somewhat quiet last night; no soldiers came in. Every day, military police come to inspect and see whether Japanese soldiers come and go. Vautrin is really good-hearted. Yesterday afternoon, on her way out for dinner, she met an old woman at the gate. The woman told Vautrin that her daughter was being taken away by the soldiers, begging her to save [the girl]. At once, [Vautrin] ran to rescue the girl. At Shanghai Road, [she] saw Mills coming, got in his car, and together they went to chase [the culprit]. Soon, [they] caught up with the soldier, who did not want to release the girl. They had the girl sit in the car. The soldier got in the car too and refused to get out. Luckily, an officer came by, but did not scold him; instead he counseled. The soldier left only after the officer said many good words to him. Otherwise, there seemed to be no way out. I advised her [Vautrin] not to chase after the soldiers if she encounters the same kind of incident outside [the campus]. I am worried that she may be hurt. Today, she was lucky to have Mills [at her side]; it would be even more difficult if she were alone.

There was one happy event today; Wei Szi-fu came back. He was held captive [by the Japanese soldiers] for eleven days, carrying things [loot], a lot of them, to Chuyung. From there to Shanghai, and then [the loot] was either sold or shipped back to Japan. Later, [he] was driven to Hsi Pu Pu Lane, so close to home, but he could not come back. Staying there for two more days, he was again [ordered] to carry things to Chuyung. After being there for several hours, they [Wei and other Chinese men] were ordered to return [home]. Originally, there were twenty-three men, but only three remained. At first, Wei was ordered to remain and was released only after saying so many good words [to the Japanese].

On the way home, they met a lot of soldiers. Bless their hearts—it was not easy for them to reach Chenshang Street, where again they met soldiers and were forced to carry their loot. Then, several hours later, he [Wei] was released and came back. It is still lucky [for him]. [Although it was] only for several days, he was so frightened and much thinner. He will be all right after resting for two weeks. They [the Japanese soldiers] are indeed robbers. They take everything. Nanking is an empty city now; only seven or eight buildings on Taiping Road are not burnt, and all [the buildings] in the Confucius Temple area are gutted. Half of Fu Tung Street was burnt and so was Chen Ming-chi's store. It is almost like an ash land. Those of us who remain here are just like tortoises in the jar. The Japanese can do whatever they please. Few foreigners are here. The Japanese are not afraid of these Europeans and Americans. Even exhausting their minds and energy, they are helpless. No communication with the outside world. There is really no place to turn. Only pray to God to open a road of survival for the Nanking people.

Today, registration of [refugees] begins at the University of Nanking. The Japanese mask is put on again. In reality, [a program that is supposed] to protect civilians is to search for defeated [Chinese] soldiers and young men and women. I heard people say that there are so many defeated soldiers, one thousand [at the University]. During registration, they [the Japanese] gave sweet talks, claiming that if the defeated soldiers confess themselves, they would not be prosecuted and will receive protection. If they do not confess now and are later found out, they will be killed. One of the Japanese and one [Chinese] collaborator gave talks on the platform. Some believed [the two men] and came out to admit that they had been [Nationalist] soldiers. I heard that 200 people came out [to confess]. Later, these men were taken away. Probably all are dead. Some did not confess [because of] knowing that [the two men's] words were hooks.

Now, fewer [refugees] are here; some have gone to other camps, and some have moved inside. Some of the prostitutes have left. The top layer of the lawn is gone; grease and dirt cover floors inside the rooms. Everywhere is urine and stool. Today, the weather cleared up, which is lucky for the refugees.

No soldiers came at night. During daylight, [they] came at least thrice. Not long ago they came numerous times, so sometimes Vautrin and Twinem would not have enough time to handle them. I heard that fewer soldiers are on the streets.

Tonight, Vautrin is not feeling well; probably she is sick, which I have been so worried about. She is much thinner and aging. Yet, she has a good title. Now these refugees call her the "Goddess of Mercy" [for trying] to save people from suffering and misery.

Monday, December 27

From Vautrin's Diary

It's a day off for me. Have not been feeling well for two days so friends insisted on my stahing [staying] in bed, Mary being here made it possible and I was glad of an excuse.

The night again was peaceful, with one Embassy police at front gate. One of the foreign men also came over to stay with F. Chen. For some reason our Practice School dogs barked a good deal in the night which makes me think there may be prowlers. Do not know how my dogs have escaped bayonets of soldiers. Military police came over during day to check up and see that all is quiet. They really seem like clean, well-disciplined men, and in the main have kind faces.

In the afternoon there were a number of official callers—one a colonel Oka who will come in the morning to see me.

Destruction is still going on in [the] city, now in [the] direction of Beh men chiao [Pei Men Chiao, "North Gate Bridge"] for we can still see clouds of smoke and fire. I suspect all shops from South Gate to Beh men chiao have been looted and burned. Looting is now being done by truck, and big things taken, such as rugs and beds. People say they are being taken to Giyung [Chuyung]. Women coming in at [the] gate this morning say that looting is still going on in private homes and that even small [amounts of] money like coppers are being taken. Mary said a truck came to the college, asking for three girls; when she showed them our official letter they went away.

How Ginling looks as a refugee camp needs greater power of description than I possess. Needless to say it would not receive any blue ribbon for cleanliness. When we had our first 400 refugees we had ideals of cleanliness and tried to have rooms and halls swept every day and paper picked up every day. Not so now. With 10,000 or more here we can do nothing except to persuade people not to use main campus as a toilet. Harriet's[7] ideal of having grass walked on has been realized so fully that there is practically no grass left, and in many places—especially where they serve the rice, there are mud puddles.

The shrubs and trees have been badly used and some of the former have been trampled until they have disappeared. On every sunny day every tree and shrub and railing and fence is strewn with diapers and pants of all description and colors. When the foreign men come over they laugh and say they have never seen Ginling look thus.

To date we have had fourteen births and four deaths. Mrs. Tsen is the only nurse we have and she is terribly overworked.

From Tsen's Diary

I hear people say that some of soldiers in the south side have been transferred. Although soldiers no longer come here to take girls, they still demand girls in homes outside. If there are no girls, they just capture older women. This afternoon, a commanding officer came to ask how much rice for porridge we have. [We] replied not much. He said that he had ways to get some rice to here. It's not true; they are very tricky. [I] believed that when he came here, he wanted to get the refugees out for him to molest. When I think of the future of Ginling, there is no hope of opening the school. [We] have no way to know if there is possibility for Ginling College to exist in Nanking unless [the Japanese] do not want Nanking or the United States negotiated with [them]. Today a soldier escorted a girl to here and asked Yang Szi-fu to take care [of her], who had been molested. [The soldier] gave the girl a fur garment and several ten dollar bills. Probably [the items] were looted.

Tuesday, December 28

From Vautrin's Diary

We are now entering a new epoch—the period of registration. This morning by 8 o'clock we became the center for registration of the Fifth district of the Safety Zone. Men are to be registered first, it seems. We got our own men together; they were first lectured through an interpreter, then told if there were any ex-soldiers in the group they should confess; they would not be hurt but would be put into a labor corp. It was not clear to me whether they meant a recent soldier or former one. The man who confessed first was one of Y. H. Chen's[8] workmen. I found later he is not a recent soldier, and am now trying to get him released. The men were then formed in lines of four, given a slip for registration and then marched out to register over at Chen Chung-fan's[9] house (at Northeast corner of campus). I was interested in studying faces of men. In main it was the old, the maimed, the halt, for all young men who could do so have gone west.

In the meantime, Colonel Oka came to call, and insisted that he had promised in Shanghai to protect all Americans and he wanted us to live in one place. I told him we could not leave our particular places of responsibility. We were both kind and polite but firm, and so far I have won the battle.

Before noon our staff and servants returned unregistered, for the crowds were too great. It is snowing now and this section of Nanking is a dreary looking place—but less so than the southern section of Nanking.

P. Mills came in this afternoon and reported that practically all foreign property of all nationalities, as well as Chinese, has been looted—some more than others. The looting of our residence has been light and even that would not have taken place if I could have been in about four places at one time. Our looting, therefore, is all to blame on me, because I have been too slow!

Wish those of you who know South Hill House [Residence] could see it. You remember that all furniture was stored for the summer, either in attics or in big dining room, so painters could paint floors and tint walls. At least four chests of drawers and wardrobe were put in the dining room. They have been like honey to busy bees. One group of soldiers after another has come to that room. I've stopped many of them in their task of going through drawers. We have not tried to put things in order. The storeroom has a huge hole in the door—it was a mistake to lock any doors—and a bit of food and canned things were taken.

They say Elmion[10] is a sight. All three floors are strewn about a foot deep. Recently two beds and mattresses have been taken also.

Strange to say, only twice has the Practice School been visited. On that fatal night, December 17, one man came, and the servant served him tea in the sitting room. As far as I know nothing was taken. Once since, one man has come but did not go further than the kitchen. I think our dogs have been a great protection to us. Also the fact that we do not turn on our lights at night but use candles.

From Tsen's Diary

This morning I saw ghosts. The whole morning [the Japanese] came here to register [people]. Not many men and women on the campus [are registered]. Most [of the registered] are workers. After registering the workers, it should be the refugees' turn. But, [they] did not do so; [instead] they forced many men outside to come here to register. We belong to the fifth district. They forced all these men to come here for registration. First, they lined up the men row by row and then lectured them, asking them to return home for a good and happy life after registration. All are ghost talking [nonsense]. Also, they asked people to confess and former [Chinese] soldiers all stepped forward. Over one hundred people confessed and stepped forward. These people were either sent to the front line or killed.

Today, it began to snow. It's really impossible to sleep outside. Some [refugees] squeezed inside, and some slept at the entry door of #400 Building, which is a little bit better [than outside]. So was the patio of #100 Building. Tomorrow, we'll find other solutions. All of them do not have children and are ignorant people, pitiful but hateful. When Japanese devils come, they [the refugees] all gather around to watch them. They would not leave [even if we] asked them to. If [we] ask them to go home, they would say that they are afraid of doing so.

Today, the people who have registered only get a little slip. They have to go through line by line. If anything goes wrong, the Japanese soldiers beat them with a stick. One time, a woman's head was beaten to bleeding. [The registered people] need to take the little slip to Ninghai Road to exchange for a large slip. [So], some people went to wait in line at dawn [to get the large slip], and some did not get it until noon. Sometimes, when [the Japanese] saw young people, they asked them to remain [there]. Our workers need Vautrin to take them to register to speed up the procedures because they have no time to wait for half a day. Today, after having talked with that collaborator about [the arrangement], [our workers] will go to register early tomorrow morning.

Wednesday, December 29

From Vautrin's Diary

Registration of the men of this district and many from the city in general continues. Long before nine o'clock a long line extends far beyond the gate. Today they were more severe than yesterday. Then they asked for ex-soldiers to confess, promised them work and pay. Today they examined their hands and selected men whom they suspected. Of course many who were selected had never been soldiers. Countless mothers and wives asked me to intercede in their behalf—their sons were tailors, or bakers, business men. Unfortunately I could do nothing.

Mr. Wang, Mr. Hsia, Mr. Djao[11] (your teacher, Eva, who now lives in East court), went before seven and by ten had completed registration; the rest will go tomorrow morning at 6:30. They seemed to have no difficulty. It is reported that the Registration slip means little to the common soldier and has been torn up by them in several instances.

This afternoon I went over to the American Embassy. No foreigner has as yet returned, and they have no exact word as to when one will return. To date we are still cut off from the outside world and no foreigner from outside has been able to get in—to any Embassy or business firm, and it is more than two weeks since Nanking was entered. They say trains are beginning to run to Shanghai for military supplies.

This morning I went with a group of the men who sell hot water on the campus in order to help them get a cart load of coal—they were afraid to go alone lest they and their cart be taken. As I was standing in front of the coal shop waiting for the loading to be finished, a woman came up and began to talk. She said she was from Hsia Lingwei,[12] out near the National Stadium. She says that town has been completely burned, first partially, by Chinese military, and then completely, by Japanese soldiers. Of her family of ten, three are left—she, her husband, and one grandson. Her two sons, three daughters, one daughter-in-law and grandson are scattered, and she has no idea where they are. This is but one of many such tragedies we hear about every day.

There are fewer soldiers in the city and therefore there is less looting, although some looting and burning still continues, our refugees are slightly fewer. Rice could only be served once today because of registration. The campus is a field of mud.

Tonight we again have an Embassy police and our three watchmen are on the job.

From Tsen's Diary

Today, again [the Japanese] order men to register here. I thought that it would be women to register here today. They [the Japanese] have all the men in the whole city to come here for registration. Today, it is cold. [The Japanese] wanted fire wood. They made fires to keep warm at the front gate of #100 Building. Won't it burn that gate? There is no way that this [making fires] is just for the ones to give lectures. When Vautrin saw this, she felt too uneasy to say anything, and [instead], she herself went outside to buy charcoal to make fires. Two pans of fires were set there, so charcoal was piled on the lawn. At the place where soldiers sit, firewood is still used. Everyday, quite a lot of firewood is consumed. [We] have to [supply the firewood] fast; otherwise, [the soldiers] would use chairs and tables [for fire], and a lot of the wood which I have spared for cooking was burnt by them. [They] want to make the largest fires. At the University of Nanking, no one serves them; they freely take tables and chairs to make fire. It is really despicable. We have workers to serve them and prepare firewood for making fire.

Today, at registration, no one confessed [being former Chinese soldiers]. They [the Japanese soldiers] kept a number of young men whom they suspected, and asked female refugees to come out to identify whether the men were their fathers, brothers, husbands, or relatives. One old lady was so courageous that she came out to identify three men whom she did not know at all. She just wanted to save them. Another young lady came out to identify [one man] as her brother. Then, she went inside to change clothes and came out again to identify more men as her relatives. This person is really admirable. The ones not being identified will be taken away [by the Japanese]. Some of the ones being identified are the women refugees' relatives and acquaintances. Women stayed here [at Ginling]; men stayed outside. Thus, not many men were taken away [at the registration], and their fate is unknown.

Now, the Japanese soldiers clean up the streets and bury the dead bodies or burn them. Too many dead bodies are on the streets. Tonight, again buildings are burning outside. The sky is cloudy with light snow, which, thus, is melting. I heard [people] say that over twenty women were taken away [by the Japanese soldiers] from the women's theological college.[13] Now, they seldom come here. One of the three sheep brought here last time [by two men on December 24] died and was given to the workers to eat.

Thursday, December 30

From Vautrin's Diary

Registration for men still continues. Before five o'clock I could hear men forming in line out on Ninghai Road. I got up at 6:30 and joined out [our] staff of men, including servants, who by six o'clock had joined the line outside.

Mr. Jan Yung-kuon [Chang Yung-kwang][14] kindly took our group in early to enable them to get through so they could come back to their work for the refugees. Thanks to this special help they were back by 8 o'clock. The line for the first step in the registration was four abreast and extended far down on Hankow Road. The men in the first row said they had been there since 5 A.M.

This afternoon I went over to our Embassy again to see if I could get a cable off to New York and to Dr. Wu. There is still no way, but they hope Atcheson will be in Nanking in a few days. You should see Shanghai road! If the area outside the Safety Zone is deserted as "No man's land" certainly the street inside the zone look[s] as if a "Big Market" day is on. There are crowds, and all kinds of business is being done. They say a regular market is starting up on Shanghai road. When soldiers are few the "lao beh-sing" (people) are plentiful. On my way back from the Embassy I met a young lad who had just registered and his number was 28,700. I take it that many have registered through Ginling in the three days.

As I entered our gate a mother came kneeling before me saying that one of the soldiers on duty on our campus today had taken off her twenty-four-year-old daughter. I went at once to Mr. Jan's home with the mother to report [it]. Both Mr. Jan and the Japanese official said it would be impossible to find the girl tonight, but if the soldier could be identified tomorrow morning he would be severely dealt with. The official said that six of his men had been severely disciplined already. I think he meant "killed" but am not sure.

Tomorrow registration takes place for women between ages of 17 and 30. Just what the purpose is I do not know, but was told it was to try to get the age group that is most active in anti-Japanese propaganda. Women are all frightened about it—and I am not too sure.

We are hoping markets will soon open up for us. No meat and no eggs can be purchased, and absolutely no fruit. Our food this noon and this evening was vegetable and rice.

Mr. Wang and Mr. Djao went to attend a meeting at Japanese Embassy this afternoon. It seems there is to be a big reception or welcome on New Year's Day and people are expected to show enthusiasm. They say we are expected to have a goodly representation from each district. The "Self-Government" is in process of formation. We hear that the former five-colored flag is to be used. Will look for our old one tomorrow.

From Tsen's Diary

Today the registration is still going on. The registration for men outside is not finished yet. I heard [people] say that women above 40 and children over 15 are no longer required to register. I'm really glad. Our whole family does not need to register. Now, one benefit from daily registration here is that soldiers dare not come here to make a mess. Everyday, the airplanes fly overhead. No idea where they would go? Perhaps to Wuhu.[15] I heard that Wuhu has already been subjected to killing, burning, and raping because the Japanese soldiers first went to the city. Now, what happens outside is unknown to us; no one comes from Shanghai. We butchered one sheep because of nothing to eat. During ordinary times, I have no appetite for lamb, but today I ate it.

Friday, December 31

From Vautrin's Diary

Registration took place this morning—not of 260 college women, but of about 1,000 refugee women between ages of 17 and 30. By 9 o'clock they were lined up in front of Central Building and given a discourse—first by the Japanese military official, and then by Mr. Jan Yung-gwang [Chang Yung-kwang]—both in Chinese. They were told a number of things which I did not hear, but the things I heard were, "you must follow the old custom in marriage, letting your parents make arrangements for you. You must not go to theaters, study English, etc. China and Japan must become one, and then the nation will be strong, etc." After the lecture they marched single file, one line to south and one to north through the frames we have made for selling cooked rice. Most of the women and girls got their first tickets, but about twenty were singled out because they looked different—either had curled hair, or dressed too well. Later these were all released because a mother or some other person could vouch for them. Once in awhile I can "Count a blessing." Today the blessing was that we had no college or middle school students on the campus.

After the women were through the men were again allowed to register. Du, the gateman, said that men began to form in line this morning by 2 o'clock. At 5 I heard them out at Ninghai as far down as the Practice School. Registrations have now ceased until Jan. 3.

This afternoon I did not go to the office—did nothing but wind some yarn and that seems to be about as much mental effort as I am capable of these days.

M.S.B. [Miner Searle Bates] came in this afternoon and brought us a bit of news. Rumor says that people are being asked to evacuate from Kuling;[16] that Chiang has ordered Canton to be turned into "scorched earth" before it is evacuated. Mr. Cola, a young white Russian, has been down Tai Ping Road (Hwa Pai Lou)[17] and reports there is nothing left of it—the big stores, on both sides, were evidently thoroughly looted first and then burned.

This evening at 7 in our upper room, we had a service, to end the old year and usher in the new with prayers of forgiveness and of thanksgivings—for there have been blessings and miracles in the midst of the suffering and sorrow and these we cannot forget. After service we went down to [the] living room and had some canned pineapple.

This morning a very fine Japanese called, a Mr. Endo, who has his headquarters in what was the Metropolitan hotel. I like him very much, also the military police with him. They had kind and understanding faces. Mr. Endo said he was deeply interested in the refugee work and offered to help later. At noon Major ——called—he was the one who called at midnight soon after December 13.

What does the New Year hold in store for China, for Nanking and Ginling? We must not lose faith.

From Tsen's Diary

Today, originally, it was women's turn to register. Only after registering [women] in one building, [the Japanese] again registered men. Outside, the registration has not finished yet. People came from far away places. They [the Japanese] lectured women not on freedom, but asked them to fulfill three obediences and four virtues. [Women should] not worship freedom after just learning a little bit of English. [The Japanese] simply have nothing [meaningful] to say.

This afternoon, the registration resumed. To prepare for the New Year, the registration will be stopped for three days. Their [the Japanese] words are unbelievable and have no substance. No one knows what they would do. Their country will not be on the stage long. Their sweet rhetoric carries nonsense.

Tonight, we have a special night prayer to bid the old year good-bye. Tomorrow morning, a special prayer will be held to welcome the New Year. Workers also have a special prayer meeting. After being registered, some of the refugees can go home. Recently, the situation in the refugees' zone [Safety Zone] is improving; outside is still not safe.

Saturday, January 1, 1938

From Vautrin's Diary

New Year's Day! The first day of the year—1938.

The words "Happy New Year" die on one's lips and one can only say "May you have peace." There were nine of us at our 7:30 fellowship service—which we try to have daily now. Since we are still so completely cut off from the outside world our prayer for others is becoming imaginary—we know not in what condition our friends are.

The morning was uneventful save for a surprise breakfast Mrs. Tsen gave us—pineapple, a kind of fried cake, and cocoa were added to our regular breakfast, and were a real treat.

At noon Mrs. Tsen and Mary went over to the Buck house for New Year's dinner—it was difficult to get Mrs. Tsen to go, for she is too sad and discouraged to feel like making merry. This afternoon I took my turn at staying in my office, and before four o'clock there were two events. About three, one of the servants came in hastily and said a soldier was taking off one of our girl refugees. I went out hastily and caught him with her in the bamboo grove just north of the library. He beat a hasty retreat when he heard my voice. Later I sent off two more soldiers who had come on campus at [the] same time.

Some of the young girls on the campus are terribly foolish for they will not stay inside the building but wander out toward the front gate, in spite of all we can do.

Perhaps a half hour later three military advisers came to call. They were clean-looking men and seemed genuinely interested in, and sorry for, the plight of the refugees, which they blamed on Chiang Kai-shek! After they left I went to call on Mr. Jan Yung-gwang, an interpreter, to see if he can indirectly prevent further registration of men on our campus. We have been very careful about keeping all men—high and low degree—from bringing food in, or coming to see any refugee, but this registration of men has broken down that custom temporarily.

A great fire is burning over toward Belimen chiao [North Gate Bridge] to-night—looting continues. We believe that the raping of women has decreased, although a few days ago twenty-seven women were raped on B.T.T.S[18] compound. We were told that the military police, which seem distinctly superior—rounded up a number of common soldiers (7) today for grave misdemeanor[s] and, they think, shot them.

There was a great meeting in Drum Tower Park this afternoon at which time the new city officers were installed. Our district was asked to send 1000 representatives. There was a great array of the five colored flag and Japanese flag. I have not heard the details—but I know one of our representatives felt sick at heart about it and would eat no supper. Undoubtedly you will see the pictures of this spontaneous burst of enthusiasm for the new regime.

It is New Year's night and our Embassy police are not yet come—which worries us.

From Tsen's Diary

The Chinese Self-ruling Committee was established today. It convened at the Drum Tower with delegates, one thousand all told, from every district. They used two kinds of flags: the Japanese flag and the flag of five colors. Everyone held the flags in his hand. Tao Pao-chin of the Self-ruling Committee was originally the head of the Swastika Society. He said that Chi Hsieh-yuan would come to be a puppet. I do not believe that he would. Chen Fei-rung is the head of housing of the fifth district. He and Mr. Wang went to the convention together. The speeches were inaudible. Pictures were taken in order to use them for propaganda, letting other nationalities see how the Chinese welcome them [the Japanese]. Sometimes, they come here to take refugees' pictures, holding children. They ask the refugees to smile. It clearly shows their intention for propaganda. Shortly after they entered [the city], they demanded money from the International Committee [for the Nanking Safety Zone]. Chairman of the Committee is a German,[19] and he replied: "You want money on my dead body." It deterred them. Today, a soldier came and spotted a girl outside. He carried the girl to the bamboo place behind #300 Building and stripped her clothing. When he was about to rape the girl, Vautrin raced to there, shouting. The soldier fled. It was fortunate that the girl was not molested because of prompt action taken. That place was very dirty, filled with urine and stool. The girl's clothing was covered with human waste. Can this soldier be considered as a human being? [To rape] in bright daylight. He is simply a beast.

[Japanese] soldiers distribute cigarettes to Chinese people today. There must be cocaine inside. Soon they will sell cocaine and opium. It has been almost three weeks since they occupied Nanking. They still do not allow other nationalities to enter the city in order to prevent people from seeing the despicable things they have done. This time, what the Japanese have committed here was clearly witnessed by the Americans and Germans. They should know the Japanese's ruthlessness; in the past, they did not believe that the Japanese were evil.

During several days recently, there were more things for sale on the Shanghai Road. Bed sheets from the hospital for the wounded soldiers are twenty cents each; soldiers' uniforms [are] one hundred dollars each. All look as if they are donations by some people. There are many other items such as furniture and foods. Clothing is cheap, but salty foods and vegetables are very expensive

Now, we have more people to be fed here, adding seven more workers. We have so many refugees that the workers only have food to eat but no wages. Besides, they are under protection here. Thinking about Chinese people's selfishness and greed for money, it is a hopeless case. When the Japanese were about to enter the city, there were so many policemen who sought protection from the International Committee and they were willing to work for food without wages. But, now, they are no longer willing to do so because they can move around a bit. No wages, no work. These people really deserve to die.

4

Registration of Women and the Return of American and European Diplomats

Sunday, January 2, 1938

From Vautrin's Diary

Warm, bright sunshine day. What a blessing for those whose homes have been burned and those whose bedding has been looted.

As rice was being served this morning a car drove in with three elderly Japanese women, who were representatives of a women's National Defense Organization. They did not make many comments but seemed interested in looking about. How I wish I could speak Japanese in order to explain something of what these refugees have suffered.

At ten o'clock Mr. Li and I went over to Drum Tower to church. They had a very, very fine service—the speaker, who used to be on our Sunday school work at South Gate, then left distinctly religious work for a business career, largely selfish, showed by his sermon that he had learned a deep spiritual lesson through his suffering. There must have been eighty at the service. Religion has become a vital sustaining force in many lives; James McCallum said they had a fine service last Sunday also. The church was decorated in red, and really looked festive. This afternoon at 4:30 the English service was revived—after four or five Sundays of omission. I went to the service this morning and Mary this afternoon. We do not both like to leave the campus at the same time—in fact one of us is always here with the Japanese military police letter to drive off stray soldiers.

We have had three services on the campus today. Our 7:30 prayer service this morning, a 2 o'clock service this afternoon for women, and a 7:30 service this evening for campus servants. We have enough helpers on the campus so we can take turns—Miss Wang took morning meeting, Miss Lo afternoon and Mr. Chen the evening.

Registration of Chinese continues tomorrow in eight places in the city. People are naively anxious to register, thinking the slip will be a protection. We have already heard of several instances where soldiers have torn up these registration slips.

At 2 P.M. today five Chinese planes flew over the city and dropped some bombs. Our old friends, the anti-aircraft guns, sounded forth.

Searle has received a letter from Lilliath,[1] brought by a Japanese newspaper correspondent. Her last word from Searle had been dated November 14; although she had written him twelve times and wired six times, she had not heard from him. To date no one from outside has been allowed to come to Nanking.

From Tsen's Diary

Yesterday, the merciful Miss Wu sent us two geese and one duck to consume. She did not give them to us for nothing; she wanted to be paid. Also, it depends on when she is willing to give them to us. Now it is even difficult to buy things even if you have money. This is also a time when we become slaves of a crushed nation.

It was the Chinese New Years day yesterday, so we had geese to eat. If it were not for the two Westerners,[2] I myself could not afford to buy the geese, nor did I want to eat them. How can a refugee have any appetite to eat goose?

Today is Sunday. No incidents happened. Vautrin and Twinem cannot go outside at the same time because we have to have one Westerner here. Although Twinem is a Chinese,[3] her face is that of a foreigner.

Our country's airplanes came to bomb several places. I have no idea where.

Three Japanese women devils came to visit and they are from the Women's National Defense Assistance Committee. Vautrin took them to see various places and to meet me. I really did not want to see them and became much angrier when I saw them. Also, one more hateful thing made Vautrin and me deadly mad: when the three women devils were leaving, they gave away several rotten apples and a small amount of candies. Some middle-aged women refugees surrounded the Japanese to fight for the goodies and grab for a couple of coins in the devils' palms. They indeed lost the Chinese people's face totally. It made me angry to death, and I scolded them. So did Vautrin. Several refugees also cursed them. Those women simply have no shame. For such worthless small items, they wanted to shout and grab. Does it make others laugh at them? They are low-bred like this and have no sense what kind of people the Japanese devils are. Even if they starve to death, they should not eat food from the Japanese. It may be okay for children to do so, but definitely not for adults. Those ignorant Chinese people! China's future is dim and hopeless. However, thinking of those educated [Chinese] who even became traitors, one should be more tolerant of uneducated people's behaviors.

Monday, January 3

From Vautrin's Diary

Registration continues—supposedly at eight places, but certainly at Ginling we have the crowds. By 8 A.M. the Japanese guards had arrived, and by 8:30 the lecturing had started—first to women, and then to men. The method worked out yesterday by the Chinese of the new "Self Government" organization was completely and rudely discarded by the Japanese official in charge—at least at Ginling. During the morning I went to the University and found that they were registering there and at the Agriculture Building, but crowds are small compared to ours. For us it means cutting down rice to one meal a day which is terribly hard on the children, but I rather think men prefer to register here where some of their women folk can bear witness, in case they are taken for soldiers. We have no trouble from stray soldiers as long as registration is going on the campus. Wrote a letter or petition for five women today, trying to help them find their husbands.

Tonight Wei, the messenger boy, told me his story in full. On December 14 he was taking letters, first to International Committee and next to the Hospital. Near the Drum Tower he was stopped by two soldiers, one put a bayonet at his stomach, the other a gun back of him. The American Embassy sleeve band which he was wearing was torn from his arm, my letter was taken from him and torn up, and the chit book he was carrying was thrown away—and of course his bicycle was taken. He was forced to go to Hsia Gwan [Hsia Kwan], where for ten days he did nothing but carry loot for them, and load it on trucks. He said he saw hundreds and hundreds of people killed—some soldiers, some civilians, some old, and some young. Everywhere there were dead bodies. Very few houses seem to be left standing—he remembered the Yangtze Hotel and Episcopal Church property as still standing. He said the furniture that was not carted off was used as fuel—not in stoves, but in bonfires. The next two days he was taken to a house just west of Central University, and again continued to carry loot. At last he was made to carry things to Giyung [Chuyung], starting before dawn and reaching there long after dark—without food or drink for the entire day. After the eighteen men reached there, they were given a statement of dismissal and told they could return to Nanking. Although the journey in the dark was dangerous, they decided to risk it. Again and yet again they were stopped at point of bayonet, but finally reached Nanking. In the end all but two of them were taken to do more carrying. He said that every pond they passed was filled with dead bodies of people and animals but in spite of it they had to drink to quench thirst. He arrived home on December 28—thin and exhausted. Even now he is still too tired to get about.

Two young women came in my office this afternoon and wanted me to help find their husbands. Of the three brothers in the family two were taken on December 14. The family kept a duck shop near South Gate.

Women are gradually learning to stand in line to buy rice—and they think it is a much better method than crowding and fighting for it.

Shanghai Road today near us looked like Fu-Dz Miao [Confucius Temple][4] at China New Year. Some foods can now be bought. We have killed Dr. Yuen's[5] goat for meat for ourselves and servants. No meat can be purchased yet.

From Tsen's Diary

Today, the registration resumed again for those men yet to be registered. They do [should] not register here. The reason for this registration is that the Japanese want to know how many people are left in Nanjing. Also they want to know who they are in case some incidents occur. It is impossible to finish registration today.

Many people died in Nanking. Some dead were military men who were unable to escape. There were several thousands of [Chinese] deserters in Yen Tzu Chi [the Swallow Cliff][6] who had been starved for three days. Then they dispatched two soldiers to surrender to the Japanese. For two days, they were given some food to eat. Yet, three days later, they all were shot to death by machine guns. This was witnessed by Wei Szi-fu at the site. Some of the military men and civilians were roped together by the Japanese and dragged to the edge of the ditches. They were shot one by one and row by row into the ditches. It was really tragic.

The bodies of those who were killed at Yen Tzu Chi are still there. At some places, the bodies were dragged away by dogs. When thinking about it, one cannot help feeling sad. They died so miserably! A lot of women have become widows. Wei Szi-fu came back and said that the day when he was dragged away by the Japanese, everything he saw was horrific. The roads around Hsia Kwan were impassable, covered with dead bodies. People had to walk over the bodies, so he was scared to death.

Tuesday, January 4

From Vautrin's Diary

The Heavenly Father certainly tempers the wind to the shorn lambs, for the days continue clear and warm. Registration continuing on our campus—it seems that for men it is mostly completed. I would say that from five to ten thousand women registered today—or at least completed the first step, consisting of listening to the lecture and receiving the preliminary slip. The procedure started a little after eight and continued through four, with time out at noon. Although it was announced that women from 17–30 only were to be registered, many were both younger and older. In the main, the women were treated better than the men, but nevertheless the soldiers on guard get a good deal of amusement out of herding people like cattle and sometimes they put the stamp on their cheeks, which of course is embarrassing.

I had hoped to get my first letter off to Ruth[7] today by Mr. M. Tanaka, who was supposed to go to Shanghai at 3 P.M. Unfortunately he started at 1 P.M. and my letter is still in Nanking. My radiograms are still at the American Embassy waiting for an American gunboat to send them.

It is just three weeks today since Nanking was taken and as yet there has been no froeigner [foreigner] allowed in or out.

There are many people on the streets today in the Safety Zone and many venders are selling food. There are not many soldiers to be seen. Tonight from the South Hill House I saw two fires—one near south gate, one near east gate–but this is much less than usual. As soon as registration is finished people will be urged to go back to their homes with the promise that they will be safe. The pity is that so many have no homes to go to, or if they are fortunate enough to have a home, it has been looted, again and yet again.

From Tsen's Diary

Registration for men can be completed this noon. Several hundred pounds of firewood has been burned. Tomorrow is the women's turn to register. Vautrin wants us to register. I told her that it does not matter if we register or not, and this kind of registration is meaningless. It is a trick played on the Chinese people by the Japanese. One time, they said that only women between 17 and 40 need to register; another time they said all women should do so. Although it is more convenient for those who have registered to go outside of the city, we do not want to leave the city for the time being. However, Vautrin is not willing to let us not register for the time being. She said that we ought to be truthful. It's not easy to talk some sense into her. Besides, she cannot understand the real motives of the Japanese. She insists that we go to register. Wang, Hsueh, and Lo are also here. Vautrin is afraid that the Japanese will come here to investigate. She does not object that I do not register, but if I refuse to register, those four [three] would do likewise. So, I have to go.

Life under this kind of pressure is difficult to endure. Yet, our registration went smoothly. Several of us were not registered by the Japanese. Today, people who administered the registration were mostly Chinese. Vautrin was there too. They combined two lines into one for registration. It is pitiful that those women refugees were beaten and molested by the Japanese soldiers during registration. It was really painful for them.

On the platform, the Japanese urge people to return home to good and happy lives. As a matter of fact, the Japanese soldiers go to private residences to sleep, dragging husbands out. If husbands refuse to leave, they are shot to death. If wives refuse to obey the Japanese soldiers' sexual demands, they are shot too.

For almost one month, I did not take off my clothing for a good night's sleep until last night.

Wednesday, January 5

From Vautrin's Diary

Breakfast at 7:30 this morning (we have been having it at eight) because of registration. By 8:30 between three and four thousand women had streamed past me as I stood talking to a Chinese policeman. What a pitiful sight it was. The women came in mostly in fours, for that is the way they are required to march later. Although the announcement said only women up to 30, yet there were many, many old women. Usually there would be one of the four more energetic than the rest and she would pull the other three, urging them on as if it were a matter of life and death. One woman, who looked ill, was being carried by her husband; another elderly woman was being supported by her son, and another woman, who evidently has heart trouble, fell exhausted near me, and said this was her sixth attempt to register. By nine the official car came and to our surprise instead of registering the women they were told it was not necessary for any of them to register and off they wearily trudged homeward. Some had been standing in line since four o'clock this morning, I was told by our gateman. We still continue to furnish bonfires for heat for the soldier guard at registration but our supply of wood is about exhausted. In Chen Djing-[Chung-] fan's house tables and chairs are used for fuel. The fact that registration of women was cancelled was a great relief to Miss Hsueh and Miss Wang.

Conditions are somewhat better and the strain is released, as evidenced by the fact that this afternoon three of our helpers are in bed with colds and exhaustion—Mrs. Tsen, Blanche Wu and Miss Wang. However, outside of the Safety Zone conditions are still none too good. This afternoon P. Mills brought in a woman of fifty-six from Hubugiai [Hubu Street] who had been raped last night. This evening at the gate a man wanted to bring food to his daughter who is a refugee on our campus. When informed we did not let men come in he said "I have only my daughter left now. Three nights ago in the Safety Zone my wife had a bayonet put through her heart when she called out against a soldier, and my little child was thrown out of the window." Also this afternoon as I was in my office one young bride of eighteen days came in to see if I would help her find her husband. He was an innocent tailor taken from his home on December 15 and has not returned. And another young bride of two months came to implore my help saying her husband had been taken on December 16. Although in neither case were they soldiers, yet there is very little hope of their returning, I fear, for many young men were shot during those first days of madness. In the first case, the man was the only support for a family of ten and in the second case, for a family of eight. Such tragedies we hear constantly.

I went with Mr. Wang to Japanese Embassy, between five and six, to ask that the Embassy police be continued at our gate each night. It is a great help to have one.

From Tsen's Diary

Today, women from outside [of Ginling] came here for registration. They waited for registration since four o'clock in the morning, and the registration did not begin until nine. In fact, those who waited for registration were not registered. Because not many people came, the Japanese did not want to register them and said, "You are decent civilians, and you are excused from registration. You return home to have happy and safe lives. No matter which country's soldiers, they dare not to harm you." This is simply rubbish, pleasant to ears. Same old cliche! Each night, the Japanese soldiers committed crimes outside; they did not allow people to close their doors. If doors are locked and not opened promptly, the soldiers would instantly shoot the owners. Last night, one person who had registered returned home to stay and came back this morning. Because Japanese soldiers went to his home, he hid under the bed. For those women who had not registered, they dare not to return home because when they were walking on the street, they were asked for certificate of passes.

Tonight, the Self-ruling Committee sent a note to request Chen Fei-rung to find fifty tables and fifty people to write characters. Where on the earth can we find fifty people here? At night, Vautrin and Chen went to the Self-ruling Committee to explain that we could not find fifty people to write characters and asked them to look elsewhere. At most, we only have twenty some people, including our workers, who can write characters. This morning, the Japanese devils declared that they did not want to register people. Yet, at night the Self-ruling Committee claimed that they needed many helpers and registration is on again. Is it strangely funny? Probably, they have too many heads; this one wants people to register, but that one does not.

I heard that the American consul would return to Nanking tomorrow.[8] Yet, I have no idea if it is true. This afternoon, a Japanese officer came to ask Vautrin if she has any personal letters that need to be sent out because he is on his way to Shanghai. Vautrin replied, "Yes." She wants to write several letters in cipher to Miss Tsai, hoping that the latter can decipher them and then write to President Wu and Mrs. Thurston.[9] I do not know if the soldier will deliver the letters. There is simply no way to send out correspondence. It frustrates people to death. So, it will be great if the American consul indeed returns to Nanking.

These last several days, many people have become ill—most are coughing. From November 10 to today, all told, three adults and nine children have died. Eighteen were born. All day, from morning to night, if I'm not busy with the sick, then I'm busy with the deaths and the newborns.

Thursday, January 6

From Vautrin's Diary

Evidently the plan about registration of Chinese was altered late yesterday afternoon for we received a notice that registration of women would continue at Ginling and registration of men at the University [of Nanking]. However, it is under the civil officials this time and not the military. By eight o'clock again crowds of women were pouring in; this time they were not given the lecture but formed into about twelve lines. Near the head of each line were two tables and at the first they received the permit and at the second the registration card. All the registration was under Chinese, although there were several Japanese police, and also a guard of soldiers near, warming themselves around a cheerful bonfire—it is cold today. Several Japanese newspaper men were present taking pictures, and when the women were asked to smile and look happy they tried to do so. I received quite ready permission to bring our five workers, Mrs. Tsen's daughter-in-law and the four amahs [Chinese maids], and their registration was quickly completed, thus passing a hurdle of which the mere contemplation had made several positively ill. Blanche and one amah were in bed, but I had no difficulty in getting their blanks.

At 11 this morning three official Americans—consuls,[10] I think,— arrived, having notified the Japanese Embassy that they were expecting to come. They had tiffin, at 3 Ping Tsang Hsiang[11] and this evening are being officially entertained, at the Japanese Embassy. I know for [sic] Mr. Takatama[12] came over to see if he could get some eggs. I was able to collect ten for his dinner party and was glad to present them as a gift.

Lt. Colonel Y. Oka kindly called at 11 this morning and took a letter I had written to Mrs. Thurston, Ruth [Chester], [President Wu] Yifang and Rebecca [Griest].[13] He flies to Shanghai this afternoon so I hope Ruth gets the letter tomorrow morning. It was a most difficult letter to write. To my great surprise and pleasure, at 5 P.M. Lewis [Smythe] brought me letters from Ruth, Florence[14] and Alice[15]—the first I have received since about December 5. The letters were dated December 19 and 20. Remember that my last N.C.D.N.[16] was November 14. I never think of looking in a mail box any more. Lewis also told me that letters taken to our Embassy before noon tomorrow will be taken to Shanghai by a boat tomorrow afternoon.

This afternoon a guard of five soldiers were brought over and are now at our gate house—or rather the house family [family house] occupied by Mr. Chen. The Embassy police, whom we had for eight nights, were most satisfactory and we were rather loathe [loath] to change the method of guarding our refugees. My difficulty is that I cannot tell our guard from the ordinary soldier and therefore make the awful mistake of trying to send them away.

Mr. Tao Bao-gin, the head of the new self government association, called this morning. He is a man of 62, and the last time he was in public service was under Chi Hsueh-yuen [Chi Hsieh-yuan] (about 1924).

Our older refugees are gradually going home, but most of the younger ones are still with us. It seems to me a wise thing to do. Our hearts ache for those who have no homes to return to—and there are many such.

From Tsen's Diary

This morning, people came here to register. No Japanese officers gave lectures because after conducting an inspection of the crowd, they thought all were nobodies. So, they just used low-level people to handle the registration. Everything went smoothly today. One station issued small slips [at the start] and another issued large ones [at the end]. Only a couple of Japanese soldiers were here in addition to several Japanese student groups. Probably, most of the soldiers are going to be sent to the front line to fight. It is much easier to register than the day before yesterday, [and there were] no more beatings. During the past two days, the large slips were only issued at Chen Chung-fan's house. Those Japanese soldiers took furniture from inside to make a fire: they threw things from the upstairs windows to the ground to be burned.

This morning, the American consul entered Nanking, coming from Wuhu. As a matter of fact, he had arrived at Nanking once before but was not allowed to enter the city. So, he proceeded to Wuhu and then witnessed the sinking of the U.S.S. Panay by the Japanese bombs. I heard that this time he did not inform the Japanese here beforehand about his coming. Instead, he just sent a telegram to the Japanese officers in Shanghai, stating when he would depart for Nanking. He did not care whether he could get permission. If he had asked for permission from the Japanese, they would have definitely denied permission again.

The American consul brought us letters from Tsai [Ruth Chester] and K'o [Florence Kirk] in Shanghai. The letters were dated December 19, but we did not receive them until today. So, we know the consul had arrived here once before.

The Japanese announced on the Sheng Pao[17] that they entered Nanking on the 13th (December) and all the stores opened for business on the 15th. Is this simply nonsense, lies? People in Shanghai have no idea how the people in Nanking have suffered. The Japanese went on a rampage of looting, killing, and raping. They committed all kinds of crimes. They do not allow other nationalities to enter Nanking, and they just do whatever they please. Fortunately, there are some Europeans and Americans here, witnessing the crimes committed by the Japanese. They are prohibited to go to many places in the city because the Japanese are afraid of letting them see so many corpses in those places. Outside they are allowed only in the Safety Zone where most of the people are. On the other side of the city, there are all the Japanese devils. Nobody dares to go there. Likewise the area around the former Nationalist government [is off-limits] where it is used as the Japanese military district.

Now, the American consul is here, so we can write and send telegrams to people in Shanghai. I think consuls of other countries will return to Nanking soon.

Today, the registration is not completed, and it will continue for half a day tomorrow.

Friday, January 7

From Vautrin's Diary

Registration for women finished about three today. The methods used the last two days have been most satisfactory, and have taken the strain and fear from the women, as the work is all done by Chinese. There is only a small guard of

Japanese soldiers off at one side. A few Japanese Embassy police are on hand to cooperate with Chinese police. At noon I passed a small group of women hurrying in, who said they had come from 17 li[18] west of Nanking. They feel that if they have registered then they will be safe.

This morning a group of Japanese officers together with one military police, called. They said they were connected with the postal service. When two of them went out of my office they saw some gospels in Chinese and asked if they might have them.

Blanche is still in bed with a very bad cold but is better today. The weather is considerably colder but still clear and sunshiny. Groups gather to the south of the buildings and get warm in the sunshine.

This morning I wrote the report requested by the three Americans who arrived yesterday at the Embassy. It will help to have them back. It seems they did not wait for permission to come, but just sent word that they were arriving at a certain time. I also took over a letter to Ruth, Florence and Alice, for a ship is going to Shanghai today and will take it. It is difficult to know what to write for one does not know how drastic censorship is in Shanghai.

Today the Red Cross started a new system for serving lisi [hsi]-fan (rice)[19] to people on our campus. Heretofore it has been served at two places in our main quadrangle. From now on it will be sold at the kitchen, which is just north of and across the road from our faculty garden.

For the first time we received scraps of radio news today. It brought us word of what we have been fearing—that with these moonlight nights there are bad air raids in Hankow.[20] In such a crowded city that would be terrible. Hangihow [Hangchow][21] is reported to have become a city of horrors like Nanking. God pity the poor! May they be spared our ten days reign of terror!

I went to 3 Ping Tsang Hsiang at 4:30. Tung Lao-ban,[22] still living down at our carpenter shop, went with me—as I still think it is better not to go out alone lest something should happen. Several of the men are greatly worried about their wives, especially P. Mills and L. Smythe. (The wives were in Kuling, later in Hankow.)

The men on the Safety Zone Committee have done magnificent work, giving all their time and energy for the good of the large group of Chinese—letting their own homes be looted. The German business men have been great, too, and there has been excellent team work. Rabe, chairman, has been fearless.

From Tsen's Diary

Yesterday, there were Japanese soldiers again coming into the campus and wandering around, once in the morning and again in the afternoon. After being registered, the people were ordered to return home. Their houses were burnt. Where can they live? Some people pitched tents on Shanghai Road and on the ground opposite to the campus.

Last night, soldiers were dispatched here to guard the campus. As a matter of fact, there is no need for their presence. Besides, when they are here, we have to serve them. Vautrin dares not to offend them. We have provided them with two stoves for fires, yet it is not enough for them because they love to make large fires with wood and are used to burning people's houses. They are not happy to have only two small stoves to keep warm. Their real motive of coming here is not to guard the campus, but to investigate whether the refugees have left. At first, Miss Vautrin went to the Japanese consulate to report their soldiers' crimes. Now she seldom does so. I asked her not to because the more you report, the more they would hate you. Now those Western gentlemen [of the Safety Zone] have filed reports of the Japanese soldiers' bad deeds to their consulate. No matter how the Westerners file complaints, Japanese soldiers still continue to commit crimes. Now that the American consul is here, it is more effective to let him report certain things to the Japanese consulate.

Saturday, January 8

From Vautrin's Diary

Cold today and no sunshine. People without enough bedding and clothing will begin to suffer. Although conditions outside are not too settled, yet more and more are going home. Only about 5000 refugees left on the campus now. Tao, our neighbor to the west, who has been living with his family at East Court, came back this morning saying it is impossible even for a man to stay in his district now for the soldiers come in at any time and demand money. If they can give no money then they insist that a "hwa gu niang," or young girl, be found for them. There is nothing left in his house, he says—he went home with hope he might save his doors and windows. This afternoon we could see fires in three directions from our campus—this means that looting continues.

Searle shared his radiogram from Elsie,[23] in which she mentions having received my radiogram. She also says that on January 16th the U. of N. [University of Nanking] office and staff go to Chengtu. We long to hear from our Wuchang Unit—are fearful for their safety. Have no idea where Dr. Wu is. It is a great relief to have three Americans over at our Embassy.

In the middle of the afternoon, Takatama, from the Japanese Embassy, called to have me put in a claim for our losses—college and individual Americans. He had an interpreter with him, who made it clear they would not consider Chinese faculty losses. The college losses have been so small that I said I would not enter them—perhaps six smashed doors in all. As to personal losses, Alice Morris is the only one who has lost anything. All the possessions of other foreigners were in attics at South Hill Residence, which were not discovered—or have not been discovered yet. Having Takatama in my debt yesterday by presenting him with ten eggs for the entertainment of American Embassy representatives, I made bold to ask his help in letting our soldier guards know, in the most tactful way, that if they would guard on Hankow and Ninghai Roads, we would be responsible on the campus. Last night between 9–10 two of the guards went to our chicken yard and scared the servant within an inch of his life.

Rumors are spreading like wild fire. It is said that Chinese troops are within a short distance of city; that Japanese troops are trying to borrow Chinese civilian clothes so they can disguise and escape, etc. I can admit that civilian clothes may be desired, but I know of one or two other motives that are probably much nearer the truth. When I asked Takatama when Nanking would be peaceful enough for refugees to return to their homes, his answer was, "in about two day." Women who have come in from the country say conditions for them have been fearful—they have literally had to bury themselves to be safe at all.

From 4–5 Mr. Wang, Mrs. Tsen and I went in a car over to Miss Gray's[24] to look up Wang Szi-fu. Never have I seen such a mess as her house! Most of her things are out in the yard. We did not find Wang either alive or dead, and surmise he went to Wuhu before December 13. Later, we went down to Sin Giai Kou [Hsin Chieh Kow]. Many shops on both sides of the main street (Chung Shan Road) have been burned, and all the remaining seem to have been looted. Saw two trucks out in the road on which loot was being loaded.

After our fellowship meeting from 6:30–7:30, Mr. Wang, Mrs. Twinem and I went down to the gate house to see the guards—they are changed every day. Our main purpose is to let them infer that we are on duty inside the campus.

From Tsen's Diary

Some of the refugees have returned to their homes. Now there are only five [thousand] people left. However, some of the returnees came back again because the Japanese soldiers went to their homes. The places where these people returned are not their original homes, but the housing in the Safety Zone. People dare not go back to the south side of the city, because finding women, forcing labor, grabbing money, and looting by the Japanese soldiers are still prevalent outside. For eight or nine days, the soldiers have not come here to find women.

This afternoon, Vautrin and I went to Fu Hou Kang on the other side of the Chinese school to visit the Westerners' residences. Miss Gray's house had been guarded by our worker for the Westerners, Mr. Wang. We had no idea if Wang was still there. When we got there, we could not believe the chaos. This is the first time when I witnessed a place being looted. Things were littered everywhere on the ground: good items were all taken away, and some were broken. At first, we were afraid that Wang might have died inside, and we walked slowly into the house. There was no one there. We presumed that he might have fled. Outside, the yard was covered with things. Sadly, Miss Gray is a naturalized Chinese, and none of her lost things will be compensated. All other Westerners have listed their things being looted by the soldiers and asked the Japanese for compensation.

From Miss Gray's home, we first went to the Drum Tower and Chung Shan Road and then to Hsin Chieh Kow. On the way, we saw no Chinese, but the Japanese devils were walking there. Buildings and stores were burnt and looted. It's extremely pathetic. In the vicinity of Hsin Chieh Kow, there were soldiers moving things with trucks. Some of them were searching for things. There are troops stationed there. At first, we wanted to go to other places to see how things were, but we did not go because there were too many soldiers.

This is the first time we went to that area to see how things are. There are many people on the section of Shanghai Road near our area, but no one on the section adjacent to Canton Road. Because there are many peddlers selling old stuff lying on the ground, most of it looted. Also some sell salted foods. Some are very cheap. We dare not to buy any, nor do we want to buy the stuff which was looted.

Today, Vautrin received a telegram from Miss Pi[25] at Hankow. We had no news from her for a month.

Sunday, January 9

From Vautrin's Diary

Sunshine, but quite cold. One half inch of ice on ponds. No refugees sleeping in covered ways and verandahs, but some still in halls. Many come for the night and go to their homes for the day. Many of the problems of poor Searle at the University, Sericulture Building, and middle school we have not yet had—i.e. quarreling among Chinese in charge, and then one side reporting to the Japanese. Also bringing in of loot by refugees and then quarrels over it ensuing. Also the problem of spies within.

Mr. Wang, Mr. Li, Miss Hsueh and I went to Drum Tower to church service. You cannot imagine the dense crowd of people on Shanghai Road, mainly in the section between Ninpo Road (American Embassy) and north to Gin Ying Giai [Chinying Street]. On both sides of the road are hundreds of venders now starting up small shops. I'm sorry to say that most of the things they are selling are loot from shops. Our servants are beginning to buy it too, for the temptation is great. Church service was good, and about fifty people were out. You see much traffic on Chung Shan Road now, mainly Japanese trucks and cars. Also many soldiers in the section outside the Safety Zone.

Mrs. Twinem helped at 2 o'clock women's meeting. The South Studio was filled. Miss Lo has [had] charge of the meeting. We also have a Thursday meeting for women. Tonight at the servant's meeting the South Studio was packed, probably by many who came out of curiosity.

Fourteen of us attended the English service at 4:30. John Magee led. Mr. Espey[26] of the Embassy attended and for the first time I really learned that the U.S.S. Panay was sunk and at the same time two Standard Oil boats. It seemed to be a deliberate act on the part of Japan—why, I cannot understand. In all my contacts with Japanese soldiers and officers they seem friendly to the Americans, but invariably warn me against Russian and English. We are rejoicing over the fact that three British officials arrived today[27]—that now makes six additions to our numbers, which means more stability.

Nice Mrs. Tsen "looted" Eva's [Eva Spicer] house today—which by the way has not been entered once—and having found some extracts she had our old cook Chen Ben-li make a cake, which we had at supper. She [Tsen] intended to give it to No. 3 P.T.H.[Ping Tsang Hsiang] but when we told her they had a good cook, and often had cake and cookies, she let us have the cake. Mary and I are going to have him make some mince pies before long—for Mary found that they had not taken the mincemeat from her house.

Dr. Trimmer[28] says that a Japanese store has been opened on Chung Shan Road. Mr. Riggs spends all his time delivering coal to the rice kitchens, and Mr. Sane [Sone] spends his time delivering rice. Had it not been for their toil I suspect many would be starving.

From Tsen's Diary

Today is the first time for me to accompany Vautrin to No. 3, Ping-Tsang Lane to attend the English service. I was the only Chinese, and the rest were all Americans. Rev. Magee preached. In the afternoon, an American gunboat arrived and three people went ashore. Actually, four people came with the gunboat, but the Japanese only allowed three of them to go ashore because they only applied permission for three. They had no other way out but to comply. At the gate of the consulate there are Japanese soldiers as guards. When the consulate people come out, they are followed by the soldiers. They cannot come and go freely.

To the soldiers who guard our front gate, the two stoves of fire which we provided are not adequate. They sit at the front gate and burn fire wood, which I have spared for one month's cooking because there is no way we can buy coal. All the fire wood is probably not enough for them to burn, so we have to cut trees. It is very difficult to reason with them. They do not care about anything. If they want fire wood, you have to give it to them quickly. Otherwise, they just go ahead to burn furniture. They are very fierce and so mean that some of the workers dare not to approach them.

Today, it has been one month since refugees came to our campus. During the past several days, there were four more births and two miscarriages. Today, we slaughtered and ate Mr. Yuen's goat. Now, we, too, learn to rob from others. Mr. Yuen is not here, so it gives us a good opportunity to "rob."

Monday, January 10

From Vautrin's Diary

What a wonderful day it has been—especially its closing hours. At supper time, I found a fat letter from Ruth [Chester] waiting for me, dated January 5th, and evidently brought up by the British Embassy people. In it there was a letter from Dr. Wu of December 20 from Hankow, and a carbon of Florence's [Florence Kirk] letter to Miss [Rebecca] Griest of January 3. Right after supper we gathered around the round table in our sitting room and read and read. It is great to know that the Shanghai Unit is growing stronger, and that four new faculty have arrived and more are expected. And after the reading of Dr. Wu's and Ruth's letters how we discussed our Ginling plans! At the present moment the idea of starting a middle school on our campus is quite out of the question, but starting an industrial school for women whose husbands have been ruthlessly killed seems a great need and a real possibility. This morning Mrs. Tsen and I discussed encouraging the starting of a primary school at Ming Deh,[29] but even that may not be possible—but we shall see.

After our feast of news, Mary and I went down to the gate house to get acquainted with our new guards and try to impress them with the fact that we would be responsible with the inside of the campus if they would patrol Hankow and Ninghai Roads.

Later Mrs. Tsen came down with some cake—think of it—some home-made cake! Yesterday she "looted" Eva's cupboards, and today we had roast goose and cake as the result. Really too much of a feast in one day. Before Mrs. Tsen left we read aloud Florence's good letter to Miss Griest. Most of our unanswered questions are now answered and we feel quite caught up on outside news. By candle light Mary and I have eaten a good share of the cake. We wondered if we should save it for the future—but decided against that as we are in a hopeful frame of mind tonight.

Before 4 o'clock this afternoon I took a number of letters to the American Embassy to take to Shanghai for us. Think of it! There are now foreign officials in the city—three American, three English and three German.[30] Life seems almost normal, although the smoke in the distance this afternoon is a mute testimony of continued looting, and not far from our campus this morning two girls were raped.

This afternoon four soldiers came to look around but they were quite likable. The head traded stamps with me and proudly showed me the picture of his wife and baby. I wish we could turn all our enemies into friends and help them to see themselves as they are.

From Tsen's Diary

One child developed strep throat, and the hospital refused to accept him. I have no other alternative than to move him to the laundry room of #500 Building. The child got this disease in such cold weather when he was forced to stay in a cold place. The child's mother is here by herself with five children. I'm afraid that it will be difficult to save the child's life. There are others sick. Some only have diarrhea and are cured after taking castor oil. Some are coughing and have a fever. Since I do not have cough medicine for children, I have to purchase some from the hospital. I ask the patients to go to the hospital. Yet, some of them cannot afford to go, and some are afraid to go outside of the campus. They want to seek treatment here because it is free of charge and also nearby. Besides, they can come whenever they want to, and they do not show up at the scheduled time.

The child who had strep throat died. And his sister has also contracted the disease. All together, fifteen children and four adults passed away, two seniors and two middle-aged. The weirdest thing is that these people were not sick but simply died after a night of sleep. They had no symptoms whatsoever the night before. Yet, they were not too strong and so frightened by the Japanese. Also, during this month, they did not have much nutritious food to eat. They died of shortness of breath. All told, twenty-six babies were born.

The most delightful thing is that we received letters from Tsai [Ruth Chester] and Thurston in Shanghai. They also enclosed a copy of President Wu's letter to them. To us, receiving the letter is like acquiring a most valuable treasure because we have not received any letters for a long time. These letters were transported by the American gunboat. Now it is much more convenient. I heard that the German gunboat also came, and three Germans went ashore.

With the return of representatives from various nations, the Japanese have to restrain a little bit on certain things in order to save face. So, the situation here on the surface is improving some.

Now the Japanese have plainclothes security people and also Chinese traitors. They are very tricky. They dress in Chinese clothing to go to private residences to rob, and they claim that they are Chinese. Sometimes, their soldiers ask Chinese people to rob for them, and then they bayonet the victims to death in order to let other foreigners see that it was the Chinese, not they who robbed. On the one hand, they use trickery to kill the Chinese people, and on the other, they let other foreigners believe that the Chinese were the culprits. Yet, this time their dirty trickery was no longer working because their mask has been detected by other foreigners.

5

→ ·— ·— ◆—— ·—·

LIFE AND PROBLEMS INSIDE THE GINLING CAMP

Tuesday, January 11, 1938

From Vautrin's Diary

You cannot quite understand how grateful we are for these nights of peace—when we can properly prepare for a night of rest and feel reasonably sure all will be well on the campus for our large group of women refugees. For the last few nights we have had a guard of five newly appointed military police and before that for eight nights we had our [Japanese] Embassy police each night at the gate house. Our regular night watchman supplemented by our two former police, now in civilian clothes, whom we have turned into night watchmen, keep watch on the campus. Before that for five nights we had a large group of ordinary soldiers for guards (about 25 men)—and they worried us not a little, for in spite of all we could do they insisted on guarding the inside of the campus as well as the outside. The first night they were with us two of our refugees were raped and it was soon after that that we secured Embassy police. There were only seventeen "hsien bing" (military police) for the whole city; had there been more conditions would have been much better, for they seem like a much higher grade of military men. A few that I have met seem unusually fine.

From 9 to 12 this morning F. Chen and I were down at headquarters of the International Committee. For the first time all heads of refugees camps were called together. It was an excellent meeting. Mr. Rabe was with us at first, and expressed his deep appreciation of work done by the persons responsible for the various camps—about twenty camps, I should say—and there were about 35 present. Our difficult problems were shared and discussed. As usual Ginling's problems are much simpler than those in the camps where they have both men and women. Bad men in those camps—opium smokers, gamblers, etc., create many problems.

At 3 P.M. took a package of letters over to our Embassy. I finally persuaded Mrs. Tsen to write a letter to Mrs. New[1]—she has not felt like writing one before.

From 4 to 5 I was in my office and many women came in, imploring me to help them find their husbands. In some cases they have been gone for weeks—since December 14 in fact. It is too cruel to tell them I think their husbands will never return, but that is true of many of the younger men who were taken. They were shot during those terrible first days.

This evening after supper I went to the gate with Mr. Wang to talk with our guard. We feel it is wiser to get the name of the head of the group and to let them know we feel responsible for order inside the campus. The sky to the northeast is all aglow. Another house being burned.

After that I went with Miss Hsueh to take the census in the Arts Building. In my original estimate I assigned about 490 to that building, and some people thought I was crowding them. At our peak I'm sure there were 2000 in one building.

From Tsen's Diary

Another child died of strep throat. Fortunately, no one in other rooms contracted the disease except the brother and sister.

This afternoon, I was deadly busy with the dead and the new born. I had to get a coffin for the dead and deliver the one to be born. As a matter of fact, I found out that there are still some people in the dead child's family here so I refused to get the coffin for him. And later, the family members carried a coffin to the campus. As to delivering the baby, I found a midwife to attend the woman giving birth.

In the afternoon, the members of the International Committee joined in the meeting by the Self-ruling Committee to discuss the problems about ordering the refugees to return home. Some of them have no place or house to return to. As to those who had returned, the Japanese soldiers went to their homes to search for girls and forced the men to labor for them. Who would dare to return home? The Japanese military district is in the city, not outside of it, and the Chinese people have no freedom to walk around. The Self-ruling Committee wanted to discuss with the Japanese enlarging the refugees' section and allowing the refugees to pitch tents in the Safety Zone. Now there are already quite a few tents pitched. Many peddlers on Shanghai Road have pitched tents; some looked as if they are building houses. There were so many people there that the road is simply impassable and also the tents made the road much narrower. If people come back here now, you will not be able to recognize it. Now so many people are unemployed, and they just wander around on the street. If people have no food to eat for a long time, they will become cannibals. The Japanese soldiers rob the Chinese people's rice and flour to sell for money. Also, they demand the Chinese people buy food from them; buy their military tickets first and then use the tickets to buy flour. Their tricks are plenty. It is cheaper to buy flour with their gray colored military tickets. People are greedy to make money and buy flour from the Japanese. So many of them fight and grab each other for the chance to buy the flour, and some of them are beaten by the Japanese soldiers. The Japanese like to sell flour to young girls. Some of them buy cheaper flour and sell it much higher. So, young girls often dress up and go to buy flour from the Japanese. Many people sell tobacco and cocaine. There are quite a few Chinese consumers. What future will the Chinese have?

Wednesday, January 12

From Vautrin's Diary

It is much colder and we are afraid it will snow. We want to get the night soil cleaned from behind the buildings if at all possible, for the snow would but scatter it. Unfortunately we cannot get lime anywhere, so we do not have that as a disinfectant. It has been impossible to get all the women to empty their toilet buckets in the holes we have had dug for this purpose. Since the rice is being service [served] twice each day outside of the campus, and since registration has stopped, the college servants have a little more time for cleaning.

This morning about 7 A.M. I saw what looked like 9 Chinese planes flying toward Giyung [Chuyung].

From 10 to 12 Mr. Wang spent in the guest room in Arts Building taking down data from women whose husbands or sons are still missing. This afternoon I sent this data over to Mr. Fukeeda [Fukuda]. Let us hope he will be able to do something. The number of people asking for the red tickets which permit free rice is increasing, partly because people have used up the money they had, and partly because poor people are coming in. A large number are also asking for bedding.

This afternoon Mr. Wang, Mr. Djao, Mr. Hsia, Mr. Chan and I went over to the temple north of the American School to see if we could get some rice for their use and for college use. We could get the rice but had no way to get it transported. Down the crowded Shanghai Road we saw scores of venders at side of road selling looted materials—clothing, bedding, cloth, dishes of all kinds, vases, brassware, etc[.]; and we also saw men carrying wood to use as fuel—parts of good wooden beds, window frames, doors, furniture. All the lawless elements are at work and there is no restraint. Naturally the Chinese police—the few that are left have no power and the few Japanese military police cannot restrain their own soldiers much less the "lao beh sing" (populace). Many people are going back to their homes from the Safety Zone even before it is safe, for that is the only way to save the frame work of their houses and doors and windows and floors.

Mrs. Tsen, F. Chen and Mary Twinem are laid up with colds today. Everyone has worked too hard and the strain has been terrific.

George Fitch and Lewis Smythe called this evening to bring me some butter— from the manager of the Met. Hotel[2] which is now a Japanese headquarters of military police. It is none too fresh, but it is butter.

This evening when Mr. Wang and I went to get acquainted with our new guard of four, we found them very intelligent and friendly. The sergeant is a graduate of a middle school. Each evening we make a point of getting the name of the head of the group. I think all will be peaceful tonight. I still keep my fountain pen in my tooth brush holder instead of in my table drawer.

From Tsen's Diary

Quite a few older refugees returned home. The younger ones who have returned home came back [to the campus] again. I do not have a definite number. Few people want to handle business here. Nor do Chen Fei-rung and Mr. Li want to work hard. I have no idea if they are too disappointed with the situation here to do anything.

This winter is not very cold. It only snowed once, not too heavily, but it melted immediately. Today is cloudy, very windy, and cold. I'm afraid that it's going to snow. So many people here have colds with coughing. Only a few physicians are at the Drum Tower Hospital; there are not many patients there. Most of us have colds and are coughing. When spring arrives, more people will become sick.

If it snows, vegetables and food will be more expensive. Now we do not serve rice porridge to the refugees inside the campus. They need to get it from outside [of the campus gate], and the order is improving a little bit. It is more convenient for the Red Cross workers to run the rice kitchen and make money. For those refugees who have money, they pay for the rice porridge from their own pockets. For those who do not, they are given a red slip attached to them and are given free food by the servers. All have gone through investigation to determine if they are indeed poor. Yet, some of them are not genuinely poor.

Last time, we received three goats. One was eaten by the sick workers, and we only ate one. Because the workers at the rice kitchen claimed that the goats were given to them, we let them eat the third one.

Thursday, January 13

From Vautrin's Diary

A month ago today the city was entered. Some progress made:—Looting and burning less, slightly more sense of security, only a few soldiers—especially in Safety Zone, raping of women practically stopped in the Zone. Outside we only hear talks and do not know facts. Looting going on, not only by soldiers but also by "beh sing" [civilians].[3]

Spent goodly part of morning trying to work out problem of five young women—short course nurses—who came to us for shelter and protection. Did not feel we could take them all—endanger them as well as other refugees. Selected five camps, including our own, and let them draw lots. Later wrote letters of introduction for them and sent a servant with them. Wu [Wei], our messenger boy, since his bitter experience, is afraid to go outside our gate.

This afternoon spent almost four hours trying to get rice delivered to the college. Finally succeeded in getting in twelve bags. The International Committee has given over the handling of it to the Autonomous Government and they are having all sorts of difficulties. They have had their sales depot over near Hillcrest but now will be forced to move it out of the Safety Zone—why, we do not know. They are now getting rice from the Japanese—formerly Chinese military rice. Heard Mr. Riggs say that today he went to seven coal shops and there is no coal to be had. Fuel is a growing problem. Houses and furniture will increasingly be used for fuel unless somehow it can be brought in from outside.

Food that will keep people well is also a problem. Practically no green vegetables left anywhere in the countryside. With 70,000 soldiers living off the land for a time there are few or no chickens, pigs, or cows left. Donkeys are being killed for meat, and horses also. Some one saw horse meat for sale today. An effort is being made to get beans, peanuts, and green things from Shanghai.

Mary, Mrs. Tsen and Blanche still in bed with colds, and Mr. Chen up, but not out.

Two hundred attended Miss Lo's meeting for women this afternoon—the fact that there was to be a meeting was kept very quiet. Wish there was a good person here who could give whole time to this work.

[Note: There are no entries in Tsen's diary for January 13 and 14 because she was sick.]

Friday, January 14

From Vautrin's Diary

Again we are having sunshine and fairly warm weather—an untold blessing is continued.

I have spent the day trying to get twenty-eight bags of rice from a storehouse in temple near Hillcrest to the college. If Riggs cannot secure a truck for us we shall have to spend the day transporting by means of a wheelbarrow and a heavy cart. Just as we had given up hope at about 3 P.M., Riggs turns up with it.

This morning at 11:30 Mr. Wang and I again went to gate house to get acquainted with our new guard. The head man is a farmer, another a mechanic and still another works in a munition factory. We feel that this method of getting acquainted, although it takes time, is worthwhile, and thus far our various guards have caused us no trouble. We would feel much better if they would select four good guards and make them our permanent guard instead of changing each day.

The electric light is now on in at least one section of the city, and we are beginning to hear radio messages again. News has come of a great concentration of Chinese and Japanese forces near Hiuchowfu [Hsuchow].[4] How I pity the common folk in that district!

Tried to purchase a live pig today, but was told by a man who knows that there are none for scores of miles around Nanking. Horse meat, mule meat and even dog meat are on sale but not pork or beef.

Radiogram from Elsie [Priest] today saying Dr. Wu is in Chengtu.

When conditions become peaceful—if they ever do—somehow I would like to reward our watchdog at the Practice School with a "distinguished service medal" of some kind. He certainly is a faithful night watchman.

This afternoon and evening saw two large fires—one in the northwest and the other to the east. Looting and burning, its aftermath, continue. A fearful amount of loot is appearing on streets. The lower elements of the population are having their opportunity—those elements that are released when the police force are not present.

A military police and a common soldier were found looting in a foreign house today.

Saturday, January 15

From Vautrin's Diary

Between six and seven this morning, ten planes went over Nanking to the southwest—and we thought with dread of the bombing that we thought would probably occur in Kuikiang [Chiukiang],[5] Hankow or Chengsha [Changsha][6] a few hours hence. The planes were all lighted and looked as gay as if they were carrying a merry group of passengers off for a holiday.

(This morning Jan Yung-gwan, the Chinese ex-preacher who interpreted for the Japanese military official at the time of registration two weeks ago, came quietly into my office alone this morning and I think wanted to ask if he and his family could come and live on the campus, and he [would] help with evangelistic work. It seems that he is now in danger, due to fact that the above mentioned military man married a young Chinese woman living in his home and other officials do not approve of the marriage, through jealousy or other better reasons, and so they are not pleased with Jan. Evidently he is enough afraid and thinks it best to move from his present location and to give up his present work. How much of his story to take as authentic I do not know.)

Forster came in this morning and says his workers can give us five days a week for meetings. We must work out the plan; they will prepare the topics, and give the talks. Will begin meetings on Monday next. He also reported to me that Chen Yueh-mei's[7] piano and victrola have been taken, as well as their beds.

This afternoon I reported to Japanese Embassy the cases of twenty-six women whose husbands or sons have been taken and have not returned. In every case the husband had not been a soldier, and in many of the cases he was the only wage earner in a large family. I wonder how many of these men were killed in those first ruthless days of slaughter. Every shot I heard in those days I felt meant the death of some man—probably innocent.

For the first time in many days a soldier came onto our campus—paid no attention to gateman and was found by me entering a room in southwest dormitory where there were refugees. He was willing to leave when I escorted him out.

Had a gift today from the American Embassy—two chickens and some eggs. They got them from farmers who came up to side of the U.S.S. Oahu. Also received the good news that our case of valuables has probably been recovered in toto—by a Russian diver from the sunken U.S.S. Panay. They cannot raise the boat, as it is fast being buried by silt in the bottom of [the] Yangtze. For Mrs. Thurston's sake I'm especially glad as her wedding silver was in it—she had left it in the college vault.

Tonight Rabe, Kruger [Kroeger],[8] Magee, Bates, Smythe, Bauer, Trimmer, Mills and I were guests at [the] Japanese Embassy. We had a pleasant evening and our lips uttered jokes, though often our hearts were heavy. I think it was worthwhile to come to know each other better. Tanaka, Fukuda and Fukuei[9] were the hosts. The dinner was as international as the group, being Chinese, Japanese and western foods.

We have no guard at the gate tonight. May all be well with us!

From Tsen's Diary

January 13, 14, and 15: Because I'm sick and bedridden, I have not written anything in the diary. No accidents happened outside. It is usually unavoidable to have the Japanese soldiers coming. Yesterday the Japanese devils did not come. However, the situation is better than before. The refugees still come and go. No more Japanese guards at the front gate. Probably all left and were suddenly transferred to the front to fight.

There is bean curd for sale, 240 cents for one square. It is really expensive. Today, another child died.

Sunday, January 16

From Vautrin's Diary

Again the blessing of a warm sunshiny day. The snow which has been threatening seems to have changed its mind about coming. As usual early this morning we heard many planes start out on their work of destruction of cities and railways. The campus is such a busy place these days—women washing clothes and hanging them on every shrub and tree; others going out to the rice kitchen for soft rice gruel; still others going home for the day who expect to come back for the night. The big road leading out of the campus always seems crowded. We still do not let men in on the campus and they accept the regulation as reasonable for they know we are trying our best to protect their women and children—and their words of appreciation show how grateful they are for that. Fires continue every day but not as many as formerly.

You should see Ninghai, Hankow and especially Shanghai Roads. Little shops are now being built along the sides and there are literally hundreds of people selling everything from food to looted garments and dishes; fish, 40 cents per pound; cabbage, 10 cents; carrots, 3 cents; etc. Prices are gradually going down. Not many soldiers now in Safety Zone. The University and our guard have been withdrawn. Church this morning was well attended. Mary stayed at home this morning while I went to Chinese church, and I stayed home this afternoon while she went. Searle came home with her and I gave him a bunch of Ruth's and Florence's letters to read. He does not know where his wife is. She was supposed to leave Japan the first week in January but she has not arrived in Shanghai.

This afternoon our servants finished making a net, and later we took 23 fish out of one of our ponds. Three of them were 4-pounders. We shall share with our friends as well as have enough for servants and staff. There are still some big ones left in the pond, for we saw them escape from the net.

Tomorrow we are beginning a series of evangelistic meetings. Tonight distributed 200 tickets to those in Recitation Hall who really want to go. Not admitting children and do not want people to go just out of curiosity.

The new rulers have large posters now posted outside the Safety Zone urging people to go home. The picture shows two soldiers, a farmer, a mother and children. The soldiers seem very friendly and kind, and the people in the picture seem very grateful to their benefactors. The words imply that the people should go to their homes, and all will be well. Surely there is less tension in the city and many people, especially old ones, are experimenting on going home. At first they go only during the day and if nothing happens they remain. Young women are still very much afraid.

From Tsen's Diary

Last night, the Japanese consulate invited the members of the International Committee for dinner. Vautrin was also invited. I think the Japanese invited them as "kitchen gods" because the Japanese want these people to say good things about them.

It has been cloudy for three days with a little bit of light snow. Today it is sunny. Now we have meat to eat, and so do the workers. They eat whatever we do, but there are more of them.

Monday, January 17

From Vautrin's Diary

Raining today. The sunshine which has been such a blessing has left us. Mud-bed—you should see buildings.

For several nights now we have not had a soldier guard at the gate, nor even an Embassy police. Last Saturday I reported this at Japanese Embassy but nothing has been done about it. Not many soldiers seen in Safety Zone. Unfortunately the Chinese police now have little power.

Wasted whole morning. No creative energy left. Have many things to do but cannot seem to get them done.

This afternoon at 2 we began a series of meetings at which the workers from the Episcopal Church are helping us. Five days a week they will come and give the same talks to five different groups. Last night in the Arts Building we distributed 200 tickets to the women who really wanted to come. They are not to bring children, and no girl under 14 is to come. They were so orderly and the ushers had no difficulty with them. They learned to sing the simple hymn very quickly and very well. Tonight we distributed 200 tickets to the women in the Science Building and they will come tomorrow afternoon. They listened most attentively this afternoon. The South Studio was well filled. I am so glad there are enough workers in the city to carry on such meetings. Have sent to Shanghai to N.C.C.[10] for new tracts.

Tonight we have been watching the great clouds of smoke to the south— probably outside the south gate. At times the dark sky is aglow with the flames. Destruction still continues. How much of Nanking will remain depends on how long the looting by soldiers and populace continues. People are being urged to return to their homes but how dare they do so. The older women are gradually going, but the young girls remain.

No soldiers have come to campus today. Mary and Mr. Forster went down to South City and also to the Foreign Cemetery. The latter has sustained no other injury than a hole in the surrounding wall. Of all the streets they visited Tai Ping Road seems to be the most completely and ruthlessly destroyed.

A month ago tonight the 12 girls were taken from our campus. Will we ever forget the horror of that might?

From Tsen's Diary

Outside, law and order is not yet restored. The refugees still dare not return home. Now we have over 5,000 here. Fortunately, the Japanese soldiers who had been here were all transferred out. Yet, the newcomers always molest the people; looting, burning, and searching for girls. Some older refugees went home, but the Japanese soldiers demanded young girls from them. If they replied they had no girls, the soldiers would order them to find girls. If they refused, they would be bayoneted to death. Therefore, even the old men dare not return home.

Starting today, we have sermons for the refugees at 2:00 every afternoon. It is a good chance to invite people from the Episcopal Church to give sermons. Also, it is a good chance for the refugees to hear sermons to soothe their spirit and let them know that there is a real God in heaven.

Tuesday, January 18

From Vautrin's Diary

We hear that soldiers in [the] city have been changed. Four came this morning while I was out. Mary received them and took them around. She felt they were not very polite.

From 9–12 Francis Chen and I attended meeting of refugee camp heads at 5 Ninghai. Most of the time was spent discussing a questionnaire which is to be made out for the very poor—those who have had their livelihood taken from them.

Mr. Wang has been giving from 10–12 each morning to taking down data from women whose men have been taken and have not returned. We shall probably have to stop trying to take this data, as more than 100 came during the last two days, and today the crowd was so large that we are fearful that it may cause trouble. It seems that December 16th was the worst day. I fear many were shot, and even their bodies can never be found, as they were probably burned. So many feel that we can help them, but as a matter of fact we can do no more than hand in the names.

The evangelistic meeting was for women in the Science Building. About 160 attended. Again it was a very quiet, orderly meeting, and I feel sure many were helped. The pastors are inclined to make their talks too difficult. We have cleared out the Science Lecture Hall this afternoon and will begin meetings for children tomorrow at the same time.

Saw no fires today and heard few aeroplanes. People are still afraid to go back to their homes. Older women are being urged to try to go back for fear there will be nothing left—for looting is proceeding by the common people as well as soldiers. I wonder if the loot from homes in Nanking will eventually find its way to homes in Japan. Thinking I might save Mrs. Han Lih-wu's [Li-wu's] piano and victrola I asked Mr. Forster to investigate. He reported that both, together with beds, had been taken.

From 9–12 this morning I attended the second meeting of the heads of the refugee camps. Most of the morning was spent discussing a questionnaire which we are to use for those refugees who have no means of support. It will be difficult to do this fairly as many will desire help even if they do not really need it—the number who must be helped will be very great.

The weather is slightly warmer. As yet we do not have snow. We still have between five and six thousand refugees at Ginling. Mrs. Tsen who has been ill is now up but must stay in her room.

From Tsen's Diary

This morning, once again, three Japanese soldiers came to inspect. They come to Nanking to change guards. Their real motive for coming to the campus was to look for girls or to take things. They all are highwaymen. Every time the soldiers change guards, the civilians will subsequently suffer a new round of atrocities. Each day, we are living in fear. If we do not die physically, we will die of anger. I simply cannot look at the soldiers. As soon as I see them, I become angry. So I do not want to see them.

These past few days, we began to have meat in our diet. However, the diet is not good; yet, we have meaty dishes every two or three days. Under the circumstances, it is a really difficulty job for staff like me who are in charge of the board. Sometimes, we have meaty dish once daily; other times we eat only beans for two or three consecutive days. Yet, no matter what, we always have a dish of beans every day. Once, for more than a month, we did not have pork and beef to eat. Yet, we, including the workers, ate three chickens, ten geese, and two goats. Today, out of Miss Wu's[11] mercy, she sent a small chicken to us. I did not taste it. In the future, we have to pay for it. Naturally, we have to pay for the geese and chickens raised in our own school. If the Japanese soldiers did not want to take them away, we would not have eaten them. We have two Americans[12] working here, and there is no way that we would not let them eat a slightly better diet. It is alright for us to suffer, and the Americans do not have to remain here. Yet, Miss Vautrin has done a lot for us this time. If she was not here, we definitely would suffer more. Will there be any chickens alive here?

Yesterday, the Japanese embassy sent two chickens and twelve eggs to Vautrin. The eggs produced on the campus are only enough for them [Vautrin and Twinem] to consume. My small grandson has one egg each day. The rest of the eggs are saved for Miss Wu to breed new chickens. It's not bad for us to have this kind of diet, and we should not be considered as genuine refugees. I'm concerned that we may not have food to eat in the future. The good thing is that the International Committee will try its best to prevent it from happening.

Wednesday, January 19

From Vautrin's Diary

Rained steadily most of day. You can imagine what our roads are like. The tens of thousands of people who registered on our campus more than two weeks ago tracked in the earth and now the rain has turned it into mud. It is impossible to do anything with the buildings for the mud is being tracked in by thousands.

This afternoon we had two excellent meetings. About 170 carefully selected women from Central Building filled the South Studio. Miss Wang taught them the song and Mr. Paul Tang[13] gave the talk. The women came in and marched out in an orderly way, and, since no child under 14 was allowed to come, the meeting was very quiet. There is excellent attention. At the same hour we had a children's meeting, for children from 9–14 in the Science Building. About 150 came. They were so happy when they learned to sing the first verse of "This is My Father's World." And how they enjoyed the story Miss Hsueh taught them. It is a wonderful time for such meetings for everybody is hungry for comfort.

This morning Mr. Wang and Mr. Djao continue to receive the data from women whose husbands or sons have not returned. One woman had her husband and four sons taken and none have returned. So many women are imploring us to help them that we are afraid their coming may attract attention and bring danger to the college and its refugees.

We have heard no news from the outside world today. As you know we have no radio and we do not always get in touch with the few foreigners who do have—John Magee, The International Committee, The Hospital, and 3 Ping Tsang Hsiang. Mr. Kruger [Kroeger] came today to see us and says that no boat has come from Shanghai recently and he is not sure when he will be able to get out.

Tonight our group of workers met in Mrs. Tsen's sitting room and finished numbering and stamping the 1500 tags with which we expect to identify each of our refugees. We expect to sew the tag on the garment of the head of each family group. We do not want refugees to come to us from other refugee camps simply because it is more convenient here—we hear they are doing so. It will also help the men in charge of our Rice Kitchen to see that our people get their daily portion of rice.

It is 10:30 and my bedtime.

From Tsen's Diary

Today we ate fish, which Vautrin asked people to catch from the pond in the middle school. The ponds in the college are all so dirty that no one dares to eat [food from] them. We have not had fish for two months. This time, all personnel on the campus have fish to eat, even including people at the American embassy and No. 3 Ping Tsang Lane. All the Americans in Nanking live at No. 3 Ping Tsang Lane, not in their own homes. So, their own homes have been looted because they are not there; they stay in the office during the day time. These two days, it's not bad because we have a little bit of something to eat.

During the past two days, I did not step out of #400 Building because I was coughing and the weather was cold.

Today another child died.

Thursday, January 20

From Vautrin's Diary

Snowing today, but not too cold. You can imagine what buildings look like with mud and slush being tracked inside. Am not sure we shall ever be clean again.

Mr. Wang and Mr. Swen continue to write data for those women whose husbands or sons were taken and have not returned. One woman has just told me that her husband of 38 and son of 17 were both taken on December 16 and that only she and her little daughter are left. I doubt if she could have saved them had she stayed at home—those terrible days—but who knows? Mrs. Tsen does not think I should hand these in to Mr. Fukuda—that we must never forget that China is the hated enemy and Japan does not care how much she makes her suffer. In a day or two I will see Mr. Fukuda and tell him about the many women who are employing me to help them and ask if there is anything that can be done.

This morning I spent beginning a report to the Board of Founders.[14] So much has happened that it is difficult to condense into a brief report. In the midst of my writing I was called to my office to confer with a young Japanese officer who was about to leave Nanking and who wanted us to take two young Chinese girls, one of 20 and one of 14, who are now living over near the Wai Giao Bu.[15] He said it was quite unsafe for them to live there—which I thought interesting, since refugees are being urged to go home! I explained very clearly how uncomfortable it is here as a refugee and let him see how the women are living. It will be interesting to see if he brings them. I really hope they do not come. My guess is that he has become interested in the older girl and is afraid to leave her in her own home outside the Safety Zone.

A radiogram came from Rebecca today and was delivered to me from the American Embassy. Will send the answer tomorrow. Have been informed that our Embassy has a sending station now.

Meetings this afternoon were splendid. The one for the women was attended by about 170 and that for children by about 150. Tonight Mary and I distributed tomorrow's tickets in one of the dormitories and some of the women begged for them. We still have too many people on the campus to do anything constructive.

Those of you who remember Shanghai Road as wide would scarcely recognize it now. This afternoon I counted 38 newly constructed shops on the right side of Shanghai Road as I went between Hankow and Ningpo—the latter is just north of the American Embassy. Of course they are rudely made of either matting or wood but they seemed to be doing a thriving business in selling food or looted materials of various kinds. Some were tea shops and others were restaurants. Very few people are brave enough to live outside the Safety Zone as yet.

Mr. G——[?] of Red Cross Society said that when he went out to get rice on January 17 he saw great heaps of bodies of men outside the Han Chung [Hanchung] Road. The people in vicinity said they were brought there about December 26 and killed by machine guns. Probably the men who admitted at time of registration that they had been soldiers at one time and were promised work and pay if they confessed.

From Tsen's Diary

It has been cloudy for two days. Today begins to snow. Probably, tomorrow will be sunny. Telegram came from overseas via ocean. It's so much more convenient to have an embassy [the American] here. Vautrin sent out a telegram overseas on the sixth and received a reply today.

Two [Japanese] officers came to see Vautrin and wanted to send two girls here under her care. These two girls have worked [for the Japanese]. The officers will be transferred out of here shortly. Later, they sent the girls here by car. How can one believe that these two young girls really worked for them? The quilt covers they brought here are all good ones. They stayed there [the Japanese officers' place] for over thirty days, one for each officer. These two girls have no shame to come into the campus by car. Several refugees cursed them. Vautrin could not understand and, instead, praised the officers. They wanted Vautrin to know that because she received young women [at Ginling], they sent two more here. What can Vautrin do? It really makes one mad.

Friday, January 21

From Vautrin's Diary

Today the weather has been almost mild in spite of the snow on the ground. Mud is our problem now. The hundreds who go out to the Rice Kitchen to purchase rice and the other hundreds who bring in food to their relatives here, bring into buildings more mud than we are able to cope with.

Soon after the noon meal, as I was going over to the northwest dormitory to announce the afternoon women's meeting, several refugees came running toward me saying there were soldiers on the back campus. I went toward the back gate just at the right time, for four soldiers saw me and released three girls whom they had taken from the refugee huts that are near Farmer Tsu's house. The soldiers disappeared over the hill. A very short time later a group of military police came on the campus and I was able to report the incident to them. Still later two officers came—said they were stationed out at Nanking.

During the last few days sad, distraught women have reported the disappearance of 568(?) husbands or sons since December 13. They continue to hope that they have been taken off to work for the Japanese Army but many of us fear that their bodies are with the many charred ones in a pond not far from Gu ling Temple, or among the heap of unburied, half-burned bodies outside the Hau Djung Gate [Han Chung Gate]. On December 16 alone 422 were taken—and that is the report of women mainly on our campus. Many young lads of sixteen or seventeen were taken, and one boy of twelve reported as missing. All too often the one taken was the only bread earner in the family.

Our afternoon meetings for women and children continue. We are beginning on plans for a rehabilitation school for women without support.

At five went over to our Embassy and had a most satisfactory talk with Mr. John Allison, senior secretary. He is anxious for us to report any violation of American rights. Cannot convey to you what it means to poor old Nanking to have the official representatives of Germany, England and America back to plead and act in our behalf. Mr. Allison seems very understanding.

In the new newspaper that is being published called "Sin Shun Pao" [Hsin Shen Pao][16] in the January 8th number there is an article entitled "Japanese Troops Gently Soothe the Refugees. The Harmonious Atmosphere of Nanking City Develops Enjoyably." There are 25 sentences in the article, 4 sentences are true, one about the sun, the Drum Tower, military police and the position of the Japanese flag; one is half true, 19 are false and one is unknown to me. Not a very high score on a true-false test!

Sent a radiogram to Rebecca today.

Last night at En Tiao Hsiang [Er Tiao Lane] within the Safety Zone — soldiers went four times to the home of Mr.Wang's relative. They tried to take a young girl, who was able to make her escape, and three other times they did petty looting. You can see why we cannot persuade our women refugees to go home.

From Tsen's Diary

It is a clear day. Fewer Japanese soldiers are on the street. Yet, they still burn houses to make fires every day.

Today another child died. All together, eighteen have died. These couple of days, I only see a few patients because I do not feel well, and also there is no more medicine left. We need to buy some. I do not know where we can get the money. Further, it is much easier to walk on the street now, and there is a hospital on Hwachao Road for refugees, which is very inexpensive. If I send a note to the hospital, the refugees here can get free treatment. So, I asked them to seek treatment there. The Drum Tower Hospital is more expensive. Probably, all the medicine used at this refugee hospital was looted from other places or hospitals in the rear areas. It's a good cause to use the looted medicine for saving refugees' lives, better than being robbed by the Japanese.

At noon, once again, four Japanese soldiers came to find girls and ask them to take off their clothing. Actually, the soldiers wanted to molest the girls. Fortunately, Vautrin was at #700 Building to find refugees to attend the service, so she chased the soldiers away.

Every day, there is a service at noon. Two hundred people gather in the music room for the service, and the children are in the lecture room of #200 Building. Hsieh Yu-jen and Mr. Li led them in song and told them stories. These two adults were sent here by the Episcopal Church.

Today, there is one more refugee [newborn] here.

Saturday, January 22

From Vautrin's Diary

Cold but clear today. A goodly number of our young refugees from the immediate neighborhood are now going home for the day and coming back for the night. Two Japanese whom I have spoken to today said they hoped that by February it would be peaceful enough for all to go home.

This morning as I was trying to get a letter typed, four men came, an officer and three soldiers. One of the soldiers spoke English—said he had studied in a Mission School in Kobe. When I asked if he was a Christian he replied that he was not, but his wife was, and that his two children went to a Mission School. He interpreted for the officer. His first statement was that they were sorry for the things that had happened in Nanking and they hoped conditions would soon be better. Mr. Li and Mr. Wang took them around for inspection and then they came back to my office where I served tea. When the officer asked if soldiers came on the campus I had a good opportunity to say none had come today but yesterday four had come and started to take off three girls. He asked me to report this to the office of the military police which I was able to do this afternoon.

(Just previous to this a young officer brought in two Chinese girls whom he wanted to stay at our refugee camp. I really did not want to take them, but did not know how we could refuse them. The girl who is 24 years old was a student at one of our Mission Schools and knew Mrs. Gish[17] and Miss Kelly.[18] I will be glad to follow up this case later.)

This noon just after we started dinner, we received some packages of food from Shanghai and a fine bunch of letters—our first answers to letters written since December 13. Tonight after supper I read them all to the group and how glad they were to get news from the outside world. The food will be a most welcome addition to our limited diet. The letters were written January 16 or 17 and were brought up by a Domei truck.

This afternoon most of us spent several hours writing letters which I took over to the American Embassy by 6 P.M. They will go to Shanghai by a military train tomorrow—will be carried by Mr. Kruger [Kroeger], a German who is the first Nanking resident to get out of Nanking since the fall of the city, excepting the four foreign correspondents who left soon after December 13. Think of being shut up here for 37 days with little news from the outside world and little opportunity to send news out.

Conditions surely are improving at least in [the] Safety Zone. We no longer have that terrible fear of the night, and although we still use heavy curtains at our windows we at least do not thumbtack the edges and use only candle light.

John Magee came this afternoon with radio news.

From Tsen's Diary

Today, I'm really happy. We got letters from Shanghai. In addition, we received the salty meat sent by Miss Yen En-wen. It's really unexpected. Hwang [Chun-mei], Liu [En-lan], Wang [Ming-jen], and Yen[19] had arrived in Shanghai. In addition to Yen's salty pork, the other three sent us salty fish and fried pork. To have these delicacies is like receiving charcoals in the snow. Also, I received letters from my family [from Hupei].

We have not had delicious meat to eat for a long while. When we saw the meat, we all put on a happy face, in contrast to the long faces during the ordinary days when we had no good food to eat. When reading this page of my diary, one would know that everybody here is longing for delicious foods. Honestly speaking, receiving letters [from Shanghai] makes us even more elated than food. Things recorded in my diary are all unhappy except today. Some people also gave Vautrin foreign plums. Now, we share our belongings with each other. If one gets some food, we all will eat, not allowing only one to enjoy it. You see how fair we are.

Sunday, January 23

From Vautrin's Diary

An uneventful day. Weather quite cold. Mary went to church at Drum Tower this morning and I went to English service at 3 Ping Tsang Hsiang this afternoon. We still feel it better to have one foreign face on campus all of the time. Plumer Mills led the service this afternoon and his subject was "Being victorious even in tribulation." Surely it is difficult to be hopeful in days like these.

This morning the nephew of one of our refugees came over to see me. Said he returned yesterday after an absence of 34 days. He was taken on December 18 with about 400 others. He carried bedding to Changhsin[20] for a "dui-djang"[21] and also did his cooking for him. He worked for this officer eight days and then was released and told he could come back. On his return journey he got as far as Ihsing[22] when he was taken by another officer, who kept him until January 14. This second man liked him and was kind. When he let him go he escorted him outside the city gate and told him to keep off the main highway. It took him eight days to walk the 520 li back. Said that cities like Huchow had no "beh sing" in them and were about seven-tenths burned. Said that there was little left of Gwangdeh [Kwangde][23] for it had been fought over so long and fiercely. He reported that in one section the villages were being protected by the "Great Knife Society" from bandits, Chinese and Japanese troops. Said these men carried large knives on their backs and had a strange look in their eyes. Villagers respected them and burned incense for them as well as Kowtowed to them. He reported that towns like Li Shui, Li Yang,[24] [and] Ihsing were all practically destroyed, and it seemed to him it would take 30 years to rebuild them. The man said people along the way were very good to him and gave him food and let him spend the night in their homes. How I hope many more such men will be able to come back to their families.

Miss Wu Ai-deh, the Presbyterian evangelistic worker who works with Miss Hyde,[25] told the wonderful story of her escape at the women's meeting this afternoon. She was in hiding for about forty days from soldiers when they were looking for girls. She hid under piles of grass, in pig pens, on boats, in deserted houses, and finally hearing of Ginling she decided to try to come in. She disguised herself as an old woman, borrowed a little boy of six to carry on her back, borrowed a cane and trudged in. Each obstacle seemed to clear away, and she reached here safely, just as we were in the midst of a meeting. It was her voice that sang out so lustily that afternoon—and I wondered who it was. She is living on the north verandah of 500 [Building] with other refugees.

From Tsen's Diary

Today, two Japanese soldiers came, and there was no incident. In the afternoon, I went to Ping Tsang Lane to attend service. Rev. Mills presided and gave the sermon. Because of illness, I have not been outside for ten days. The situation outside has been improving. There are more tents pitched on Shanghai Road, all for conducting trade. [The same is true for] the area from Ninghai Road to Shanhsi Road. These two roads are the busiest. However, on Chungshan Road, there are no pedestrians except for the Japanese soldiers. You may say that even ghosts can beat people to death there. It's very much deserted, and looks very sad.

Monday, January 24

From Vautrin's Diary

This morning started typing informal report but did not get far when Mr. Forster came in with a good deal of news. He told us the facts about what happened at the Embassy last Saturday evening.

It seems that Mr. Allison and the others were at dinner, George Fitch and P. Mills being guests, when one of the servants came in and reported that two soldiers were in the #3 garage. Mr. Allison went out and he found them there playing mah jong.[26] He told them to leave, and later, as he returned to the dinner table, he felt he had perhaps been a bit severe, and wondered if he had done the right thing. He had no more than gotten seated when another servant came saying that his daughter had been taken—he and his family living in the #5 garage. Mr. Allison said surely he must be mistaken for he had just ordered the two soldiers to leave the compound. But the servant said it was a third soldier and that at first he had wanted his youngest daughter but the parents had absolutely refused. Mr. Allison then started out to look for the girl, and met her coming back. It seems that the soldier with the girl had been met by the two soldiers and the latter had said the he must let the girl go as he had taken her from the American Embassy. Although I do not wish to harm anyone, yet I have been glad about the shooting of Sir Kuat Hugeson,[27] the bombing of the Panay, with the wounding of the Italian and American officials, and the taking of the girl from the American Embassy. At least such things catch the attention of Japan and Western nations.

Our afternoon meetings continue.

Right after the noon meal I went to our Embassy for a car which took me to the Japanese Embassy. In a conversation with Mr. Fukuda, I told him of the large number of women who had been imploring me to do what I could to get back their men folk, some of whom were taken on December 13. He told me to bring him the data and he would do all he could, for he too felt sad about the situation. He will be surprised when I take him 532 data cards tomorrow.

When I was leaving our gate to go to the Embassy a young girl came up telling me that three soldiers had just entered her home and were carrying off young women. I went with her and found that the soldiers had already left, and the girls they had tried to get, being nimble and quick, had succeeded in getting out a back gate and running down to Ginling. As we walked back together the girl told me that when the soldiers first entered the city her father of sixty-seven and her little sister of nine had been bayoneted to death.

A good many aeroplanes—bombers—have gone westward today. Fires in the city are fewer, but they continue—one or two each day.

From Tsen's Diary

Recently, several children have contracted pneumonia. One died today. Perhaps they were too cold from sleeping on the ground. Anyway, it's better than sleeping in the straw tents outside the campus.

This afternoon, seven Japanese soldiers came; four of them gave talks. Probably they came to inspect, and left shortly.

Now we have started to conduct a survey to find out the poorest among the refugees and the ones who have no homes to return to. The Japanese ordered the refugees to return home. It seems that the International Committee would let the homeless stay here, but they have no way to control the matter. So, they have to conduct a survey of refugees and make a list. As a matter of fact, they know the refugees cannot go home now because Japanese soldiers are still committing crimes even in the Safety Zone, and there is no need to talk about the areas farther away from it. The soldiers commit crimes day and night. I heard people say that Shanghai suffered the same fate for six months. If the Japanese do not have bedding, they just take them from people's homes, and there is no end in sight unless the war ends. The civilians suffer to death, and they are furious but dare not seek redress or have no place to seek redress.

Tuesday, January 25

From Vautrin's Diary

We are adapting ourselves to new conditions. For a time we closely curtained all windows and covered all lights with black shades—now we think it wiser to have lights to show that a place is inhabited.

Last night two servants foolishly shut all windows and put a coal ball stove in their room. This morning they were unconscious from carbon monoxide.

Mrs. Tsen and I and all the others here worked to arouse them and by this evening they are considerably better.

From 9–12:30 there was a meeting of heads of Refugee Camps held at 5 Ninghai Road. If only there was an experienced social worker at the head of each camp or in each camp to study the needs, so that we could work constructively. It is so difficult to get at the true condition of each family, so easy to make people dependent instead of independent. Each camp is now working on an investigation of the most needy families. Encouraging word has come from Shanghai of funds raised, and of extra medicine like cod liver oil.

Wu Ai-djin, an evangelistic worker of the Presbyterian Church, who is a grateful and happy refugee here, started a phonetic class this morning for twenty girls. She is also helping with the afternoon meetings. If we had more workers and vacant classrooms we would begin some Bible classes.

This afternoon I took 532 blanks over to Mr. Fukuda and reported same at our Embassy. We also went to the secretary of the "Automatic Government"—the name given by Mr. Chen to the Nanking Autonomous Government, to see him about the possibility of excluding from the Safety Zones the shops that sell loot. The fact that hundreds of little shops are starting up along Ninghai and Shanghai Roads means that more and more looting is being done each day by the poor. They would not have dared to start it if the Japanese soldiers had not led the way.

How we devour the bit of news that comes to us each day from the foreign men. They very generously write down the broadcasts they hear and send them to us. How we wonder about the friends who evacuated to Hankow, Wuchang, Changsha, and Chungking.[28] It sounds from the broadcasts as if Chungking is having air raids, too. It all seems like a hideous dream—the scattering of friends, the breaking up of schools, the terrible destruction of life, and property. Can it be true?

Rickshas? I haven't seen one on the street since December 12, I believe it was. Many without tires or wheels can be seen hidden away but none are plying the streets. We walk, or go in cars.

Went with Mrs. Tsen over to Grace Chu's[29] home this afternoon—but not to a tea. The house is filled with refugees—and you cannot imagine the condition it is in. Mrs. Tsen brought home some of the things still left—most of her things are gone—radio, dishes, etc., some taken by soldiers and the rest by refugees.

From Tsen's Diary

Last time I saw meat but did not eat it until today. Today, I ate the salted meat sent by Miss Yen. About fifty days I have not eaten pork, and it tasted exceptionally delicious. We are the lucky kind of refugees and several times better off than other refugees.

Today, there is another newborn in #600 Building.

Today, I saw a refugee who told us that his next-door neighbors have two brothers. The younger brother's wife is more attractive than the older one's. One day, a Japanese soldier came to their home, and the brothers treated him cordially with tea and pastries. They thought the soldier would not molest their wives. Yet, they had no idea that he wanted to take away the younger brother's wife, who flirted with him and served him liquors. The soldier thought that the younger woman favored him and was willing to leave with him. Then, when the soldier was drunk, the two brothers beat him to death and threw his body outside at night. The following morning, they all fled to the Safety Zone. It's really great! To kill one [soldier] to vent our anger is also an awesome idea.

6

THE JAPANESE DEMAND TO CLOSE REFUGEE CAMPS AND VAUTRIN'S DEFIANCE

Wednesday, January 26, 1938

From Vautrin's Diary

Several bombers went westward again this morning and returned later this afternoon. They evidently start from Gi yung [Chuyung]. We are fearful for cities like Hankow, Wuchang and even Chungking.

A number of our refugees today have asked for bedding. Some of them have tried to stay at home but find soldiers are still coming in asking for bedding, and "hwa gu niang" (young girls). Mr. Wang's brother and mother-in-law had their bedding taken night before last—they are trying to live down in their home near Shui Hsi men [Shuihsi Gate].

This morning, and part of the afternoon, I have been trying to write a report "A Review of the First Month," but the interruptions are too many to do it justice. Sometimes in one paragraph I have three or four.

Having worked until almost five I decided to be bold and take a walk to the street west of Ginling—the one called Hu Gi Gwan [Hu Chu Kwan]. The houses were all closed and boarded up and the streets were almost deserted. The first person I saw was Mr. Atcheson's cook's mother. She is staying with an acquaintance across from her home—is afraid to enter her own home for fear the soldiers may come back. She keeps watch so the "lao beh sing" will not loot the little that remains. I went to the Gung [Kung] home—the one bestowed on that family by the first Ming Emperor.[1] It is a mass of charred wood and scorched tile and brick. The old caretaker came out to greet me, and gave what he thought was the cause of the burning. Soldiers had stolen a cow and taken it out to this house to cook it. Naturally they built a big fire in the middle of a room, and when they left they did not put it out. The charred wood and the skeleton of the cow verified the truth of his explanation. And thus one more interesting and historic landmark has gone.

When coming away from the ruins, I met a woman I know, and she asked me if I knew of the large number of bodies over in a pond in the Yang valley. I told her I had heard something of them and would like to go over, whereupon she offered to go with me. Soon we met her husband and he said he would go with me and my servant. We found the pond. At its edge there were scores of black charred bodies and among them two empty kerosene or gasoline cans. The hands of the men were wired behind them. How many bodies there were, and whether or not they were machine gunned first, and then burned, I do not know, but I hope so. In a smaller pond to the west were perhaps 20–40 more charred bodies. The shoes I saw on several men looked like civilian shoes, not soldiers[']. All through the hills are unburied bodies.

From Tsen's Diary

This morning several refugees came back [to the campus] because last night Japanese soldiers went to their homes. They dared not stay there and were afraid that the Japanese would return again.

Today, I went to see Hsieh Wen-chiou's house. Originally, I intended to see the place several days ago, but my illness prevented me from doing so. I heard that all belongings in the house had been stolen by people. Some were taken by the Japanese; most were taken by the refugees who had stayed inside. Because no one guarded the house and Old Liu was not willing to go there. Fortunately, the piano and refrigerator are still in a small room which is occupied by a refugee. When the Japanese soldiers came, they took away everything on the third floor. If I had not moved several beds and chests from the house, they would have all been stolen. The most despicable thing is that the refugees pour human waste in the bathtubs. Two bathtubs are full with stools. I was furious and scolded the refugees. There is not even a tea cup left intact in the house.

Thursday, January 27

From Vautrin's Diary

Aeroplanes have been very active today, many of them flying to the northwest—some of them heavy bombing planes. Rumors of all kinds are rife in the city, and some people feel that the Chinese soldiers are quite near. With the severe cold, soldiers who are underclad must be suffering.

The Swastika Society[2] gave us $300 today for vegetables and oil for the red-ticket or free-rice group—a China New Year gift.

We are planning to open a bath house in the bathroom of the northeast dormitory. It will mean extra work, but it will bring joy to many. Getting the coal will be the first problem, and getting reliable people to manage will be the second.

Have finished writing my "Review of the First Month." Interruptions have been innumerable, and tonight I feel it is not worth the time it will take to read it.

The vast amount of loot being brought into the Safety Zone worries me. At first the Zone saved lives, now it has become a haven for storing and selling loot. Streets are lined with little shops or stalls. It means that the "lao beh sing" are growing bold, and are going to all the houses outside the Zone and taking what they want to sell and to use. Mr. Sone said today that doors were being taken from his house just on the edge of the Zone. It seems to me that the Zone should prohibit the entrance of loot—but that would take more power than they have. Mr. McCallum says he is putting people into the Chung Haia [Hwa] School to save it from further looting. I wonder what the next few months will bring forth—for all the evil elements in society seem to have been released—as a bomb bursting in the sea would stir up all the dregs and filth.

From Tsen's Diary

These two days, we have been busy with the survey of the poorest of the refugees. The International Committee will allocate some money to help them.

Today, we ate the fried shredded pork and salted fish that were given by Liu En-lan, Hwang Chun-mei, and Wang Ming-chen. Now, we have delicacies to eat but are longing for more. Previously, when we had none to eat, we got by. These two days, no Japanese soldiers came here. My nerves are calmed down a little.

There is meat for sale on the street, but not plentiful. I heard it was eighty cents for a pound; even dead chicken sells for a dollar a pound. It is really too expensive. We cannot afford to buy it until the price drops. However, both the sellers and buyers on the street are robbed by the Japanese soldiers who encounter them.

Today, one child died and one was born.

Friday, January 28

From Vautrin's Diary

Much aeroplane activity all morning. Heavy bombers that are carrying death and destruction pass over our heads in a northwesterly direction. It seems to us here that all of China is being destroyed. I wonder so often what has happened to Lu Chowfu.[3]

Spent all morning working on letters to the outside world. We have an opportunity to get them off on U.S.S. Oahu if we get them to the American Embassy by 9:30 tonight. I will leave here by 5:30, for I do not go off campus at night—have not done so for years it seems—as a matter of fact since December 12.

This afternoon there was a meeting of heads of the districts in the Safety Zone called at the headquarters of the Automatic Society—the name used by Mr. Chen and which we think too exact to change. A Japanese officer was present. The plan was announced that all refugees in Zone must go back to their homes by February 4 and that all the mushroom shops on the streets of the Safety Zone will have to be taken down after that date. Order is to be maintained in the city, and plans have been worked out so that soldiers found misbehaving can be reported and dealt with. Soldiers are to be in a restricted district. We devoutly hope this may come to pass as announced.

Three philanthropic societies in the city are planning to distribute 1000 bags of rice and $2000 in money to the most needy. We were granted—upon our request—$200 for vegetables and oil for our "free rice" or red-tag group, now numbering about 1000 including children.

This morning about 10, a large envelope of mail was delivered at our gate, brought from Shanghai by one of the foreign ships. How famished we are for news of our friends! This evening after supper we had quite a party in Mrs. Tsen's sitting room reading the letters addressed to the group and such others as are of interest to all. So far we have had no foreign mail.

Among our refugees are four blind girls who are now living in a room in Mrs. Tsen's dormitory. They are such happy, eager girls and wait so eagerly for us to come to see them. They know our footsteps now. Took them to the service on Sunday afternoon and ever since they have been asking what certain phrases in the Lord's Prayer mean. Sometimes I hope we can send them to Shanghai to Blind School.

Lights go out at 8:30 since we received our refugee family, so much of the evening I write by candle or lantern light. City electricity is restored in certain sections of the Zone. City water also on again, at least in Zone. No telephone service yet.

Lt. Col. Oka called this evening for a friendly visit. He took my first letter through to Ruth in Shanghai.

From Tsen's Diary

It seems that the refugees are preparing for celebrating the New Year. No matter how much they have suffered, they still cannot forget about celebrating the lunar New Year. Under the circumstances, people have no food to eat, but they still want to celebrate the holiday. Now, some of the poor have become well-to-do. Just talking about it, I begin to feel sad again. Under this persecution [by the Japanese], I cannot help thinking of the happy, busy time during New Year in the bygone days. This year the families are painfully separated. Many refugees are suffering: some husbands were bayoneted to death by the Japanese soldiers, and some were taken away by the soldiers, whether alive or dead is unknown. Some of the mothers cried for their sons' fate. How can one celebrate this kind of New Year?

Letters came from Shanghai. Mrs. Liu bought a fountain pen for me; my old one was taken away by the Japanese soldiers. President Wu also sent a letter to us from Hankow. Plenty of news came. Receiving letters is the happiest thing to us.

Saturday, January 29

From Vautrin's Diary

Snowing today but not cold. Nothing seems able to prevent preparation for China New Year! There is an expectancy in the air—and an extra supply of food on the streets—also an increase in prices—although prices are unusually high.

Men brought over more letters this morning and several December ["] Christian Centuries["] as well as my January "Atlantic." Where is my mail from U.S.A.? I trust not in the post office in Nanking.

Mrs. Tsen, Miss Wang, Miss Hsueh and I spent about four hours today trying to get some blanks finished for the International Committee. Upon our recommendation depends the help that some of our poorest refugees will get out of relief funds from Shanghai and abroad. Many of our statements for women with little children read—"if her husband returns there is no problem, if not let her enter industrial or homecraft school, which we hope to conduct at Ginling from March 1 to June 30." For many we recommend a small loan until [the] woman can get in touch with their husbands who are in West China; for some an outright gift of $5 to help them get started again. It is so difficult to know how to help people to become independent again. Would that our Sociology Department and their majors were here!

Mrs. Tsen and I made final arrangements for the Vegetable-oil-rice dish which is to be served to the "free-rice" group tomorrow evening—New Year's eve according to the old calendar. The fund given us ought to furnish about ten such meals—and will help a little in keep[ing] up health.

Have not seen a soldier or officer today—so you can see conditions have changed.

An amah who served us in old Ginling[4] came in from the country to beg us to receive her 14 and 18 year old daughters. She says conditions in country are still very bad—everything is taken from them by soldiers, and their young girls and women are in constant danger. She will take responsibility for disguising them and trying to get them in, as no foreigner is yet allowed out of [the] city.

I heard that Mr. Rosen[5] of [the] German Embassy had insisted on going out to [a] Golf Club, but I cannot verify this.

Chang Nan-Wu,[6] head of [the] Swastika Society, told me this afternoon that their society had buried 2000 bodies. I implored him to bury those charred bodies out near the temple. They haunt me.

From Tsen's Diary

Today, we add two more refugees [newborns], and one and a half deaths. When you read this diary, you may feel strange and question why [I say] one and a half death? Because a middle-aged, five-month pregnant women died and her unborn counted as a half. Today, it snowed heavily the entire day. The woman died at 5:00 P.M. It's too late to take the body out, and there is no place to lay it. She originally stayed on the third floor at #300, and her family members all slept at her side. There were still 100 refugees there and [they] accompanied her. Now it is difficult to find a coffin for the dead, not even four wood panels, because of so many deaths. The Red Swastikas Society has buried a large number of bodies without coffins. In Nanking, there are seventy or eighty thousand people dead. Where can you find so many coffins? While alive, these people could not have a restful life. And after they died, they still could not be restful.

Tonight, we seemingly had the New Year's Eve dinner. People from Hu Chu Kwan, who stayed at the East Courtyard, saw that we had no special dishes to celebrate the New Year, and they sent us four dishes: salted meat, salted fish, salty duck, and a vegetable dish mixed with ten vegetables. All are special dishes for the New Year. In ordinary times, we only have three dishes but tonight, we have six [seven]. Is it like eating the New Year's Eve dinner? Under the circumstances, it is indeed to celebrate the New Year. You may say that it is [a celebration] even if only for [the] taste buds.

Sunday, January 30

From Vautrin's Diary

No aeroplane activity today.

Occasional fire crackers heralding the China New Year give us a start—too near the time when guns and bayonets held sway.

Church service this morning not so well attended. Can it be that people are staying home to prepare for China New Year? The streets between here and the University were dense with the crowd that packed them.

Afternoon service was by ticket, and only for women and girls who are either Christian or have attended Christian schools. Every seat in S.S. [Sunday school] filled. Miss Lo gave a good talk on "Preparing for the New Year"—not in homes but in hearts. At the same time there was a Sunday school for the children. Four lovely bouquets of poinsettias and pussy willows gave a festive look to the room.

Mary's turn to go to English service at #3 Ping Tsang Hsiang. She learned that George Fitch went to Shanghai yesterday by [the] same boat that took our mail—a British gunboat. He is the second person allowed out. In imagination we followed him to the service at the Community Church. How eagerly those women with husbands there, pressed him for news. He received promise that he would be allowed back. I wonder? The men at No. 3 [Ping Tsang Lane] have provisions from Shanghai—milk, butter, baking powder, canned goods. How their cook must be rejoicing after these lean weeks for the larder! Cakes or cookies were an impossibility for a good many weeks.

The service for servants this evening was in the form of a New Year's Eve service—forgiveness for the past, strength for the new and its unknown road. There is a fine spirit among the servants. They have been loyal, and they have had heavy work.

The International Committee sent two gifts of money—which we are using as tips for the extra servants who have had only their food, and for extra food for all. Pork is 70 cents a pound today. Extra vegetables and oil for the free rice group was served.

From Tsen's Diary

Today, it is snowing again. I could not attend the church service. Some of the refugees returned home for the New Year. It's the Chinese people's tradition—no matter what, they would celebrate the New Year. The Japanese soldiers still go to private homes [to loot and look for girls].

Now, we are preparing rice porridge with vegetables for the poorest [of the refugees] because they have not had oil and vegetables to eat, and only have one meal daily. Miss Wu becomes merciful because it is the New Year; she sent two geese for the workers and two chickens for us to eat. It's very pleasant to the ears. Yet, the chickens and geese are not gifts from her because they belonged to the school, and also we have to pay for them. They are also very expensive!

Monday, January 31

From Vautrin's Diary

If fire crackers have the power to drive away evil spirits and usher in a New Year of prosperity, then surely the coming year will be one of great happiness and bounty. Early, long before it was light, the fire crackers began to go off; not singly, but in boisterous confusion; and they continued more or less through the morning. It is a dismal, muddy day for which I am sorry, as it seems that China New Year ought to be one of sunshine. While you do not feel like using the old set phrases of "Congratulations, may the New Year be as you like it," "May you grow rich," I found I could say with deep meaning "May the New Year be one of peace!"

After the women and children's meetings this afternoon, the old gardener and I started out to see if we could purchase some sprays of "lah mei" or "twelfth month plum" from the farmer from whom I got such glorious branches last year. We went north on the road west of our campus. On our way there we passed two unburied bodies—one has been there since the middle of December. The country to the west of the road is a veritable no-man's land, with no sign of life. Every little house has windows boarded and doors barred. When we reached the temple district it looked too deserted for us to venture past it to the farm house, at some distance beyond, even for a spray of "lah mei," and so we turned back. When we came almost to our campus we turned up the hill, and there were still the bodies of the three men whom I heard [were] shot about December 16, and who looked to me like civilians. At the gardener's home he insisted on serving me a steaming bowl of chicken soup and poached egg. He, too, should be a character in a Book of Earth,[7] for he is so typical of the industrious farmer of China, so close to the soil.

When I arrived on the campus several large groups of young girls crowded around me begging to be allowed to stay after the 4th of February, the day set by the "Automatic" Society for the return of refugees to their homes. What a dilemma they are facing!

From Tsen's Diary

Today, I do not have many things to write about. Yet, we have another addition of a refugee [newborn]. It is really suffering for a woman to give birth here. She not only has to sleep on the ground, but also has no food to eat. These past several days, the situation is a little better because the number of refugees has decreased and everybody can sleep in the room. When there were more refugees here, women in labor had to give birth on the patio.

Now the Self-ruling Committee wants people to return home. Who does not want to go home? What can you do about lawlessness? They order that all people must return home by February 4. Naturally, it is not the Self-ruling Committee, but [the Japanese] behind it who issued the order.

Tuesday, February 1

From Vautrin's Diary

Day fairly clear and mild. Again there is areoplane activity—heavy planes to the northwest. The blimp is also up today—over near Pukow [Pukou].[8] Why so near we do not know.

At nine this morning in the six refugee buildings we began our own registration of refugees for we want to find out more details about each family before they go home. There are two of our helpers in each building doing this work. It will take two days to complete the work. Mr. Wang and Francis Chen went to the meeting of heads of Refugee Camps. It seemed best for Mr. Wang to go in my place since they are discussing the important problem of the return of refugees to their homes. The greater part of meeting was filled with reports of outrages on men and women who have tried to go to their homes. How the young women can go to their homes is more than I can imagine—and why the heads of the military want them to do so also passed my comprehension, for the stories of mistreatment and outrages will be greatly multiplied. The people at the meeting felt that since a high military official is coming that it might be possible to get the date postponed.

Just before noon a woman of thirty-nine came at 6:30 [?] to talk over her troubles. This morning she persuaded a man, who worked in the family where she worked, to go back to their home to get things that might still be there. The woman was seized and raped by 5 soldiers, and the man was slapped and relieved of $9.00. The woman's husband was taken on December 27 and has not returned. Just after this woman left my office, another of fifty-seven came in. She and her husband had gone home on Sunday. Her husband had been forced out of the home and two soldiers had mistreated her. Women do not willingly tell me these tales for they feel the disgrace of it too deeply. How can young girls be asked to go home? Again today, every time I went across the campus a group would gather and implore me to make it possible for them to stay. How my heart aches for them!

This morning, thanks to John Magee for loan of his car, Mary and Mrs. Tsen took two old men down to Christiana Tsai's home to see if they can protect what remains of that fine old residence. It has already been badly looted, but some of the heavier mahogany furniture was still there. Blanche Wu and I at 1:30 went over to the National Research Institute in the eastern part of the city. What a sickening sight it was! Houses and shops everywhere are burned or looted clean. We saw practically no one about but soldiers. In the Institute, three of the five major buildings were burned and we could see the charred remains of the great herbarium—the work of years. The biology building had been looted but not burned. We went to Dr. Ping's office and tried to collect what seemed to be the remains of his research data. We shall try to get some old and reliable men to go over there to be caretakers and preserve what is left. After we returned Mrs. Tsen and Mary went out again—this time to Mary Chen's home. What a sight it was—everything looted and mutilated. What will be left of old Nanking by spring?

Tonight we had a special meal for our staff, and at the end we each had half of a honey orange and some chocolates.

From Tsen's Diary

The things mailed from Shanghai arrived. Most of them were brought by Mrs. Liu at our request, and some were given to us by her. All are foods. If the current situation drags on for a prolonged period of time, we're afraid that it may be impossible for us to buy foods here.

Tonight, we had delicious foods for dinner, given by the International Committee. We did not consume much of them for only one meal.

Because of having a lot of money [given by the International Committee], we gave most of it to the workers and staff who have helped us and asked them to buy meat to eat. We only spent several dollars to buy vegetables for ourselves. Also, tonight, we ate three good things given by the people from Shanghai: apples, orange, and candies. As refugees, we are able to eat three such delicious foods. Are we privileged refugees? They're really tasty. I have not eaten an orange for a long time, and I really miss it.

Wednesday, February 2

From Vautrin's Diary

Although dismal and cold, this morning there were many aeroplanes carrying death and mutilation to the northwest.

At 10 o'clock went with Ernest Forster and James McCallum first to our Christian Mission Compounds in S.C. [south of the city] and then to American Church Mission. The Indiana Building is not badly damaged externally but has had a thorough looting, especially in the apartment on top floor. The school buildings in the west compound were burned. On Chung Hwa Street it seemed to me that 80% of the best buildings were burned. The Y.M.C.A. was among the first to be burned. For the first few days after the entrance of the Japanese Army there was not much burning but within a week the policy of deliberately looting and then burning was started and carried on for days—the result I saw this morning. The Chinese army did little looting before it left—excepting for money. Strangely enough we were not prepared for this. Many of us had been afraid of a long siege and of looting by Chinese soldiers—we were rather confident that the Japanese would be too well disciplined to loot and burn. The American Church Mission was in about the same conditions. Missionary houses completely looted—although well protected by American and Japanese proclamations; the school had been largely destroyed by a bomb, but the church not badly damaged.

Tai Ping (Peaceful) Road has practically been burned store by store—to cover up the evidence of very thorough looting. Army trucks took out the loot. If the Japanese business men are later expecting to occupy the city it will require a vast amount of capital to build needed buildings. Not a store was in existence save a few opened by Japanese.

At 11:15 I went to [the] Japanese Embassy to see Mr. Fukuda who has just returned from Shanghai. He received the data I gave him concerning 658 missing men—husbands or sons of our refugees. The large majority were taken on December 16. He said he would do what he could—and I believe he was sincere, for he realized that such women without their husbands are dependent on society—and there is no society. Talked to him briefly about the order that had gone out forcing all refugees to go to their homes, and gave him some incidents of the raping of women that had taken place in [the] last three days. He said he wanted more facts. After this call, I went to the Swastika Society headquarters to report the unburied bodies in the vicinity west of us—especially the charred bodies on the edge of the two ponds. They have placed more than 1000 bodies in coffins since the occupation.

From 3–5:30 was in my office—but not to work. Several women came in to tell me their tragedies—accounts which seem unbelievably cruel and beastly. Some day I would like the women of Japan to know some of these sad, sad stories.

Our own registration of refugees is going on in all six buildings by our own workers. It is a big piece of work but will be of great help to us later. The afternoon meeting for women was very good.

As Gwah-Chiang [Kuo-hsiang][9] and I distributed tickets for the meeting tomorrow afternoon, young girls begged piteously for me to do all I could to keep them from being forced to go home on February 4. Said they would rather starve on our campus than to be forced to go out.

From Tsen's Diary

Now, we have plenty of cod liver oil and milk powder shipped from Shanghai for refugees' children and babies. Today, we began to distribute to them. Many have registered for the cod liver oil and milk powder. Each afternoon, from 1:00 to 3:00 P.M., we check if they are taking them regularly. I have to prepare the formula from milk powder before giving it to them. Several babies were born on the campus and have no milk from their mothers because the adults have nothing to eat and how can they produce milk to feed the babies? Every week, we weigh the babies once and see how much they have grown. I found three educated women among the refugees to help me to deliver milk powder and prepare formula. We have to deliver it to six rooms.

Thursday, February 3

From Vautrin's Diary

Snowing steadily. Quite cold. Finished our local registration in all but the two academic buildings where there are perhaps more than 900 per building. Lewis Smythe called this morning and again this afternoon, to discuss methods of distributing cod liver oil and powered milk to the babies and sick children. He also says that the Safety Zone Committee want all of us in charge of Camps to remain at our posts tomorrow—the date set for refugees to go home.

What a fearful decision is before the people—to go to their homes, where they are still in very grave danger of being robbed or stabbed, and the women of being raped. Part of our strength today was used in urging older women to go home—in spite of risk and danger—and thus make it safer for the young girls to remain here.

Mrs. Li—former matron of [the] women's dormitory at Seminary was sent over by young women in Seminary Camp. When that camp is disbanded they want to come over here. They have heard a fantastic tale that we are going to take all the young girls to Shanghai on a boat.

Mr. Forster called and brought radio news which he and John Magee have kindly written out for us. Also told us that a Mr. Bishopric of the International Export Company, who has been in the city for a number of days, is going to Shanghai tomorrow morning by car, and will take mail which will probably be placed in an Embassy sealed envelope. This is another opportunity to get letters off—if we have time to write them.

I have a sore, inflamed eye tonight which Mrs. Tsen has treated and bandaged. I now have more sympathy for the four blind refugee girls. How can they be so cheerful?

From Tsen's Diary

These past several days, I have felt very frustrated, and I do not know what to do. Should we ask the refugees to return home? We are sure that it is not a good idea to ask them to do so. Yet, if we do not, we are afraid that trouble may arise because the Japanese push us to urge refugees to go home.

Today, it turns out to be a clear day. If it was snowing, we could use it to request an extension of the date to send the refugees home. It is most unfortunate that we have no place to redress our suffering.

Today, the Japanese soldiers came three times, twice for inspection and once for propaganda. When they came, they were accompanied by a Chinese. This Chinese was a Nationalist petty officer and he was saved by the Japanese from jumping into the river. Now he is working for them. When the Japanese were not at his side, he talked to Vautrin, asking her not to send the young women home now. While talking, his tears were rolling down on his cheeks. He said that he had no alternative other than accompanying the Japanese. In the future, he plans to escape.

Friday, February 4

From Vautrin's Diary

This is the day of terror for the poor women and girls—the day when they should go to their homes. What the day will bring forth we do not know. We are not expecting to force people to go home—they must take the responsibility.

During morning five girls came over from B.T.T.S [Bible Teachers' Training School] saying that camp was disbanded yesterday, that they had gone to their homes, that soldiers had come in the night, that they had scaled the wall of their home and run back to B.T.T.S. They want to come here. We are fearful about taking them lest we have a deluge which will bring added danger to the 4000 or more that we still have. Later in the day we decided to let them come. If in the next few days girls who have gone home from other camps find they cannot remain at home, we will have to receive them and take the consequences.

At ten and at 12:30 two military police called and inspected some of the buildings. Said they had come to see if we were all right—although they may have had an additional purpose. We explained that many had gone home—we had ten thousand, but now only about 4000. We also tried to make it clear that some of our refugees are from Shanghai and Wusih and other places and cannot go home until communications open up; that others have had their sons or husbands taken, the breadwinners of the family, and have no means

133

of support; that still others have had their houses burned and have no homes to which to return.

At 3 P.M. two Embassy Police and a Chinese came and asked us to get all the refugees together so they could explain to them the plan of returning to their homes. We suggested that we get those in the Science Building into the big lecture room and they begin with that group and thus take building by building. This plan they approved—but stopped with the first building. It is no easy thing to make a group of refugee women understand. The three points were:

1. All must go home. Military police, ordinary police and special district organizations will protect them. (There are four special districts in city.)

2. If husbands have been taken or homes burned, or if they are very poor, they should report to the Special District Organization.

3. Hereafter there will be no protection for Safety Zone—only the four districts will be protected. You must not bring property back into Safety Zone.

The Chinese man lingered long enough to let us know in a whisper that he felt young women were not safe and that they should remain with us.

At 5:30 P.M. Plummer [Plumer Mills] came to talk over plans for Relief, also reported no forcible eviction in any camp. At 5 P.M. about 200 young women came to Keh-tow [kowtow] and beg to remain. We have had no thought of forcing them to go. Later when Plumer went they had quite a demonstration in front of his car, weeping and keh-towing. Poor youngsters.

From Tsen's Diary

Today, we asked the older refugees to return home. For the young women, they can return home if they want to or stay on for several days. As a mater of fact, in our heart, we do not want them to go home now. When you are in this kind of dilemma, you feel helpless. The young girls all beg Vautrin to let them stay, not forcing them to go home. She does not want to do so either. These last couple of days, you simply cannot see the young girls because whenever you see them, they beg you [to let them stay].

This evening, around five o'clock, Rev. Mills came to visit Vautrin. When he was about to leave, the young women had quite a demonstration in front of his car and begged to remain. They cried and kowtowed in the mud. No matter how Mills leveled with them, they would not listen. Finally, Mills had no way out but left his car and stealthily walked home. The young women did not notice that Mills had already gone and continued to kneel on the ground until I told them what happened and asked them to get up. They are so worried and desperate. It is really pathetic to see them wail like this! If people go home, women will be raped and men will be forced to serve in the military. Even the old will be molested. Where is humanity? [The Japanese] are indeed beasts.

Saturday, February 5

From Vautrin's Diary

Spring started yesterday according to Chinese calendar. Today the sunshine is quite warm—snow has all melted.

Because of inflamed eyes and a touch of tonsillitis, I have been in my room all day. Mr. Wang has been in my office all day—to receive guests, and to classify the missing men according to professions. If possible I want to see Mr. Hidaka[10] about the matter. Rest of staff have been working on classifying the data which they have spent three days of this week in securing. Relief from the International Committee will depend upon our recommendations. How inadequate the staff of trained workers in Nanking is to cope with this huge problem! Five of us spent three hours this afternoon making the recommendations for our group.

Four of the women who went home yesterday came back this morning. One of these, a woman of 40, in going out of city gate yesterday was relieved of $3.00 by the guard, and a little farther on in her journey led off by another soldier to a dugout. When her captor saw a woman of twenty coming across the field, he released her. It is not strange that even the old women prefer to starve on our campus than to venture back to their homes—or the remnants of homes. Some prophesy that within a week all will be back in the Safety Zone. Poor, poor women—what a dilemma to be in!

A good many young women have slipped in without even the gateman being aware of it. They are from disbanded refugee camps. Yesterday we tried to prevent a rush from other camps to ours.

Today we think we have about 4000 refugees still on the campus—the large majority being young women. To date we have had 37 births and 27 deaths, five of the latter were adults. Today we are trying to send girls from lower hall of Arts Building to rooms upstairs—and this will enable us to clean the hallway—which it certainly needs. There are girls still occupying the glass enclosures under the stairway—people living in glass houses.

This afternoon the warning siren sounded quite distinctly—and what memories it recalled! Chinese planes were probably going to Giyung [Chuyung].

From Tsen's Diary

It is snowing again. The refugees cannot go home. It is wet from head to toe. How can they leave? Two military police came to inspect. Some people left, but not too many. We have no heart to ask them to leave, and it is hard on us. Among the ones returning home, some young women came here for refuge. We have to accept them because we cannot let them be molested outside. If the Japanese use weapons to force them to leave, we will be helpless to intervene.

Now, there are many babies, about thirty, taking milk powder. Several of them were not born here [on Ginling campus]. One three-month-old baby was fed with rice porridge and is skinny like a tiny cat. Really ugly! Some babies take milk powder and cod liver oil too. There are already several dozen adults and children registered for cod liver oil. More applicants are coming. The International Committee asked me to start the program here [to distribute cod liver oil], and then it will give the supplement to other camps.

Sunday, February 6

From Vautrin's Diary

Spring began February 4. Somewhat warmer. Sunshine. Some new spring birds chirping about. Seems too sad to have spring return.

Staying in today because of eyes. If it were my left hand it would be better—then I could at least read and write.

Only one soldier called today—Mr. Wang took him around. They say people must leave campus, by February 8. I doubt if they will do anything drastic to us—because our camp is different—mostly young girls now.

Fine meeting this afternoon. Miss Wang spoke on story of Prodigal Son. How the young girls love to sing—they begged Miss Wang to teach them.

Yesterday Blanche and Mr. McCallum took two of our old men refugees over to the Science Research Institute to live to see if they can prevent the remaining biological specimens from being destroyed. The men were quite willing to go and are so old that they can hardly be accused of being young radicals. Think of the work lost when that great herbarium was destroyed!

Lewis called this morning and gave instructions on proportion of milk and cod liver oil to feed to undernourished. A little later Plumer called and gave us $300 for use of refugees—$100 to be used as gifts and $200 to apply on a loan fund which will later be $500. The Committee[11] feel that direct relief is needed so badly that they cannot set a fund aside for a school although they approve of the idea.

Many heavy bombers have been flying over city today.

From Tsen's Diary

These last couple of days, Vautrin has had eye problems. I asked her to rest in her room. Every day, young women come here. I have no time to check them.

There is fish for sale on the street, very inexpensive. So, we have fish in our meals daily, and my small grandchildren are very happy. When they have fish, they eat more rice and faster.

The report has said that the tents on the Shanghai Road have been dismantled and will be moved to places assigned by the Japanese. The Japanese want
them to return to the city south so the soldiers can do whatever they please. This
area is in the Safety Zone, and many foreigners are here. The Japanese soldiers
cannot do as they please. All the tents are ordered to be dismantled by the
eighth [of February]; otherwise, the Japanese will dismantle them themselves.

Monday, February 7

From Vautrin's Diary

This morning there was a meeting of our women workers to reconsider our
plans. We have assigned one person to each refugee building—her purpose for
the week being to get better acquainted, to comfort, to work out best means of
giving direct aid, and to talk informally about starting a class in home making
and hand work—we are calling it a "class" and not a "school."

Mr. Wang came down this morning to report on cases of mistreatment to
older refugees who have gone home. The head of one of the disbanded camps
brought his two daughters over today. He and his wife are trying to live down
at Hubugiai [Hubu Street]. Said that yesterday soldiers drove up in a truck and
took all the good bedding from his neighbors—fortunately his was not new
or very clean so his was spared. It seems that in several homes out near West
Flower Gate the soldiers, failing to find young girls, are using teen age boys.

So far the classified summary of the men reported missing by our refugees are, Business men, 390; Gardeners, farmers, coolies, 123; Artisans, tailors,
carpenters, Masons, cooks, weavers, etc. 193; Policemen, 7; Firemen, 1; young
boys (14–20 years)[,] 9; Total, 723. The large majority of these were taken on
December 16 and have not yet returned.

Typewritten radio news was brought to us this afternoon by John Magee.
It looks as if Hofei is being endangered. How I wonder what conditions are
up in the country!

From Tsen's Diary

Some of the old refugees returned home, but we received a number of young
ones. Some, in disguise as beggars, came to the city from Shang Hsin River.

Probably the Nationalist troops are not far from here. Lots of rumors circulate
on the street, some of which claim that our troops have entered the city. People
on the street are about to take off their Japanese armbands.[12] I have not seen
anything actually happen yet and am anxious to see our troops' arrival. People
on the street complain a lot. On the one hand, the Japanese ask people to return

home. Yet, on the other, when people return, their soldiers drive them out of their homes. If they do not, the soldiers will rape young women. If the family does not have young women, they will molest young men as if they were women. You see how despicable they are! Both men and women are molested by them.

Tuesday, February 8

From Vautrin's Diary

Why such a beautiful day should make one sad, is difficult to explain. The pine trees and rose vines outside my window were covered with glistening and somehow the chirp of the birds, even though it was quite crispy cold, gave me a feeling that spring is here, or not far behind. But who is here to enjoy the glorious beauty of spring? The sprays of "Welcome the Spring" and wild daphne, the daffodils and roses, will but remind us of our friends who were with us a year ago and who now are scattered to the four winds. It will but recall for us our work and our play of the happy years that have gone and probably cannot return during my lifetime.

At 10 o'clock one of the servants came to tell me that there was a soldier up on our South Hill. I hastily put on rubbers and coat and started on the run. Found him with a young girl back of Eva's [Eva Spicer's] bungalow. Tried to get his number but failed, and then ordered him off. He looked daggers at me, but went. Later the girl said that she and four others were washing clothes in the pond near the south boundary. The four other girls made their escape but this one was caught. After the soldier pointed his dagger at her and tore at her clothes, she reluctantly unbuttoned them—and she was in this process when I appeared. My first impulse was to snatch his dagger—which I had a good opportunity to do, and call on the group of servants which had congregated by that time, to help me catch him—but I decided that was not the part of wisdom so did nothing worse than to make him climb over the fence.

At 11 A.M. went over to Japanese Embassy with a report for Mr. Hidaka, acting ambassador. Was fortunate in seeing him for 5 minutes, just before he was leaving for Shanghai, and being able to petition his aid in behalf of the 738 men who have never returned—husbands and fathers and sons of our refugees.

Three soldiers came at 1:20 to look around but did nothing worse than take pictures of children. At 2:30 another group came—an officer and military police. They had with them one who spoke Chinese fairly well. It was difficult for them to believe the 10 o'clock affair, in fact they did not.

At 2:45 Mr. Rabe and Lewis came to take me to a band concert at the Japanese Embassy. None of us had the heart to go but felt that we should. The director of the band of 20 had arranged a really good program of music—but I could not lose myself in it. When they played the overture "Light Cavalry," my mind would not leave that procession that passed our gate on December 14—that group of one hundred or more civilians with bound hands, walking behind the Japanese soldiers and cavalry—the group that has never returned; and when they proudly played "Warela no Guneai," "Our Army," the destroyed cities, desolate country side, raped women and girls, kept ever before me—I don't think I heard the music. Perhaps twenty westerners were present representing German, English and Americans[,] and the Japanese Embassy men tried to help us forget.

H.M.S. Bee came in this afternoon bringing a Netherlands official—and we hope some mail.

From Tsen's Diary

Today, almost all of the tents on the Shanghai Road have been dismantled with help from the Japanese. Some women came back here because the Japanese soldiers went to their homes once they returned there. For some families, the soldiers entered their homes, chasing the husbands out and sleeping with the wives inside the house. They slept there until the next morning, not just for a little while. If the wives do not obey, the soldiers will stab them to death.

This morning, a Japanese soldier chased a girl in the workshop from the South Hill. That girl ran as fast as she could. When she reached Miss Sze's[13] place, she was caught by the soldier. As the soldier was about to rape the girl, Vautrin got there and chased him away.

In the afternoon, two Japanese soldiers came to inspect. Vautrin told them about the soldier's attempt of rape in the morning. They asked her if the soldier had a red banner on his hat. Vautrin replied negative. This morning, seeing the soldier refuse admitting any wrongdoing, Vautrin went to the Japanese embassy to file a complaint report.

Also, in the afternoon, the Japanese consul gave a concert and invited the foreigners to attend. Some of them did, but some did not. Vautrin went. I laughed at her, saying "These days, you have been suffering bitter days in the hell. Today, you want to relax in the heaven." The Japanese asked the prostitutes to serve the guests at the tea reception. I think that no other countries would do likewise. Diplomats from the Dutch embassy also went. The German consul[14] declined to attend the tea reception on the pretext that he had to give the Dutch embassy people a ride first. This German consul dislikes the Japanese most. The Japanese soldiers follow him wherever he goes. In fact, they spy on him. He told us that he hated the Japanese soldiers following him. Sometimes he went to Ping Tsang Lane for fun and sat there deliberately for a long, long time in order to make the soldiers miss meals. Sometimes he went to Ping Tsang Lane to attend Sunday service and lingered on after the service. [That was] also intended to starve the soldiers. Yet, recently, no soldiers followed him. During this period of time, both the Germans and Americans helped the Chinese a lot.

7

※✦※

SLOWLY RESTORING LAW AND ORDER BUT SOLDIERS KEEP SEARCHING FOR *HWA GU-NIANG*

※✦※

Wednesday, February 9, 1938

From Vautrin's Diary

This morning prepared a report for the American Embassy giving an account of the incident on the campus yesterday. Took it over this afternoon, but just before doing so Lao Shao came in to tell that soldiers had been up at his home—and that they had been rougher than usual. He wanted to know if he could move down again. In the course of the morning Mr. Gee [Chi][1] and Mr. Forster were in for a long visit. The latter brought us some mail from Shanghai of February 4th, also some fruit for which we are most grateful. The former told us some of his difficulties as the head of a refugee camp. They sounded strangely familiar.

At the Embassy I could find nothing further about Helen Boughton,[2] about whom we are much distressed. They could tell us nothing about Luchowfu [Hofei]. In imagination I can see the despoiling of that great inland plain—the looting and burning of homes, the widespread killing of men, the violation of women, young and old. This is a war to win friendship and cooperation!

For the first time I went through our rescued treasures from the U.S.S. Panay. Must say things were rather sorry looking—but perhaps better than we might expect from having been soaked for weeks in Yangtze water. The money and all other papers had been dried out and the former can still be used. Allison seemed discouraged because conditions seem to improve so slowly in Nanking.

141

Matsumoto, Manager of Domei, called for a few minutes. He was planning to fly to Shanghai so could not stay. I should have liked to get acquainted with him.

As I came home from Embassy about 5 P.M. I met two groups of women—the first a mother bringing back her two daughters. Said they had gone home two days ago but could not stand it. Soldiers came frequently looking for young girls and they have to hide continually. Naturally we let them come in, for how long we do not know. The other person made me terribly sad and depressed. She was the wife of a former teacher in one of the big schools in Nanking—she came from a family of scholars. Before the trouble they had evacuated to the country—had spent their all and decided they would have to come back to Nanking no matter what the conditions. And what a pitiful tale that return journey was—her daughter of 14 and a niece of the same age had taken off shoes and stockings and walked out in the fields in order to avoid soldiers, but in spite of that the niece had been raped three times, the daughter once—as she tried to come in the City Gate. Girls of 14! The mother's mind was confused as to time—suffering had been so continuous. She did not ask to come in—said she could stand it, but begged that the young girls be allowed in. And again the Ginling Gates opened. I would we could do more for them.

From Tsen's Diary

Today was very uneventful, nothing special for me to write about. The weather is not too good. Many people entered the city. There is more meat supply, a little bit cheaper. Every day [now] we have meat in our diet. Many people have fled.

Today, we went to visit other refugee camps. Originally, there were twenty-five camps but now only about ten remain open.

Thursday, February 10

From Vautrin's Diary

Our men['s] faculty houses and the Neighborhood Center are a sorry sight. They are still crowded with refugees. Mr. Chen and I went over this morning to investigate. Again we pled with older people to go to their homes outside the zone, for the sake of younger women we begged them to do this—but they only say, "yes," "yes," and do not go. Both of the double residences have been crowded with refugee families—several families to a room. The floors and walls are in terrible condition. To make bad matters worse an opium fiend and his wife are in one of the rooms and they have collected exorbitant rents—saying we had asked him to act for the college. None of us is clever enough to cope with an opium fiend.

This afternoon we had four callers: John Magee who came to bring us the broadcast news, Mr. Bates who came looking for Dr. Smythe, Lewis who came to talk over the problem of feeding powdered milk to babies—he has plenty of the powder, but not enough competent people to teach women how to use it for their babies; and Dr. Tang[3] who came in after the afternoon service.

Between 5 and 6 Wei Szi-fu and I went west on Canton Road. I had not been down there since December 11th, when we put up Safety Zone flags. What a silent, but vivid, testimony of the havoc of war. Even the little huts are mostly deserted—some were burned. In only a few houses were people living—and these were old people. When asked how they were getting along they said that soldiers were not coming often—some were decent, some searched them for money, some insisted on and searched for "hwo [hwa] gu-niang" (young girls). On the road we passed a fair number of people going back into the Safety Zone for the night.

In one house there were four men. They would not have admitted it, but we could see they make their living by going over to West Gate region, still largely uninhabited, taking out doors and floors from houses, and making it into bundles of fire wood which they will sell to refugees. We passed one young man with many bolts of cloth in gunny sacks. He said he had purchased it. Perhaps he had, but it was loot. We tried to make him see how different it would be in Nanking if all of us boycotted loot in every form, no matter how tempting.

From Tsen's Diary

People who had been chased out [from other refugee camps] all came here because they cannot go home. Right now we do not have an accurate estimate of how many refugees are here because people come and go frequently. Some of them who had returned home for many days tearfully come back because they were molested by the Japanese soldiers. Some fled here from the countryside. They were either robbed by the Japanese soldiers or by the bandits. They came here empty-handed.

Today another boy died.

Friday, February 11

From Vautrin's Diary

A chance to send mail to Shanghai if we get it to Embassy by 4 P.M.

A beautiful sunshiny day—spring is not far behind. The sound of the heavy bombers this morning haunts me—I can only see the hundreds of mutilated soldiers in trenches and on battlefields up near Hsuchowfu [Hsuchow] with no doctors or nurses to care for them. There they will suffer until death releases their poor wracked bodies from pain. Poor fellows! Would that the men students now safely studying in universities and colleges would hear the call of these wounded men and volunteer to help them for they could do much. We are much worried about Helen Baughton [Boughton]. No further news has come through about her kidnapping. What must conditions be in Pengpu and Hwai Yuen[4] where there are only two or three foreigners and no Safety Zone? Hofei must be in the middle of a war area and battlefield. Am constantly thinking of my friends there. May the Father give them strength and courage beyond their own, and may they be used to shelter and comfort many!

Father Kearney is back in Nanking for a few days. He came up in a French gunboat, it seems, and is going back almost immediately to Shanghai.

At the American Embassy I found them putting in a big supply of coal. It seems one of the coal dealers out near Hansimen [Hanhsi Gate] had his supply still unlooted, and he has urged the American Embassy to take it over to prevent others from looting it. There seems to be a race on in poor old Nanking—to see who can get rice and coal first.

At 5 P.M. went to Hospital to see Blanche. Found her in a third class ward and in much pain. The Hospital is crowded but doctors and nurses pitifully few. There are still only two foreign doctors and I think two Chinese.

This afternoon about 2:30 our Embassy police and two military police called to see if we were being molested by soldiers. They also inquired about the number of our refugees, so that I could not help wondering if that was their real purpose in coming. They seemed satisfied when I reported that at one time we had had as many as 10,000 but now we have only about 3,000.

From Tsen's Diary

The weather is fine again, which is good for the refugees because it is more convenient for them to come and go. Today, there is another new addition of refugees [a newborn]. These little refugees taste suffering life right after being born. Now, there are over 200 children who take the fish liver oil.

Miss Wu is merciful again. She is ill and has gone to the hospital. She asked servants to send us two of her chickens. In fact, we do not need her chickens because we can purchase them on the market now. In the past, we asked for chickens from her because we had no meat to eat. I see that Miss Vautrin is already exhausted by too many things, and Wu herself is sick; otherwise, I would return the chickens to her. Also, people in Shanghai send us food.

It is very lucky for us refugees to have so many foods to eat. We should be very satisfied. Furthermore, in the past, the reason for our asking Wu for chickens was that if we did not want them, they would be eaten by the Japanese soldiers. She has more than 100 chickens. Up to now, we have eaten only seven of them. If it was not for Miss Vautrin, I would not have any appetite for chickens. Wu did not want to part with them, nor do I have any desire to accept them. These past several days, we are busy in checking the numbers of the refugees and examining their family data.

Saturday, February 12

From Vautrin's Diary

Lincoln's Birthday—but we shall have no celebrations. Good weather continues.

George Fitch is back—having come in on [the] U.S.S. Oahu today. Am eager to get news from him. We hear he has brought us many packages from our good friends in Shanghai.

From 4 to 6 we had a party down at Practice School. Had oranges from Shanghai and popcorn. Celebrated the arrival of Mr. F. Chen's new son. He has had a letter from Swatow[5] telling of the baby's arrival.

At 6:30 John Magee came over with an armful of bundles—those that George Fitch had brought up for us. Mary was overjoyed to get her first letters.

Know little of the outside world excepting that the aeroplane activity makes us realize that bombing continues unabated. This afternoon there was anti-aircraft firing[,] probably practice. Rumors of all sorts are coming through so we do not know to whom Wuhu and Hangchow belong.

No Japanese callers today of any kind.

One very attractive young woman with two children who have been living for about two months on a table in the general biology laboratory came to talk to me. She says her husband has a curio shop in Shanghai but she herself has no money. Has been living here on free rice all this time. She is a graduate of the old Quaker Girls' School. She says she wants to go back to her home and feels that the soldiers will not molest her since there are a number of men in the neighborhood where she lives. I am a little fearful about her going back lest something may happen.

From Tsen's Diary

Today, another ship anchored.[6] It brought letters from Shanghai. I was elated. And my appetite is so good because we have goodies to eat, and the oranges are the best. I have not had fruits for quite some time. Under today's circumstances, it is very rare for us to have such a delicacy to eat. We cannot help thanking our alumnae and friends in Shanghai. Miss Vautrin even has chocolates to eat, and we have tasted some too.

Sunday, February 13

From Vautrin's Diary

Raining heavily this morning. At last no sound of heavy bombers. Because of cough and sore throat am staying in today.

It has been reported to us that last night about midnight four to six soldiers went to Farmer Tsu's, near our laundry, and pounded loudly on his door, demanded "hwa guniang." The door was not opened and they finally went away. I suspect those girls will be moving back to the college tonight.

About 3 P.M. two officials, a soldier and about four Chinese from the "Automatic Society" came on the campus and asked if we could find four washer women for them. Want women between 30 and 40. Will pay them in rice. They will come back tomorrow morning for them. In the meantime we shall do what we can to find some. I have also told our laundry man, who is quite willing to go if he can come home at night. Strange to say before I got back to the Practice School one woman came and applied for the work. I happened to know she has been raped by three soldiers. She certainly has courage.

George Fitch is back and has a promise of $200,000 for refugee relief. The question in my mind is how we can distribute that amount wisely.

More letters came in today and more packages from Shanghai. Our friends are too good to us. If we ask them to make purchases for us they make gifts instead. Quite a post office system is being started. Think I must have sent 20 letters for refugees yesterday—mostly to relatives in Shanghai asking for money.

A good letter from W.Y.F.[7] today which was sent from Chengtu on January 27 and another from Catherine [Sutherland] in Wuchang dated Jan. 28.

From Tsen's Diary

During the past couple of days, the situation outside is improving, calming down a little bit. Yet, the Japanese soldiers still enter people's homes. Quite a few houses were burned down and belongings looted.

Not many things worthy to be recorded. I myself am busy in writing "thank you" letters for sending us so many good foods. We ought to tell the senders about the situation here during the past several months. Therefore, I have little to write in the diary.

Today, we have another addition of little refugees. Two Japanese soldiers came to inspect.

Monday, February 14

From Vautrin's Diary

Cloudy this morning—no sound of planes. Tsu farmers [*sic*] came in to report the 1 A.M. visit of soldiers yesterday. 7 or 8 came, pounded on door, but were not allowed to enter. Later they went to Yang home next to Tsu's, forced door open with bayonets, insisted that they must be given hwa gu-niang. Were angry when told there were none, and flourished bayonets. When one of the men said they would report their presence, they left. "Ce-men yai bao-gao."[8]

At 12:30 or perhaps one o'clock, the laundry man's wife came running for us saying the soldiers were in their home. When we arrived they had gone. They too were looking for "hwa gu-niang." The laundry man tried to serve them tea but they did not wait for it.

This morning we were able to find only one woman between 30–40 years of age who was willing to go to the military headquarters to do laundry work. Our laundry man and an assistant would have gone but fortunately the officers did not come back for them.

About three o'clock "Big Wang" and I went over near the Model Prison. Our main purpose was to find out if possible if there are civilians in the prison but incidentally we had many interesting experiences. Chang Ging Lou,[9] the upper end of Beimenchiao [Pei Men Chiao, or North Gate Bridge], which you remember as a bustling business street, is pitiful indeed. Here and there we found a brave soul who had gone back to his shop or restaurant—a watch repairer, two restaurant keepers, a maker of "shiao-bing."[10] Their main purpose was to save the remains of their store or shop. The street was almost deserted. All the stores had been completely looted, and the best ones burned. There was practically no trade. A little farther to the east we found an old lady of 65. Says for almost 2 months she has been coming back to her home by day. The Japanese looted first for valuables, but her presence has prevented the common people from taking all her other property. A husband, wife and son soon caught up with us and the wife bemoaned the fact that three of her sons had been taken off by the Chinese troops. Her husband tried to comfort her by saying they had a chance to return, but most of those who had been taken by the Japanese would never return. In two houses that we passed were Japanese women—Geisha girls, I take it.

Having had the report concerning civilians in the Model Prison reaffirmed we went to see Mr. Rabe and turned over to him a letter or petition from the men in the prison. It is not easy to do anything in their behalf because the wrong thing might mean death to them all.

Saw my second ricksha today since December 12. Where all the rickshas are, I do not know. Bought some port [pork] this afternoon at 45 cents per catty.[11]

From Tsen's Diary

These last several days, the weather is very warm. Each day, we wanted the refugees to wash the floors and windows. Some were willing to do so, but some not. We had to force them to do it. The thing we dread most is that epidemics will come with the spring. Even now, so many are sick.

[The International Committee] plans to distribute the cod liver oil and milk powder to other camps. Mr. Smythe wanted me to go there to help, but I am tied up here. I cannot even find enough time to handle chores here, so I asked Mrs. Twinem to go for me. She went by car, and I rode with her to see the situation outside. If there was no car, I could not make the trip. Yesterday, I went to see city south and the Confucius Temple. Two thirds of the buildings in Nanjing were burned down, and the rest were empty. Some buildings only have skeletons left; some have no floors or beams. The buildings in the Safety Zone are mostly intact, not being burned. The areas burned most severely are the Confucius Temple and Taiping Road. It's really despicable, so ruthless. The city of Nanjing is a completely empty shell now. I heard that Wuhu was also burned severely.

Tuesday, February 15

From Vautrin's Diary

Spring birds are here. "Welcome the Spring" is opening in my living room.

This morning we have a group of refugees moving newspapers and magazines back to the attic of library—all that work of cleaning the attic happily was in vain. Reason for moving is that we need to get at the bookcases which have been covered. Later Mr. Li and I spent about an hour back of Central Building trying to work out a better method of getting rid of night soil. We have trench after trench filled with it—and it is everywhere. It has become an everlasting problem which haunts us—and people say our camp has solved the problem more successfully than others! If we do not get lime soon, we shall all be in our graves from disease before the end of summer.

Yesterday I invested one dollar in pork which we had for dinner this noon. My, it tasted good!

One would like to know just how many Chinese soldiers were sacrificed in the attempt to hold Nanking. This morning a report came to me that the Swastika Society estimate about 30,000 killed around Hsia Gwan [Hsia Kwan], and this afternoon I heard another report that "tens of thousands" were trapped at "Swallow Cliff"—Yen Dz Gi [Yen Tzu Chi]—there were no boats to get them across the rivers. Poor fellows!

A few weeks ago I told you how the many shops, tea houses and restaurants went up along the sides of Shanghai Road almost in a day, like mushrooms after rain. Today they are disappearing in the same manner, for the order has gone out that if they are not down by night they will be torn down. Good naturedly people are taking them down and carrying them away. I saw "The Happy People Tea House" disappear. Most of the things sold in them was loot, which some of us thought should never have been allowed in the Zone. I would like to be head of the Sanitation of the city for a month or two and have a good corps of coolies under me in order to clean up the roads.

We hear that Mr. Ritchey,[12] former Directorate of Posts for Nanking, is back in the city, and is to try to revive the postal service. Our only connection with the outside world is by way of gunboats.

Mary and I are planning to have a farewell tea for Mr. Rabe on Thursday. My living room will hold only 8 people, so we can have but five guests and for any refreshments we would like to serve we find we lack the most essential ingredients.

From Tsen's Diary

Several Japanese soldiers came to look for women to wash clothing for them. Miss Vautrin was not at home. I answered them that we cannot find women to do their laundry on short notice, and it will take some time. The soldiers said that they would come back tomorrow morning. Later, I asked if any women want to do laundry for the Japanese. None of them were willing to do so. The following day, the soldiers did not show up. I heard that they had found women to wash their clothing elsewhere.

Wednesday, February 16

From Vautrin's Diary

Cold wind blowing today. Puh and Lao Wu are beginning to transplant tress, for now is the time. Again at 9 A.M. Mr. Li and I went out to see about sanitation. It is such a hopeless, tremendous task that we make no impression on it. Wish you could see and smell the hill back of the Central Building.

Miss Wang and her helpers finished replacing red tags by new yellow ones. There are 655 individuals now getting free rice. Are we too careful about giving free rice tags? If we were less careful more would be staying than at present.

We also have money from the Committee to lend and to give, but how to lend and give it wisely is far from easy. Today we made two loans, and have received rings or watches as security.

Mr. Y. G. Yan called between 5 and 6 today. Had heard that he was killed, but did not tell him so. He said he had heard that during the early days of occupation 10,000 were killed on San Chia-ho [San Chia River], 20–30,000 at Yendzigi [Yen Tzu Chi], and about 10,000 at Hsia Gwan [Hsia Kwan]. He is sure that many husbands and sons will never return. How can I tell the women who come to me so often asking if I have heard any reports from the petitions, that I am becoming convinced that their husbands will never return?

Mr. Allison brought me a package from Shanghai, two letters, and a radiogram about Stella.[13] People in America do not realize that it is almost impossible to get into Nanking.

Blanche is still ill in the hospital and Miss Lo is ill here. It is difficult to keep well—and normal.

In the package from Shanghai there was a N.C.D.N. [*North China Daily News*] of February 5—the first I have seen since November 14 when mine stopped.

Must write a report of the second month[14]—but when?

Mr. Djao has volunteered to start a lending library. Would that we had more good books to lend! He is now making the list and will open it soon.

From Tsen's Diary

Miss Vautrin would like to start a home-craft class when our campus is left with only two hundred people who cannot go home. Among the young women, some of their husbands have been killed, and some of their homes been burned. Some are young girls. Now we have 4,000 refugees left on the campus. However, there are some who could go home but are afraid to do so. [Vautrin's original] plan has changed—not to offer home-craft class because there are just too many people here. Yesterday, over six hundred registered for class. Some are at the junior high level, some at senior high level, and the rest at the third or fourth grade of elementary school. Now we offer Bible classes, and each class has seventy or eighty students because not many teachers are available. Among the teaching faculty, Miss Wang, a third-year student of the theological school with several years of teaching experience, serves as the dean of studies. Others include elementary school teacher Hseuh Yu-jen, missionary Miss Lo, who is Vautrin's friend, and two refugees. One is Ming, the high school graduate and former elementary school teacher, and the other is a newcomer from the women's theological school. They all teach Bible classes. Mrs. Twinem teaches singing, and Mr. Li also helps with the classes. Probably Vautrin and I will have to teach classes too. Most of the classes are held before noon. The classes have not started yet and are still in the planning stage.

Thursday, February 17

From Vautrin's Diary

Spring today. Much aerial activity. Anti-aircraft gun practice. Anniversary of that terrible December 17.

Again I am making the rounds with Mr. Li to try to get back campus cleaned up. Fearful condition back of Central Building at Southwest corner—but Sone says we are clean compared to many. Room 304 had a real house cleaning. Women took out all their bedding and cleaned windows and floors. Hope this will become contagious.

Two officers and a soldier with interpreter called early this afternoon presumably to look around. How easy it is for us to suspect that every caller has a deep and sinister motive.

Spent about two hours working on accounts this morning. Have neglected them badly since December 1st. Fortunately there have not been many things to buy, so items are not many.

This afternoon Mary and I had our farewell tea party for Mr. Rabe,[15] no easy thing to manage under present conditions. Guests were Mr. Rabe, Dr. Rosen, Mr. Allison, George Fitch, Mr. Ritchey and Searle. Mrs. Tsen helped us. We served a salad, opened our first box of chocolates, had oranges. The cake was not bad—kind of fruit cake made with Esther's[16] mince meat, taking the place of fruit. Not a Chinese store open in Nanking yet, so one's menu must be adjusted to the foods in one's own depleted larder, or that of her best friends.

Mr. Allison was escorted by a Japanese guard, so we suggested he leave first, because Mrs. Tsen had heard that our women refugees wanted to see Mr. Rabe and implore him to stay. We were not prepared for the sight that met our gaze when we arrived in front of [the] Science Building. Between 2 and 3 thousand women were there and as Mr. Rabe approached them they all knelt and began to weep and implore. He spoke a few words and then Mary got him away by a back path.[17] I tried to get them away so that Dr. Rosen and Mr. Ritchey could leave but it was a difficult job—Mary again got them out while I tried to divert the[ir] attention and lead them to the other side of the quadrangle. After a long time we were able to get the car out—but not until the men must have been well on their way home.

Mr. Ritchey goes by car to Shanghai tomorrow. He reports that the post office will probably open soon under Chinese management.

From Tsen's Diary

Today is a date we should remember. Two months ago this night we suffered the most. [See Tsen's and Vautrin's diary entries of December 17, 1937].

Today, at 4:00 o'clock, we invited the chairman of the International Committee [John Rabe] for tea. Also invited was the head [Mr Ritchey] of the post bureau, who plans to open the post office soon. Both the German and the American consuls came to the tea with Rabe because he is going to return to Germany. Originally he was a businessman and stayed in China for years. He is very capable and courageous. His home office wants him to go back to Germany. After he leaves, the International Committee will no longer exist and has to reorganize. Everybody here wants him to stay. When the refugees learned about his departure, they also begged him to stay. At the party, I expressed my deep gratitude to him and asked him to stay for one more month. He said to me, "It is useless to stay on. After returning to Germany, I can help you people more. Now you need people in Germany to speak out for you." I agreed with him. For propaganda, people will believe him because he eyewitnessed [what happened in Nanking].

When Rabe was about to leave the tea party, the refugees all surrounded his car, begging him [to remain in Nanjing]. His car could not move. He had to walk home.

Friday, February 18

From Vautrin's Diary

Clear spring day. Many bombers flying to northwest. Hearts heavy when we think of the cities being destroyed, the soldiers being bombed.

Spent a number of hours today in conference on Bible classes which we are beginning next week. There are 646 girls from Grade III to S.M.S. (Senior Middle School) who are interested in entering classes. No Bibles, no pencils, no notebooks available in Nanking. Three of our refugees will help with this work—Miss Rachel Wang[18] will be in charge, Miss Yang and Miss Wu,[19] graduates of Ming Deh, will each have classes.

Mary spends her morning going to the refugee camps to encourage the taking of cod liver oil and milk. The Committee has a large quantity to dispense. Mrs. Tsen is in charge of distribution on our camps, and has three refugee women helping her.

No Japanese callers today.

Mr. Ritchey was not able to get off to Shanghai today as he planned but hopes to go tomorrow. Fitch plans to go tomorrow also. It seems that the permission granted them by the Embassy had to be withdrawn.

A woman came in from the country today to see her daughter who is a refugee here. She reported that yesterday a number of comforters were taken from homes in her vicinity. We are told that stronger methods are to be used tomorrow to make men leave the Safety Zone. I doubt if women will be forced to leave our campus—but that they may be starved out by the closing of our Red Cross Rice Kitchen.

From Tsen's Diary

Today, a number of young refugees came to the campus. Because other camps have closed and they could not go home, they have to come here. At first, all the camps were ordered to close, [and refugees] dispersed. The Self-ruling Committee petitioned the Japanese occupation administration to allow several camps to be dissolved gradually, not to disperse all of them at once. The International Committee made the same petition. Now only four camps are left. They are University of Nanking, Ginling College, Ginling High School, and Women's Theological School. The rest all are to be closed at the end of April. However, one more camp at the Chemistry Institute was saved by the Self-ruling Committee itself. It is especially for receiving the refugees from faraway places in order to make it easier to send them home later. Now the Committee plans to send these people home, and the Japanese agreed.

The International Committee has changed its name to the [Nanking] International Relief Committee.[20] The Relief Committee won't be able to exist for long. Now the Japanese will strive to remove the Committee, and they do not want the third force [Westerners] to interfere with their business. Yet, the International Relief Committee refuses to comply. I'm afraid that the Committee's days are numbered.

Saturday, February 19

From Vautrin's Diary

Glorious as to weather. Spring birds are returning and making us sad as we remember the joys and our work of a year ago. In the Arts Building some of the refugees are house cleaning. Also the girls who have been living in the glass enclosures at the entrance of the building are moving out. The halls in Arts and Science and Central Buildings are now free of people—those remaining have moved into rooms. We really do not know how many refugees still remain but we think about 3000. Many go home by day and come back for the nights. Locks and fasteners and screens have had a hard time.

Listen—hear the siren warning! We do not know its meaning. Recently anti-aircraft practice. Yesterday a blimp was up over north of Yangtze.

Spent part of morning and afternoon preparing for the service tomorrow afternoon which I am to lead. It is difficult to get down to serious study.

John Magee came in for tea and reported that he had been out to the Refugee Camp at Chi Hsia Shan [Chi Hsia Hill]. Two Danes have been out there through it all and have done a magnificent piece of work for about 10,000 rural refugees. Mr. Forster is going down to the Episcopal Center at Peh Hsia Road to live. It would be great if all the Missions working in Nanking had western and Chinese pastors to go back to their churches. Each center would become a refuge of safety and comfort and teaching. Am sorry that Mills and McCallum are so tied up with general work that they cannot go back into church work. Doors and hearts are wide open now.

Today we have seen the results of hard work. On the hill west of Central Building, a new pit has been dug for night soil and all the debris dumped there has been buried. It [is] a tremendous job to make things sanitary. The odor back there has been terrific. We must get lime some where even if we have to loot it, otherwise we may have an epidemic in warm weather.

It is impossible to get good workmen now as most of them have left the city.

From Tsen's Diary

The weather is very warm. If we do not clean the places here, there will be big trouble ahead. We have to make all efforts to find lime. If we do not put lime at various places, the stinky smell will come out. Also, we must put lime in the human waste pits. Yet we cannot find lime in the city, so I told the head of sanitation that he should ask the Self-ruling Committee to tell the Japanese to use military trucks and find it outside the city. Also to tell the Japanese that the epidemic may become prevalent. They are afraid of death. If an epidemic occurs, it will be detrimental to them. If they cannot find lime outside the city, they should ship it from Lungtan by train. There is abundant lime in Lungtan. Must take actions quickly. Talk with the Japanese. They are most afraid to die. I think that they will comply. This is for their benefit too.

Now everything, rice and coal, are all in their [Japanese] control. The International Relief Committee does not want to do things in its name. They let the Chinese handle a lot of things. Also, they dare not offend the Japanese, otherwise the Japanese will not let them stay here. Even for those Americans who want to go to Shanghai or return to Nanking, they must first get permits from him [them]. They are worried that the Japanese may not allow them to

return. Mr. Fitch of the International Committee, who was originally on the
staff of the Y.M.C.A, went through a lot of arguments [with the Japanese]
and then [finally] got a permit to leave Nanking. Then he came back and left
again after staying a couple of days. I heard that he has flown to America to
do propaganda work.

Another child died.

Sunday, February 20

From Vautrin's Diary

Wonderful spring weather. Aeroplane activity continues.

Mary went to morning service at Drum Tower and I remained at home.

Soon after noon a Mrs. Chin—former refugee who spent almost two months
in Biology Lab. came back to attend the afternoon service. Her little boy
wanted to come back to see us. She reports that a number of families are living
there together, including some of their young women, and so far they have
not been molested by soldiers. We were able to lend her $15.00 from the loan
fund with which she has purchased rice and fuel. Her husband has a curio
shop in Shanghai. Wish we knew all our refugees as we know her. She is a
friendly and very grateful person. She report[ed] that many of the women in
their neighborhood were our refugees and that if we had time to call the doors
would be wide open for us.

Had charge of 4:30 English service today. Am sorry I did not have more of
a message—but time for study and thought is not frequent.

Remained for dinner at #3.[21] G. Fitch has left and Dr. Brady[22] is expected.
They have electricity, but interference was so bad that we could not hear the
broadcast.

From Tsen's Diary

We began to raise money for chicken pox inoculation. The doctors from the
Drum Tower Hospital come to inoculate. So many things need to be done for
these refugees. Miss Vautrin helps the refugees find their [missing] doctors[23]
and sons. She asked the Japanese to release the people who they had taken
[prisoner]. I heard that there are many Chinese in the Model Prison working
for the Japanese. Vautrin asked the family members of the refugees to go there
to see if their kin are there. If they are, she will go to the see the Japanese
consul. She has already written letters to the Japanese about the matter. The
Japanese promised that they would release the men, but they did not. The
refugees [who seek Vautrin's help to find their kin] are not only the ones on

the campus, but also from other places. They come to beg Vautrin to write letters [to the authorities]. Vautrin has already asked two gentlemen to handle the matter, recording their names, addresses, ages, and stamping their thumb prints.[24] About 1,000-plus refugees have gone through the process. So, people are grateful to Vautrin and call her Goddess of Mercy. She is not bothered by the trouble. Anyway, she does not handle it herself, but instead delegates others to do the work.

Monday, February 21

From Vautrin's Diary

Organization of Bible classes began today. At 10:30 the Junior Senior Middle School girls began their class in big chapel, the 6th grade in South Studio, and 5th grade in Science Building. At 2 P.M. the evangelistic service continued in South Studio (170 present) and the 3rd grade met in Science Building. The numbers will decrease, naturally, but the girls are anxious to study and until our refugee number decreases we shall continue to have the religious classes. If only we had more teachers! We still have a dream of having some kind of home-making and industrial classes for women whose support has been taken entirely away from them.

Rode in ricksha today—the 4th one I have seen since December 12. Also heard that 100 have been registered and are permitted to appear on the streets. Ninghai, Hankow and Shanghai Road are almost completely denuded of their mushroom shops. People say they are now appearing on streets south of the Safety Zone. By the way the "Safety Zone" is no more, but has been formed into the Nanking International Refugee Committee.[25]

At 4 P.M. attended the farewell reception for Mr. John Rabe held at 5 Ninghai [Road]. I went for the first part, Mary and Mrs. Tsen went for the second part—and unfortunately the talks came during the latter part. Much genuine appreciation was shown for Mr. Rabe and the unselfish way in which he has given himself to the poor of Nanking. Searle expressed for the other members of the committee their appreciation, and a statement signed by all members of the committee was given to him, to the German Embassy, and the Siemens Co. He is an exceptional type of business man—one who unconsciously wins friends for his country.

At 8 P.M. I attended another reception at 3 Ping Tsang Hsiang for Mr. Rabe—the members of the Embassy being present, including Fukuii, Tanaka and Yasui of the Japanese Embassy. Speeches were made and Mr. Rabe made an appropriate, humble and sincere reply and expressed a desire for further cooperation in behalf of the poor of Nanking. (Dr. Rosen, only with great difficulty, can be civil to the Japanese and this evening remained in the alcove away from them.)

From Tsen's Diary

Today, I went to Hwang Li-ming's[26] home to take a look. It is very chaotic inside. Two pianos were taken away, all the chests on the second floor opened, and many things broken. On the third floor, it is even worse; the floor was littered with clothing and all the good summer dresses were taken away. Luckily, there is a guard at the door; otherwise, all the summer clothing would be taken away by the civilians, who had entered the house, but not many times. So, there are still some good things left. They [the Japanese] looted everywhere.

Tuesday, February 22

From Vautrin's Diary

Washington's birthday but no reception at American Embassy today.

Spent morning and several hours this afternoon looking for books for faculty in Shanghai and getting some packed and over to Embassy. H.M.S. Cricket goes down tomorrow morning. Embassies have certainly been untiring and seemingly uncomplaining in sending packages of books and food and mail for us. In fact our refugees have quite a bunch of letters each time they hear a boat is going. How soon Chinese can go to Shanghai we do not know—many are anxious to get out of Nanking. Have heard of only two going and they at a very high cost—one wealthy man paid $1500, I understand.

Attended a farewell tiffin party for Mr. Rabe at Dr. Rosen's. How good it does seem to be approaching normal living again! Dr. Rosen is certainly outspoken in his disapproval of Japanese officials—military and civil—and yet he quite openly buys Japanese goods. It is one of the few ways I have of protesting—and I think I shall continue it. They say that there are a number of Japanese shops opening in the city, but only for Japanese, not Chinese.

From Tsen's Diary

The babies who have taken milk powder are really cute. Some have grown one pound and some half a pound. They grow fatter in my eyes. There are so many people sick. Now I see patients again. They come to beg me to see them, and I have no way out. I ask them to go to the hospital, but they do not want to. Some of them are bedridden. How can I ask them to walk to the hospital unless I find people to carry them there? I do not see the ones who can walk [to the hospital]. Yet, they say that they have no money to go to the hospital, so I have to give them the money for fees at the Drum Tower Hospital, twenty cents for registration. Also, I pay for their medicine for the time being. Meanwhile, I talked with the hospital [to ask them] to give the refugees free medicine, and they agreed. In doing so, I add additional work for myself to handle daily, writing [their] notes. Therefore, I'm extremely busy from morning to night. Sometimes the refugees come to see me even at night.

Wednesday, February 23

From Vautrin's Diary

Mr. Rabe left this morning. Took one servant with him. As far as I know this is the third Chinese who has been permitted to leave Nanking.

A mother brought in three young girls this afternoon and begged us to receive them. One is her daughter who went to the country in early December, the other two were country girls. They say it has been terrible in the country. Girls had to be hidden in covered holes in the earth. Soldiers would try to discover these hiding places by stamping on the earth to see if there were hollow places below. They said they had spent most of their days since December 12th in these holes.

This afternoon between five and six Francis Chen and I went around our campus by way of Hankow, Hugigwan [Hu Chu Kwan] and Canton Roads. We met a number of old men going back to the Zone for the night. They say that during the day the stealing of money continues. I put Mr. Chen's money in my pocket for fear we might meet the same fate. On Hugigwan I saw only four old people who were living there at nights. Most houses are still boarded up. Truly it looks deserted and sad. Not a young person in sight and no normal activities going on.

At nine this morning two young girls came running to the campus from the street between the University and Ginling saying that soldiers were in their home and they had escaped. It chanced that Lewis was on our campus in a car so we both went over to the house. The soldiers had left, but one had relieved a poor man of $7.00 before going.

The planes continue to go over us to the northwest.

Tree planting and cleaning still continues on our campus. We have made a huge trench in the back hill and are about to begin one on the hill north of the library.

Mrs. Tsen, Francis Chen and I are trying to estimate the cost of refugees to Ginling, aside from injury to the buildings. The latter will be well over $2000, I am sure. Our camp has been fortunate in many ways, but largely because we had only women and children, and because our people did not have to do cooking in their rooms.

From Tsen's Diary

Mrs. Twinem is sick, so I have to go outside [to other camps] to distribute milk powder and fish liver oil in her place. These camps have not been dispersed, and refugees refused to leave. People in our place get sick one after another. Miss Wu just recovered, but Mrs. Twinem became sick. I have to supervise the work of making covers for comforters because there are so many comforters without covers. The clothing factory operated by Mr. Smythe and others can produce cloth. We can use it to make covers for comforters and then distribute them to the refugees. I have already distributed the comforters to most of our refugees who had none, but they want more comforters for their men too.

Thursday, February 24

From Vautrin's Diary

Bright clear days continue. Our refugees are busy each morning washing clothes and heads. What a blessing they have water, plenty of it.

This morning 4 girls came in from the country disguised as old women. They have been hiding in a fuel stack for weeks. They are nice looking, strong girls, but so sad. By afternoon they were washed and clean looking and went to the afternoon meeting. What were their thoughts as they sat in that meeting?

At 11 o'clock J. Magee and Mr. Forster, and the four pastors who have been coming so regularly to preach, were over for a conference and for dinner—and what a good dinner it was, chicken, sweet vinegar fish and shrimp. The men are willing to continue. We are going to try having a big meeting each day in the chapel—and those women who desire can come to each meeting. Will follow the Life of Christ until Holy Week.

This evening we planned a statement of costs of refugees through February, and a budget for March.

Broadcast is furnished us almost every day by Mr. Magee or Mr. Forster. No electric light yet in our district, so we have no radio.

This afternoon a little boy came to see me whose father, mother and maternal grandmother and baby sister were all killed by Japanese soldiers. He saw them all killed. He and a blind woman, having heard of the Ginling refugee camp, came here. The father was a ricksha man.

Also this morning, a woman refugee came from the University to see if I could help her secure the release of her husband who was taken on December

13. She is a poor country woman and has three little children dependent on her. Her brother was stabbed on the same day, I believe. She thinks her husband is in Hsia Gwan.

From Tsen's Diary

The [Bible] classes began. There are over 600 students. I cannot help them [with the classes] because I have to go out for Twinem [to distribute milk powder and fish liver oil]. Perhaps, Miss Vautrin would help [with the classes]. Also, there are services every afternoon, two hundred attendees each time.

We want to check several friends' houses. Yet, we do not have cars, and Mrs. Twinem's car has already been taken away by the Japanese soldiers. If we had her car, it would be more convenient for us to go places. Now each car flies the American flag; otherwise, the car would be looted by the Japanese soldiers when they spot it on the street. At first, even flying the American flag did not do much good unless there were Americans in the car. Now, the situation is improving some. The Japanese took away a large number of cars. So many cars, trucks, and buses in Nanking disappeared. All the vehicles which the Japanese are using now belonged to [people from] Nanking. The Japanese also took some to Wuhu.

Friday, February 25

From Vautrin's Diary

Warm weather continues. Spring bulbs peeping through. "Welcome the Spring" is [in?] bloom in protected parts of the garden. Spent morning trying to work out new plans for camp. It is slow work, for we are so limited in staff.

Vaccination began at 2 with babies and lasted until 5:20. Vaccinated a total of 1,117. Dr. Brady came with three helpers. Place—between the two South dormitories out in the sunshine. Shall we force all to be vaccinated?

At 3 P.M. attended a meeting of Christian workers of city held over in Hospital chapel. Episcopalians had five men and three women evangelistic workers present. A fine showing compared with other Missions. All agreed that this is a time of great opportunity, and that many are eager and earnest. Unfortunately some churches have no pastors in the city.

Mr. Mills says that the city seems quieter. Mo Tsou Road is now becoming a market street. The regular business streets have not yet opened up—it will take a long time, since so many shops are utterly destroyed.

As I was going to the meeting this afternoon I passed the Anhwei [Anhui] burial ground. There I saw men belonging to the Swastika Society still busy burying unclaimed bodies, wrapped in matting and placed or dragged into the trenches. The odor was so bad that the men now have to wear masks. Most of these bodies go back to the first days of occupation.

From Tsen's Diary

There is one thing that I have to record . Although we are in this kind of peril and suffering, we gather together to pray at seven o'clock every morning. We cannot help thanking God's blessing. In our daily pray, we thank God for having our [Western] friends here. First, we pray for our nation. Besides God, who can rescue us from danger? Who can save our nation? Although we have the Americans to help in relief work, it is God's power. This time, these Westerners have helped us a lot. If Ginling does not have us here to help, it would have been looted until nothing was left. If Miss Vautrin was not here, it would not work either. It's very commendable that that they are willing to sacrifice themselves.

Now, under the circumstances, if the Chinese did not loot things, it would be impossible to get through each day. Life is difficult. We have to make efforts ourselves.

Today another child died.

Saturday, February 26

From Vautrin's Diary

Beautiful spring weather continues. Bulbs are pushing their leaves through the soil and more birds are visiting us in the early morning. Gardeners planted daffodils today, and continue to transplant trees and shrubs. It seems strange to have one part of our existence so normal while another phase of it is so upset and unnatural.

Spent the morning getting data for a radiogram to New York. How can we get estimates of cost of putting buildings into good condition when there is no contractor in the city, and the only architect we know—Mr. Gee—is so busy with refugee work that we cannot bear to ask him. How can we estimate personal losses when we have no idea what was in trunks or chests of drawers? At any rate the loss of [to] Ginling College is so small that it seems almost ludicrous to send it in.

Vaccinations continue today with more than 700 in line. Mary is ill with a heavy cold and fever.

Three neighborhood boys went with me to the west of the campus. They are as glad to go as I was to have them—it was mutual protection. We saw some of the huge dugouts which political organizations had made at high cost in the hills to the west of our campus. What a wasteful thing war is! Two months' food for a helmet, and a good sized primary school for the cost of a dugout that is used for a few months. We saw a number of poor houses that had been looted and several politically owned houses that were looted of all doors and windows and floors. In some cases all but the roofs were gone. This type of looting was done by the common people—after the Japanese led the way. The neighborhood people are very friendly.

Several Japanese visitors this afternoon when I went out—newspaper men who were not unfriendly.

From Tsen's Diary

This afternoon, vaccinations for chicken pox were given to over 800 people. [They] continue tomorrow. The weather is good, and many people participated. It can only be administered in the yard, and the order is very good. In some places, people refused to be vaccinated, and the doctors had to stand at the gate to keep people from going out. There is no other way to enforce vaccination on adults because the Chinese believe that only children need to be vaccinated, not adults. These people are not educated, and those of us here have to lecture them about the vaccination beforehand.

Sunday, February 27

From Vautrin's Diary

First service at South Gate Christian Church this morning. Almost 60 present. Second service at St. Paul's, with almost 40 present. A Japanese Christian at latter. Would there were women workers at each place to visit in homes!

Our afternoon service was held in the chapel with more than 350 present. What a challenge to see that sea of young faces! They love to sing. Mr. Wang Ming-deh preached. Hereafter we shall use the big chapel for afternoon meetings.

Invited Mrs. Li, matron at the Seminary, to come to Ginling to live, but she cannot leave her present place, for work there will be starting up soon.

Service at #3 [Ping Tsang Lane] led by Mr. Mills. Subject—Faith in a Better World.

A good deal of sickness in our group. Mary and Miss Wu are in bed here, Blanche in the hospital, and Miss Wang not feeling well.

Spring weather continues. They say the soldiers are being changed. Does it mean an improvement?

From Tsen's Diary

These two days, nothing special to be written down. Today, vaccination for chicken pox is administered to over 700 people. Tomorrow is the last day. Next month, flu shots will be given to people.

Today, people came here from the countryside again because of bandits. Now, if people have a safe resident certificate, they can come in and out of the city. However, if you have money with you, it—no matter how much—will be taken away [by the Japanese].

Even now, Chang Szi-fu's son has not come back. There is probably no hope for him to return. Chang often cries for his son.

Monday, February 28

From Vautrin's Diary

Beautiful weather continues. Refugees love to wander out in sunshine. Gathering "greens" everywhere. Gardener taking out broken and trampled shrubs and replacing with better ones. Roof of Arts Building being repaired.

Tung Lao-ban has spent the day estimating losses due to refugee occupation. They amount to $6,800, roughly, for the six buildings. All woodwork will need repairing and all floors. Most walls need refinishing. Hardware such as window fasteners has been treated badly when they could not make it work.

Spent most of the day preparing a statement to send to New York which I sent over to the Embassy at five o'clock; also preparing a statement of losses due to Japanese military. Would that other people's losses were as light as ours!

Mary went to the hospital this morning with a miserable cold and deep cough; Blanche Wu returned from an eighteen-day stay there. She insisted on living in Science Hall, and I am helpless to argue against it.

An officer and two soldiers called at 1:30 P.M. to see how conditions are on the campus. They also asked about number of refugees. I had a good opportunity to talk to them about the husbands and sons who have not returned. The officer reported that there are more than 1,000 captives in the Model Prison and they are soldiers and officers—no civilians according to his report.

About 3 P.M. four soldiers came on a sight-seeing trip. They were friendly and showed much interest in the Library. The brightest one had a map in his hand—he was evidently planning to see the sights of Nanking.

One of the men in the Swastika Society who has had charge of burying the bodies of soldiers and civilians, reported that bodies are now coming up from the Yangtze where they were thrown. He promised to give me a report of numbers.

From Tsen's Diary

Mrs. Twinem is still coughing and has a fever. Tomorrow, I'll send her to the hospital. I have no way to cure her, and it is difficult for me to take care of her because she lives in the high school. Miss Wu [Blanche] went to the hospital again after coming back for only a week. Probably, she has bronchitis and has to stay in the hospital.

This noon, we add another little refugee, and the newborn is very tiny. I'm afraid that it cannot survive.

Yesterday, I went to the Nanking University and heard that during these couple of days, quite a number of children died there. The day before, twelve, and today, seven children died. There is not ample time to bury them. Sometimes, children die too quickly to find out the cause.

Tuesday, March 1

From Vautrin's Diary

Weather too warm and spring like. We are fearful of an epidemic of some kind.

At 9 A.M. started with Mrs. Tsen in a car to call at home of a Mrs. Djao who owns two foreign style houses over near the Examination Bureau. We had hopes that her car might still be there—but, alas, both houses had been burned and were surely sad looking. Horses had been stabled in remains of one. The garage was empty—as we feared it might be. Nothing was left of any value and the houses were almost completely wrecked. From there went to Central Research Institute where we found a Japanese truck, one Japanese man—not a soldier—and a number of Chinese taking off the biology specimens. I said the material had been given to Ginling College, that we had put two watchmen there to take care of it, that we would have moved it long ago had we had the trucks. They were removing things to the Geological Institute for safe keeping, they said. We went with them to the latter place and found the head man there who said they were storing all science materials in that building for safe keeping. He thought we could get the specimens later, but he was not sure. If we wanted them taken to Ginling we would have to get permission from military at Sin Giai Kow. To the latter place we went and then Mrs. Tsen left me. Strange enough I found two young men there who went with me in their car to both the Research Institute and Geological Institute and gave orders that specimens were not to be removed, and later took me back to their office and gave me a letter of permission to move the things to Ginling.

On my way home stopped at 3 Ping Tsang Hsiang and arranged for the ambulance and truck to begin to transport this afternoon. By 4 P.M. two loads had come over. Hope to continue good work tomorrow. Cannot account for good fortune, for there were any number of places where the plan might have been blocked. It pays to be friendly and kind, yet persistent.

Have been sickened this P.M. by a sight in the Practice School campus—my dog Laddie had brought in the head of a little baby—the body had perhaps been thrown out or only partially buried.

Neighborhood women report that it is still not possible for them to remain in their homes as soldiers came and insist on their finding "hwa gu-niang." Also sums as small as 20 coppers were taken from people yesterday.

In eastern part of city, when we went this morning, we saw no Chinese except people carrying loot—the process continues. Many soldiers and many military vehicles were seen—tanks, armored cars, ammunition, etc. Saw no stores open excepting a few conducted by Japanese. It would be a bold merchant who would open a store under present conditions—and this is two and one-half months after entry.

From Tsen's Diary

Mrs. Twinem entered the hospital, and my responsibility is lessened. But, everyday I have to go outside to do work for her such as distributing milk powder and checking if the mothers give it to their children. Also, I have to teach them how to mix the milk powder. Some people do not give fish liver oil to children because the latter do not like to take it. The mothers do not understand the benefit of taking the supplement. So, I have to explain it to them. Even though it is free of charge, they do not want to take it until their children become ill. Then they become worried. Now there are so many children coughing and many will have chicken pox in the future.

Aftermath

Law and order began to be restored in Nanking in late February of 1938.[1] Yet, acts of rape, looting, and murder still occurred in the city, on a smaller scale, even in 1939. Incidents of Japanese soldiers' brutalities were prevalent in the occupied city, and people lived in fear under the military rule. For instance, on March 15, 1938, Minnie Vautrin and Rev. John Magee went to the south side of the city to take pictures of a woman of forty-eight who had been raped eighteen times and her seventy-eight-year-old mother who had been raped twice. On May 9, two soldiers forced their way through a window into Liu Lao Tai's home near San Pei Lou. They demanded Liu's two daughters-in-law. When the old lady refused, the soldiers stabbed her to death. Another example: During the New Year's holiday of 1939, a Ginling student returned to her home for a three-day vacation. Soldiers came to her door every day looking for young women. She was so frightened that she spent the entire three days in hiding.[2] Japanese soldiers still looted things from private homes, even in the poorest neighborhood. One old nun told Vautrin on May 23, 1938, that the soldiers had come to her nunnery more than one hundred times, taking all her bedding, cooking vessels, and kitchen knives.[3] Also, Japanese soldiers beat and even killed civilians on the street at will. For instance, on May 10, 1939, four soldiers killed a rickshaw man for no apparent reason. The following day, a carriage man was severely beaten by a Japanese army truck driver solely because the man did not get his vehicle out of the way fast enough.[4] After continually hearing tragic stories daily in Nanking, Vautrin recorded in her diary of May 13, 1938, "One cannot wonder that people ask you pitifully, 'How long will this terrible situation last? How can we bear it?'"

On April 6, 1938, the International Relief Committee hired several hundred workers to help the Chinese charity organizations bury dead bodies. Because there were still so many unburied bodies piled on the streets and because soldiers still committed crimes, the Japanese military authorities prohibited foreigners, except for some medical personnel and diplomats, from returning to the city until June. It was then that some of the Ginling faculty members started to return to the campus.[5]

The International Relief Committee closed the remaining six refugee camps on May 31, 1938. Vautrin decided Ginling would continue to protect 800 young women, who were either the neediest or lived in areas that were often preyed upon by the Japanese soldiers. The committee agreed to subsidize only the young women's living expenses. If Vautrin wanted to offer classes for them, she would have to raise the funding herself, and she did. She offered a ten-week session to enhance the young women's knowledge and refine their minds and bodies. The curriculum was modeled after the Danish-style people's school, including such subjects as Chinese, music, arithmetic, and history. Because of a shortage of teachers, both Vautrin and Tsen had to teach some of the classes themselves.

In September of that year, with Tsen's help, Vautrin started two six-month projects, a homecraft-industrial project and a secondary education project. The former was designed for the neediest women who had no skills to make a living; the latter for the high-school-age girls who had been staying in refugee camps or hiding in the city. All the funding was raised by Vautrin from various sources. She even went to Shanghai and other places to find the best qualified people to teach the classes.

For the homecraft-industrial project,[6] only one hundred of the neediest women were chosen because of limited classrooms, teachers, and funding. These women altogether had thirty children, and Vautrin set up a separate nursery school for them. The curriculum of the project consisted of three parts:

1. Learning to live together: The students were taught how to cook for a large group of people and how to take care of their living quarters. They took turns cooking for the rest as well as cultivating and salting vegetables from their own garden.
2. General education and home training: The students were divided into six groups according to their educational background, ranging from illiterate to the sixth grade. They were taught Chinese, basic arithmetic, Bible study, hygiene, child training, etc.
3. Training in homecrafts and industrial work: Students were taught how to sew, knit, and weave, how to plant vegetables and flowers and raise poultry, and how to make and sell soy bean milk. The students operated a small cooperative store to sell their products.

During the last three months of the six-month program, students were directed to focus more specifically on their chosen area in order to make a living later. Meantime, arrangements were made for them to practice their skills. In addition, Vautrin established a fund to loan to graduates of the program to help them start a small trade.

In the experimental secondary education project,[7] 145 high-school-age girls were admitted. They were divided into five classes, from freshmen to juniors, according to their ability. The students of the lower two grades were assigned to clean dishes and rooms. The three upper classes were required to teach the homecraft-industrial classes and the nursery school. The curriculum differed from regular secondary education because of the shortage of teachers and school supplies in Nanking. For instance, in chemistry class, students were required to do experiments and make such items as dyes, soaps, hand lotion, and ink. Raising vegetables and flowers and curing fruits were used as substitutes for part of the requirements for the biology class. They even raised silkworms to make silk.

All students of the two projects got together every Saturday morning to see one class demonstrate what they had learned that would be valuable to them all. They were expected, not required, to attend religious meetings and Sunday school weekly. Awards were given weekly to encourage students' creativity. Vautrin organized two separate choirs for the homecraft-industrial and for the secondary education students and taught them to sing religious songs.

The day before Christmas of 1938, all classes were cancelled. Students thoroughly cleaned the dormitories and decorated the auditorium. In the evening, a short play was staged by teachers, students, servants, and children of the nursery school. Students then recited selections from the Bible. The two choirs sang religious songs. On Christmas day, students attended brief prayers first in the morning and then a joint Christmas service in the auditorium. In the afternoon, gatherings to sing and read selections from the Bible were held for the women and children in Ginling's neighborhood. The attendees were treated with candies and cards made by the homecraft students. In the evening, students held separate parties with their respective teachers and ate goodies they had made. Ginling's servants and their families received gifts made by homecraft students. All of them apparently had a wonderful time. Vautrin was so pleased to hear the students, especially the destitute women of the homecraft-industrial project, chatting and laughing at the parties.

When the six-month homecraft-industrial project ended in March 1939, Vautrin held a banquet and also a farewell party at graduation. Guests were invited to attend the party and buy items made by the students. All proceeds of the sale went to the fund established by Vautrin for loans to students to start their small businesses. Among the 100 graduates, 53 had job offers waiting for them. For the rest, some returned to the homes of their friends or relatives.

Two of them remained to teach future homecraft-industrial classes at Ginling or at churches.

Vautrin hoped that the homecraft-industrial and the secondary education projects would become a permanent part of Ginling's curriculum. She dreamt that someday she could offer courses to train young village women in the economic skills necessary to make a living. She also dreamt of establishing a permanent Danish-style people's school in the vicinity of Ginling to educate the underprivileged neighbors. She even purchased a piece of land behind Ginling campus out of her own pocket as the site of the future school.[8] But before her dreams could become a reality, Vautrin would have to leave Nanking.

At the time, seeing that there was no school for the children in Ginling's poor neighborhood, Vautrin hired a former teacher to open a small school for them. She paid the teacher a monthly salary from her own meager salary.

When she heard from several women refugees that their missing husbands and sons were held by the Japanese military at the Model Prison in the city, she immediately decided to investigate. She asked these women and others in the same situation to sign a petition and sought various channels to seek the release of the missing men. After months of effort, on May 18 Vautrin was informed by the Japanese embassy that the Model Prison would begin to release the Chinese prisoners. Two weeks later, some thirty prisoners began to be released intermittently from the prison.[9]

In addition, Vautrin took time to help the residents of Nanking redress their grievances and solve problems. Under the Japanese military rule, people lived in terror, with no protection for their life and property. Inflation was skyrocketing, and a severe shortage of necessities hindered daily life. Also, the Japanese military was responsible for selling narcotics in Nanking, which further impoverished and demoralized the society. Vautrin condemned the selling of narcotics and personally helped some of the Chinese opium addicts. She imposed a one-person boycott against stores operated by the Japanese nationals in the city. Although she was longing for Western foods that were only available in the Japanese stores at the time, she chose not to eat them rather than let the Japanese make money selling them. Once, she even boldly rejected the request by the Japanese military to use several of Ginling's buildings. Her best friend Eva Spicer called her a "silly ass" because few people dared to refuse the Japanese's requests and it might generate a reprisal against Vautrin and Ginling.[10]

Vautrin was deadly tired. Her colleagues and friends became increasingly worried about her health. They urged her to return to the United States to rest for a year. She steadfastly declined, afraid that once she left Ginling, her projects for the neediest women, particularly the homecraft-industrial and the secondary education programs, would be discarded. She felt that Ginling needed her. She also wanted to stay in the city to help the suffering civilians.

Eventually, on May 2, 1940, Vautrin decided that she could no longer bear the heavy workload at Ginling. She told Tsen, Matilda Thurston, and one other American teacher in her office about her decision. Thurston, who had been Ginling's first president, took over Vautrin's administrative duties. Vautrin still refused to return to the United States for medical treatment. One night, she almost went down on her knees to beg Thurston to offer the homecraft-industrial and the secondary education projects in the coming fall semester. Only after Thurston assured her that she would do so did Vautrin agree to leave Nanking.[11] Finally, in the company of her friends Rev. John Magee and Katherine Schutze, Vautrin left the city on May 14, 1940.

Tsen remained in Ginling until June 19, 1942, when the Japanese military took over the campus.[12] Nanking was continuously under Japanese military rule until the summer of 1945. On August 6 and 9, 1945, the United States dropped atomic bombs on Hiroshima and Nagasaki, respectively. Five days later, on August 14, the Japanese Empire surrendered unconditionally to the Allies, ending both the Second Sino-Japanese War and World War II.

Within days of the surrender, the Japanese military evacuated from Nanking. The city was returned to the Nationalist Chinese government.

APPENDIX
NOTES
SELECTED BIBLIOGRAPHY
INDEX

———— ■◆■ ————

REPORTS BY MINNIE VAUTRIN ON THE RAPE OF NANKING FROM HER CORRESPONDENCE

———— ■◆■ ————

A Review of the First Month: December 13, 1937–January 13, 1938

An Informal Report to the Board of Founders, Board of Directors, President Wu, Mrs. Thurston and Members of the Staff of Ginling College.

Confidential. Please do not publish.

Explanation: My hope for days has been to write a very carefully worded report, but that hope has been given up due to the many interruptions that come each day. Each time I put aside a morning for this work it is finally used for other matters which seem at the moment more important. Have decided that if I am to get any report to you at all it will have to be a very informal and probably disconnected one. Please forgive lack of unity and coherence. M. V.

Background: December 1, 1937–December 13, 1937.

Our President departed from the College on the morning of December 1, although I think that her boat did not finally sail from Hsia Gwan until December 3. It was difficult for her to leave and even more difficult for us to see her go, but we at that time felt it was for the best and certainly conditions since have proved that it was a very wise decision. For the twelve days following her departure we worked at top speed for there were many important things waiting to be done. Before our President left she had appointed an Emergency Committee consisting of Mrs. S. F. Tsen, Mr. Francis Chen and myself, and this small committee has carried the responsibility through these difficult days.

It was fortunate that the committee was small for we could make decisions quickly—and we had to do that many times. Meal time—for we all eat at the same table—was often used for meetings and trying to think out the next step. Below I will give some of the many tasks that we performed during those twelve busy days, and something of the conditions in the city during that time.

Putting up flags and proclamations: All day of December 1 we gave to selecting strategic places for the American flags which Gwoh, the tailor had made for us, deciding where the proclamations furnished us by the Defence Commander of the Municipality of Nanking and also those that had been furnished us by the American Embassy should be posted. In the end we had 8 flag poles put up on the outskirts of the campus, and the posters were posted at the gate and on all the outlying buildings such as the South Hill Residence, the laundry, the faculty houses for Chinese men and even up on the little house on the west hill. The large thirty foot American flag was still used in the main Quadrangle to let the aeroplanes know that the property was American owned. Previously Mr. Chen and I had finally found the old college sign boards used in the old Ginling and had them repainted—those boards that said "Great American Ginling College." One of these we hung at the gate and one is in front of the Central Building. These we did not actually use until the Japanese entered the city but used their reverse sides which merely said "Ginling College."

Putting buildings in condition for refugees: For days and days our faithful staff of servants worked hard carrying all furniture to the attics or storing it in one or two rooms on the first floor. It was a tremendous job but later proved a very wise preparation. Altogether eight buildings were prepared, including the Practice School and the 400 dormitory. These latter two were never occupied because by the time the first six buildings were filled we had probably ten thousand refugees on the campus and did not have strength enough to manage more than that. Our ideals were very high in the beginning for we got out in poster form a carefully planned set of regulations that would help to make for healthful living, we trained a group of young people to act as scouts or ushers, we made a plan of the buildings and according to regulations furnished us we had room for 2,700 refugees [2,750, as stated in Vautrin's Diary of December 7, 1937] in the eight buildings. On December 8 we received our first group—people who had previously evacuated from Wusih and Shanghai and other places along the battle front and also those who were living just inside and outside of the Nanking city wall, as they were forced to leave by the Chinese military for military purposes and later many of their houses were burned. We could well have used a few more days in getting the buildings in order for after the deluge came we had no time to do any moving of furniture, or to plan regulations for living.

Burning of papers and hiding of valuables: The college vault gave us many anxious moments for if there was a long siege of the city there would surely be thorough looting of valuables and any soldier would know that all institutions like Ginling would have a vault. We therefore decided to clear out the vault and leave the doors of both the vault and inner safe open. Many of the things we hid—I shall not tell you where for we may want to use the place again. Our money we divided, keeping part of it on the campus and packing the larger part in a case and sending it with some other valuables over to the American Embassy. We knew later that when the American officials at the Embassy would leave these things would be taken down to the U.S.S. Panay. Our Emergency Committee decided that Mrs. Thurston's wedding silver should be placed in this same case although we knew that Mrs. Thurston would not want her things protected by a gunboat. You can imagine our consternation later when we heard that the Panay was in the bottom of the Yangtze. Everything has been recovered by Russian divers since so we can smile about the matter now but we did not smile then. Of the new Terrace House Building file I made two copies and hid them in different places.

The college incinerator was kept busy during those days of preparation. Mrs. Tsen spent about two days in the President's office clearing out papers that might be misunderstood, and she also spent many hours burning the receipts of the organization of which Dr. Wu had been the treasurer, lest that also be misunderstood. The Municipal New Life Organization which had rented our Neighborhood House for a few months in the autumn left us a rather big piece of work to do for they evacuated quickly and left all their teaching materials for us to destroy. Gwoh, the tailor who lives in our neighborhood also rented rooms to them this past autumn and when they left they stored a large number of boxes in his little shop. They looked innocent at the time but as the Japanese army came nearer to the city the tailor became more and more afraid of what might happen to him if these things could not be explained. Just two days before the army entered he came over to see if I would go to his house and look into the boxes. This I did and later I called in Mr. Fitch, who was executive secretary or director of the International Committee for the Safety Zone. The two of us decided that it would be better if he destroyed all of the things. I shall never forget that picture of Gwoh and his good wife on December 13th. All day the two of them and all their relatives carried load after load of books and pamphlets over to our incinerator and there burned them. It was not until late in the night that they finished their task—but he was spared from possible misunderstanding and the thrust of an angry bayonet. On the night of December 15th we buried late at night what we had considered burying before—the garments that had been made by women in the city for wounded soldiers. We had been loathe [loath] to burn them because we felt that the poor of the city would need them during the winter—but on that night that need did not seem so great to us as the need to get rid of them.

Conditions in the City during this period: For weeks and weeks people of the city had been evacuating. The movement began with the wealthy and during that period every truck and car was used and tens of thousands moved up river to Hankow or on further to the westward. Then the middle class began to evacuate and finally the poor and for days and days you could see rickshas going past loaded with boxes and rolls of bedding and people. All who could possibly do so got out of the city, the poor going into the country, especially taking the sons and daughters of the family, leaving the old to take care of their homes. I have often wondered what has happened to these people who evacuated into the country districts for from the reports that we hear these days, the suffering and destruction in the country is even worse than it has been in Nanking if that is possible.

During these twelve days there were constant air raids, and as the Japanese army came closer to Nanking there were no warnings—the planes just came and dropped their bombs—sometimes the whole rack at a time. During the last few days before the entry the shelling of the city was also terrific, in the southern part of the city especially. From my room in the Practice School it seemed to me that there was a fierce pounding on the city gates and the city wall—so fierce that it did not seem possible for the age old wall to resist the onslaught of modem military machinery. It was also during these days that burning began—first outside the city as the villages were evacuated and burned for military purposes, and then the houses inside and outside of the city wall were burned, again for military purposes. I often wondered if this method prevented the Japanese army from entering by a mere twenty four hours if it was worth the while and the terrible suffering that it caused, not to speak of the loss especially to the poor. Each night the sky was red with flames as these houses skirting the city wall were burned and it was during that time that our first refugees came. Within the city—it was Sunday, December 12, I believe that the Ministry of Communications was burned—they did that rather than to let the Japanese occupy that beautiful building. There was some looting by the Chinese soldiers, mostly of money from the stores. None of these calamities reached us in our peaceful little valley and we continued our preparations for the refugees.

On November 23, Dr. Wu took me to the reception which saw the formation of the daily Press Conference which took place until Sunday December 12. At these meetings which took place in the headquarters of the Chinese-British Cultural Association on Peiping Road, there were of course western representatives of the various news agencies and papers; representatives of the police department, the defence commissioners office and of the mayor's office. The mayor himself came to many of the meetings. I started going to these very interesting meetings on Sunday evening, November 28, and each night after that found Mrs. Tsen and me present for through the meetings we could keep in touch with events in the city and also have conferences with people whom we wished to see. I should have mentioned that a goodly number of the missionaries of the city also attended and also a fair number from the business community and the various embassies. It seems to me now as I look back over those meetings that most of them were spent in making announcements either by the military or the chairman, director and secretary of the International Committee for the Safety Zone. The latter committee members kept pushing the Chinese military to get all military organizations out of the Zone as quickly as possible so that the Safety Zone flags could be put in place and cables be sent to Japan and to the world that preparations for such a zone had been completed.

You will have learned from other sources of the formation of the International Committee which in turn proposed, carried out all the plans for the formation of, and later maintained the Safety Zone in Nanking. To this group of men—business men and missionaries, the large group of Chinese in the Safety Zone owe a great debt of gratitude—for what measure of safety and protection they have had during these weeks of terrible strain and stress have been due to them. And I find that the thoughtful Chinese are not unmindful of this great benefit and are deeply grateful for it. Mr. John Rabe, a German business man, has been chairman of the committee and has been fearless and untiring, and Dr. Lewis Smythe of the United Christian Missionary Society and a member of the faculty of the University of Nanking has been the secretary. I cannot go on to mention all the other members of the committee and their splendid work which has been carried on day and night since early in December.

The First Ten Days of Japanese Occupation. December 13–23

When the first group of Japanese soldiers entered the walled city, we do not yet know exactly. We have heard that as early as December 10 a small group entered the old Tung Dzi [Tungchi]Gate, now known as the Gwang Hwa [Kwanghwa] Gate. There was very severe fighting in that section of the city for days and we are told that the Japanese troops entered the city and were repulsed a number of times and that the loss on both sides was very high. A young Japanese official told me that the army actually entered at four o'clock in the morning of December 13. All during the night of the 12th retreating Chinese soldiers passed our gate, some begging for civilian clothes, others casting off their uniforms and firearms into our campus. From the ominous silence we knew that something had happened. About two o'clock in the afternoon of December 13 the servant in charge of our South Hill Faculty Residence came running down the hill to tell me that the J. soldiers could be seen on our west hill—the one outside of our main campus at about the same time another servant came running to tell me that a soldier had found the Poultry Experiment and was demanding two chickens. By means of sign language I tried to make clear that the chickens were not for sale and the man left. From the back of the campus I could see a number of men back of our campus. They were asking the people in the little huts back there to cook vegetables and chickens for them. No one on the campus slept that night and in my imagination I could easily interpret the sounds of the firearms and the machine guns as the killing of the retreating Chinese soldiers. How many thousands were mown down by guns or bayoneted we shall probably never know for in many cases oil was thrown over their bodies and they were burned—charred bones tell the tale of some of these tragedies. The events of the following ten days are growing dim, but there are certain of them that a life time will not erase from my memory and the memories of those who have been in Nanking through this period. Some of the most vivid of these scenes I will try to reconstruct for you.

For fully ten days if not more from ten to twenty groups of soldiers came into our campus daily; a few coming through the front gate but most of them breaking open side or back gates or jumping over our fence. Some of them were fierce and unreasonable and most of them had their bayonets out ready for use and on not a few of them I could see fresh blood stains. Our loyal staff of servants were on the job and as soon as a group came in they would run for me. My days were spent in running from the gate to the South Hill or the back hill or to the poultry experiment or to one of the dormitories. Although an American flag or an American Embassy proclamation did not seem to deter them, yet the presence of a foreigner was of great help and many were the groups that I escorted out of a dormitory filled with refugee women and children or from the South Hill Residence. It finally took so much energy that we decided that I should use my strength to save lives and not try to save things. During these days they often tried to take our servants saying that they were soldiers, but in every such case I was able to get the men from them excepting the keeper of Mr. Miao's home—the son of the Djang Sze-fu who works in the Biology Department. I was not there when he was taken for I could not leave the campus during those days.

The night of December 17 none of us shall ever forget for it is burned into our memories by suffering. Between four and six o'clock, since Mary Twinem had come over to see us, it was possible for me to escort two groups of young women and children over to the main campus of the University of Nanking where they were opening their dormitories for them. We were so crowded [at Ginling College] and so taxed in strength that it did not seem right for us to take in any more at that time. During my absence, two soldiers came in on bicycles, angrily tore the big American flag from its stakes in the main Quadrangle, and started to carry it off. Finding it too heavy they threw it on the ground in front of the Science Building. Mary was called and as soon as they saw her they ran and hid in the Power House from which place she sent them off the campus very much flushed and embarrassed. When we were just finishing our supper—we had persuaded Mary to stay for the night since it was late—the servant from the Central Building came running to the dining room and said that there were two soldiers at the front door trying to get in. Mr. Li and I went to that door and found the men pulling at the door and demanding that we turn over the soldiers[,] "enemies of Japan." They refused to believe me when I said there were no soldiers, only women and children and they insisted on searching. I did not know but later learned that other groups were searching in other buildings at the same time. Finally by a very clever trick they succeeded in getting almost all of the servants and those of us who were responsible for the refugees out to the front gate and there they carried on what we realized later was a mock trial. They made us feel that they were searching for soldiers, but as a matter of fact they were looking for young women and girls. Fitch, Smythe and Mills appeared unexpectedly on the scene, the latter expecting to spend the night on the campus, and they greatly complicated the mock trial but did not defeat it. A little later they sent off these three men and proceeded in their search for soldiers. Between nine and ten o'clock through a side gate they took off twelve women and girls and the officer at the gate with us took off Mr. Chen. It was not until they were gone that we realized that the trick was to take off girls. I did not expect to see Mr. Chen again for I was sure that he would be shot or bayoneted. That closing scene I shall never, never forget. Mary, Mrs. Tsen and I standing near the gate, the servants kneeling just back of us, Mr. Chen being led out by the officer and a few soldiers. The rustling of the fallen leaves, the shadows passing out the side gate in the distance—of whom we did not know, the low cries of those passing out. Mr. Chen was released at the intersection of Shanghai and Canton Roads, and six of the girls came back at five the next morning unharmed—both of these we believe were wrought by prayer. I think now I might have saved those girls but at the time it did not seem possible. Those of us at the front gate stayed there in silence until almost eleven for we did not know but what there were guards outside ready to shoot if any moved, and then we left for the back part of the campus. Almost every building on the campus had been entered and there was some looting beside the taking off of the twelve. That night I stayed down at the front gate house and you can imagine that there was no sleep for any of us the rest of that night. When I reached the Practice School before going to the gate house, I found Mr. Chen there and also Miss Lo. Soon the other helpers came in for they with Mrs. Tsen's daughter-in-law and grandchildren had been hiding among the refugees. Never will I forget the little prayer meeting we had that night in that room at the Practice School. From that time on Mary has stayed with us and helped to carry the responsibility—especially of sending off soldiers. In addition to the twelve girls taken that night, 3 others have been raped on the campus and nine others have been prevented from the same fate by the appearance of a foreigner at the psychological time. I would that we could have prevented all such tragedies but compared with the fate in most refugee campus and private houses this is an exceedingly good record.

Another vivid memory was the military inspection on December 15 by an officer and perhaps one hundred men. They too were looking for soldiers and inspected us thoroughly. A machine gun was placed on the main road leading to the quadrangle, and had any soldiers been in hiding and tried to escape you can imagine what would have happened to the women and children on the campus. We were told later that there were a number of machine guns and men on the roads surrounding the campus. We had been exceedingly careful not to let any men come on the campus excepting those of a few families whom we know and they are living down in East Court, and therefore we had no difficulty in passing this inspection. It is true that they tried to take several of our servants who had close cropped hair something like a soldier's, but in the end after identification they were released. The officer in charge of this inspection left us a letter signed and sealed with his stamp and this was of great use until it was torn in shreds and thrown on the ground by the petty officer who came on the night of the 17th and carried out the tragedy that I described above. This destroyed letter was soon replaced by another which was furnished me by a military attache in the Japanese Embassy and this has been invaluable in getting soldiers out of the buildings and off the campus. If I go off the campus I leave this letter in Mary's possession and if she goes I have it.

Another phase of these ten days and the days that have followed has been the visits of the many civil and military officials. Invariably the former have tried to help us to the extent of their power and at times they have sent us Embassy police to help protect the thousands of refugees and ourselves by night: for two different periods the latter have sent us a guard of soldiers, and these have not always been a safe guard although they have helped. Our first guard consisted of 25 soldiers whom we placed down in the row of rooms occupied by Mr. Chan the assistant registrar—who had long since vacated them for a safer place. After the period of the Embassy police we had a guard of 4 soldiers each day. Each day when the new group came Mr. Wang and I and sometimes Mary would go down to get acquainted, to get the name of the petty officer in charge and to try to make it clear that if they would guard on the outside of the campus, on the big roads, we would be responsible for the inside of the campus. The method worked very well and only on one night did we have any trouble. During this period, the J. Embassy also furnished us with 30 proclamations in Japanese and these we posted on all of our property and at the gate. These have helped a good deal but have not completely prevented soldiers entering buildings on which they were posted. In fact the many groups who used to love to go into the South Hill Faculty Residence had to go past two American flags, two American Embassy proclamations, three Japanese proclamations in order to get inside. We have kept one night watchman and our two former police now in civilian clothes on duty each night to report in case anything is amiss.

The Period of Registration: The registration of the people living in Nanking began at the University of Nanking on December 26 and lasted through the 27. All the men and women who were refugees on the main campus of the University registered during those days. Our registration started on December 28 and by inference we thought it was to be of the women living on our campus. That was not our fate, however. It lasted for nine long days and men and women came from all sections of the Safety Zone and even from the country. Tens of thousands came in four abreast, listened first to the lecture on good citizenship and then got the preliminary slip which enabled them to go to one of Mr. Chen Chung-fang's residences for the final step at which they were given a stamped and numbered registration blank with their name upon it. For the first few days it was limited to men. They formed in line out on Hankow Road and Ninghai Road as early as two o'clock in the morning and all day long they marched through the campus. It had snowed and you can imagine the amount of mud that these tramping feet brought in. This registration at first took place under the military officers. Two guards of soldiers came each time and each group had to have a blazing bonfire and for the officers we furnished two coal ball fires. At first I thought that it would be better to protest this registration of men on our campus for this meant flinging our front gates wide open, and for the sake of the women we had been so careful to exclude stray men from coming in. However at the end of the first day it seemed best to endure the process for when men were selected out of marching lines and accused of being soldiers, their women folk were usually present and could plead for them and thus many innocent men were saved. Although in the announcement the men were clearly told that if they would confess to having served as soldiers they would be pardoned and given remunerative work to do, we are not sure that the promise was kept but we rather suspect that their bodies are in the large mounds of unburied bodies outside of Han Chung [Hanchung] Gate which we know were brought there about that time. Finally only 28 men were taken from the tens of thousands that registered at Ginling. I shall never forget how anxiously the women watched this process of registration and how bravely they would plead for their husbands and sons. Although the registration of women began on Monday, January 3 yet it did not take place solely for them until Wednesday of that week and closed on Friday. How they feared the rough treatment of the soldiers, and how they cringed as they passed them to get the preliminary blank. A number of women were suspected of being prostitutes—and it was at that time that they were trying to start up the licensed houses in the city for the Japanese soldiers—but each time when the women could be identified they were released. During the last two days of registration of women it was put under the civil officials and was carried on in a decent and orderly way. All the writing was done by Chinese men and the entire process was carried on in our main quadrangle. I was given permission to bring our group of workers, both staff members and amahs, out in a group and the registration was quickly finished—and thus an ordeal which they had been dreading was passed. Women have found since to their sorrow that the registration blank does not mean protection to them and men have found that it does not prevent them from being seized. Ginling has never had such a large registration in its history.

Ginling College as a Refugee Camp for Women and Children: As I mentioned before[,] we began to take in our first refugees on December 8 and they were of two types, those who had come to Nanking from cities like Wusih, Soochow along the line of the advancing Japanese army and those who had to evacuate their homes due to the orders of the Chinese military. By Saturday, December 11 we had 850 living in the Central Building and one of the dormitories and we thought that our estimate of 2,700 was far too large. Up to that time the people had brought in their food with them and the rice kitchen which we had hoped to have was not yet functioning. By Thursday, December 16 we had more than four thousand and we felt that we were as crowded as we could be—we did not have the staff to look after more and we felt that it would be better for the University to open dormitories and take in our over-flow, and it was on the following day that I took about 1000 over to the University campus. But we did not stop at 4000, for we began to realize the terrible danger to women if they remained in their own homes, for soldiers were wild in their search for young girls, and so we flung our gates open and in they streamed. For the next few days as conditions for them grew worse and worse, they streamed in from daylight on. Never shall I forget the faces of the young girls as they streamed in—most of them parting from their fathers or husbands at the gate. They had disguised themselves in every possible way—many had cut their hair, most of them had blackened their faces, many were wearing men or boy's clothes or those of old women. Mr. Wang, Mr. Hsia, Mary and I spent our days at the gate trying to keep idlers out and let the women come in. At our peak load we must have had ten thousand on the campus. The big attics in the Science and Arts Buildings which we had cleared were favorite places for the younger women. Stairs and halls were so crowded that it was impossible to get through and even the covered ways were packed as well as all of the verandahs. People did not ask for a place inside but were content to sleep outside if only we would let them come in to the campus. We realized that young girls of twelve and that older women of fifty and even sixty were not free from mistreatment. I shall never forget the faces of the fathers and husbands as they watched their women folk enter the campus. Often times the tears were streaming down their cheeks as they begged us to "just give them a place to sleep outside." Women were faced by a terrible dilemma in those days—it might mean that in saving themselves from being raped they were risking the lives of their husbands and sons, who might be taken away and killed. Even during this period of danger, we tried to persuade the older women to remain at home with their husbands and sons, even if it meant mistreatment, and let the younger women come to us for protection. This fearful and beastly treatment of women is still going on and even in the Safety Zone. Two days ago a young girl came running to me just as I was going out of the gate and plead with me to go to her home as there were three soldiers there at the time she ran away and they were look-ing for girls. Fortunately the girls were good runners and knew a short cut to our campus so by the time I arrived at the home the soldiers had left without having found the girls.

I suspect you wonder how we fed this vast multitude. The Red Cross on the day that the city was turned over started a Rice Kitchen just north of our campus and that is still furnishing two meals of soft rice each day to our large family. For a number of weeks they brought the steaming rice in to the campus where it was served in two different places on the main quadrangle. We had serving frames made and tried to teach the women not to crowd but to learn to take their turn but it was a difficult lesson for them to learn. Recently the method has been to serve it out at the kitchen and that is a much more satis-factory method as it gives the women and girls exercise twice each day and it enables them to get the rice hot at any time they wish it. If they can afford it they pay three coppers a bowl for it; if they really have no money their case is investigated and they are given a red tag which means free rice. Many of the refugee camps have not been as fortunate as we in having a well managed rice kitchen so near at hand. As for hot water, very early we were able to get two men with big hot water stoves to move into our campus—they were [glad] to do so for it meant personal protection—so our women have had hot water at all times of the day. The cost is low so they can afford it. For those who were without bedding, fortunately we had a supply of comforters on hand, and these have been given to those who are in greatest need. Sanitation has been our biggest problem, especially when we had our peak load. We were non-plussed by this problem for a time for it seemed insurmountable but we are gradually working it out so that the campus does not look as it did in those early days—especially in the mornings. If only we had some lime it would help. Dr. Reeves will be sorry to hear that the fish in the pond back of the Central Building have had a hard time surviving for that is the place where the women wash their toilet buckets. As for laundry, every morning and most of the day you can see the women washing out clothes especially for the children. Every bush and tree and every fence is covered with the washing during most of the day. Many would not recognize the campus if they came at this time.

Meetings for Women and Children: Religion has become a reality to many of us during these days of terror and destruction. Jesus becomes a friend who walks by your side as you go forward to meet a group of fierce men whose shining bayonets are marked with fresh stains of blood. From August on to the present time, every Wednesday evening and Sunday evening we have had a service for the campus and building servants. How they have loved to sing "O save my Country, Lord" and "We love our native land." During the peak of our refugee load and during the time of greatest danger to refugees and to men we did not hold these meetings but soon they were started again. They are now held in the South Studio for the Science Lecture Hall was occupied by women and children for a good many weeks. It was also in August that we started our Wednesday and Saturday morning prayer group for staff members. These meetings have now become daily meetings excepting for Sunday morning. Words cannot express the value these meetings have had in strengthening and binding us together and giving us power to meet the difficult problems of each day. How real and vital prayer has become. About twelve are now attending the staff meetings. Our regular Sunday afternoon and Thursday afternoon meetings for women have been continued by Miss Lo. This week with the help of speakers from the American Church Mission we have started regular afternoon meetings for women. Each afternoon at two o'clock sees a group of about 170 women—mostly young—gathered in the South Studio. Only those over fifteen are admitted and no babies in arms are brought in. We take the refugee buildings by turn and admission is by ticket which we distribute the previous evening. Never have I attended more earnest meetings. At the same hour we also have a children's meeting over in the Science Lecture Hall which we have now cleared of refugees, by distributing to other buildings. The day school teacher conducts these meetings.

At Christmas although we were in a period of great danger and we did not know what each day would bring forth, we had a number of special Christmas services—one for Mrs. Tsen's grandchildren whom we have learned to love and who have helped to keep us normal; one for the adults who have been helping carry the burdens of the work and we included their families; one for all the college servants; one for the neighborhood women and still one other for the young people who acted as scouts in those early days. Mary decorated a north facing room on the second floor of the Practice School and made it so beautiful that some say they will never forget it. There was an altar with a Cross, a little Christmas tree with colored lights, a great bouquet of Heavenly bamboo with bright red berries, several large pots of poinsettias, the red Christmas cut-outs and the Christmas scrolls. Fortunately I had a heavy green curtain for the one window, and by putting a thick cloth over the transom we could not be seen either within or without the building. It was not always easy to keep our voices low when we sang the much loved Christmas carols but we were not disturbed in any of our meetings. Later we were loathe [loath] to take down the decorations. The staff member in charge of each of the above groups planned the meeting so that no one person carried all the responsibility. We also had light refreshments for the children and young people although such things are not to be purchased these days and there are no stores open in the entire city and all our regular stores have been looted clean and many of them have been burned.

Without the work of a fairly large group of loyal helpers the work that we have been able to do would not have been possible. Mrs. Tsen has not only had charge of the food and general management of dormitory servants but she has been our nurse for the large groups of refugees, has distributed the bedding to the poorest. and has been a wise counsellor in meeting intricate and difficult situations; Mr. Francis Chen has had trying experiences because of his youth—in a situation where youth was a handicap—but he has always been willing to do all that he could to help; Mr. Li, his assistant has been willing to help in any way that he can—from supervising the sale of rice tickets to being general sanitary manager of the compound. He too had to remain in the background during the most dangerous days when young men were being taken out of the city. Mr. Wang, my personal teacher, has really acted as my secretary and has been invaluable in going with me to the Japanese Embassy on many trying visits and also in talking to the guards who have been sent to us from time to time. He also helps when high officials come for inspection or to visit. Just now he is giving most of each morning to writing data given to us by women who have lost either their husbands or sons. To date we have prepared 592 of these slips. You will be interested to know that 432 of these men were taken on December 16. Whether or not the handing in of these requests will be of any avail we do not know, but we can only do our part for these heart broken women. Miss Wang, the only member of the student body of the Seminary who remains in the city, has been an invaluable help in many ways. She has been responsible for investigating the cases of those asking for free rice. Miss Hsueh, the Homecraft School teacher, closed our little school just a few days before the entrance of the J. troops and since that time she too has been a great help in all the investigation work and with the meetings. Miss Lo, the evangelistic worker who used to live west of the campus is now living here and giving all her time and strength to helping and the fact that she knows the neighborhood women so well has been of great assistance. Mary Twinem, whom I mentioned coming on December 17, has been here ever since that time. One of us is always on the campus with the special letter given us by Mr. Fukuda. If in the night we have to go to the front gate she is with me. She and the three women just mentioned live with me down at the Practice School and the little sitting room there with the comfort of the stove is a place of relaxation and retreat. Blanche Wu lived in the Science Building until the noise from the refugees became too much for her and then she too moved down so that makes six of us together. Besides being busy with her poultry project she also helps with refugee work when it is possible. Mr. Hsia who lives at the front gate is very good in talking to the soldiers and he often escorts a party around. Mr. Djao, Eva's teacher, who lives with his large family at East Court is very willing to help whenever we need him. Mr. Chan now lives at East Court and does writing for us when needed, but the sight of a soldier is almost too much for him. These are the members of the staff of workers. In addition there are the servants, who have been working hard through all the time of danger—what we would have done without them I do not know. They have willingly taken on the extra work—and no one not living on the campus can realize how heavy the work has been for them and how trying. We hope to give them an extra month's pay when it is over—if it is ever over. In addition we have had to take on extra servants so that we have two in each dormitory—many of these have been willing to work for their board because they felt they were safe here, but we hope to give them a tip. I might add that Tung Lao-ban the carpenter has also lived on the place as a refugee and has worked freely for us whenever we needed him.

The staff members have eaten together in the dining room of 400 and that has been a source of strengthening too—I mean all those who do not have families here. We have been in a quandary as to food. Before the fall of the city we did not put in too much food for fear everything would be looted and now we wish that we had put in more stores. For a number of days, at least two meals a day consisted of two kinds of beans and green vegetable. At no time have we been hungry although I shall be glad when we can get nourishing food to add to the diet for all the workers. The Poultry Project has furnished us with a goodly number of geese and a few chickens which have helped out a good deal, and we have killed Dr. Yuen's goat and three others that were entrusted to us by Mr. Riggs. One of our Practice School Ponds furnished us fish for the whole staff once, which was a treat.

Destruction of College and Private Property: There was no looting by Chinese soldiers before they left the city, and so far there has been no looting by the "lao beh sing," the common people. The J. soldiers entered the South Hill Residence from ten to twenty times and found great joy in the four chests of drawers stored in the large dining room. Again and yet again we have found them there looting and have escorted them out. Dr. Wu, Dr. Chen of the Biology Department, Dr. Chang of the Psychology Department, and Alice Morris, librarian, were the unfortunate owners of the property looted, however I do not think the loss was great as they had packed their best things to take with them. Although they went to the third floor of that house a number of times, yet they did not see attic doors which had been covered by wardrobes. We are hoping that the things stored there will not be touched. Mr. Miao's house was looted and also Chen Er-chang's but how much the loss I have no way of knowing. Those houses are now occupied by refugees. Mrs. Tsen lost some things—her favorite fountain pen among them and some of the rest of us lost pens and gloves. Mr. Li had $55.00 taken from him while he was on the campus and also Mr. Chan's trunks and Mrs. Tung's trunk were searched and some things taken. Those are about all the personal losses—and compared with the loss of many in the city they are very light. The total college loss due to looting by the Japanese soldiers is perhaps less than $200.00 and consists mostly of smashed doors and windows. Our greatest loss is due to the occupation of the refugees. Ten thousand cannot crowd into six buildings without injury to these houses. Walls will have to be refinished, wood work repainted, screens replaced, locks and fasteners replaced or repaired. Trees and shrubs and lawns have all been injured largely by the daily display of washing placed upon them. Our foreign friends have often laughed when they entered the campus and compared it with its former neatness. However the mothers with little children have had to do this washing and we have not wanted to prohibit it. Fortunately in this part of China, nature heals such scars very quickly and in a few years we shall not miss the shrubs that have been trampled or broken, although I have felt sad when a shrub that we have nursed carefully for more than ten years has been badly broken. We have also had some loss due to the nine days of registration which took place on the campus. Some chairs were broken and tables injured and shrubs trampled down. I would estimate this loss at about $100.00 but have not yet found the time to figure it accurately.

Wei Szi-fu, our college messenger boy, was taken on December 14, and did not return until December 28. His bicycle was also taken at the same time as he was on his way to the University Hospital with a message to one of the doctors there. At the time he was wearing an arm band furnished for our servants by the American Embassy. We greatly rejoiced when he returned safely. The son of Djang, the head servant of the Biology Department was taken on December 16, and he has never returned although we have made repeated requests for him. He too was wearing one of the arm bands at the time and was in the house which was clearly marked by an American Embassy poster and flying an American flag. The father has been broken hearted for in addition to this loss he does not know where his wife and four other children are as they were down near Wusih. I am fearful that the young man will never return as there were a good many men killed at that time, especially young men.

Surely we have much to be grateful for as we look back over the past months. The fact that we did not open college in Nanking was a great blessing. During these days I have said again and again I was glad that there were no students on the campus and that Dr. Wu had been persuaded to leave the city when she did. I am grateful too that Ginling has been able to shelter and serve the women and children of this great city as she has during these days of intense danger and terror. What the future holds we do not know, but I am confident that if we seek to know God's will for the College, he will guide us into still greater fields of usefulness in the bringing in of his Kingdom.

Respectfully submitted,
Minnie Vautrin

As a Refugee Camp: January 14–March 31, 1938

Informal Report: Confidential. Not for publication or broadcasting.

A. Conditions in the City and Countryside:

The Self-Government Association which was inaugurated on January 1st in the shadow of the old five-colored flag to take its place beside that of Japan, has now been followed by the formation of a second government. It was scheduled for March 15, but was finally consummated on March 28. Tang Shao-I is reported to be the head of the new government, but he was not present at the inauguration. Just what the relation of the new government is to that which has been established in Peiping we are not certain. Some have said it is to supersede that government and be the future central government of China, others tell us that it is to be under the northern government, and still others say that the two governments are to be independent of each other. Dr. Macklin and Dr. Bowen would know the members of the new government far better than we do as many of them date back to the previous generation and are men who have not been active in the New China.

The International Safety Zone was formally abolished some time ago and the committee which controlled it has been changed into an international relief committee the members of which keep exceedingly busy. It has taken on a large staff of Chinese workers which is busy distributing relief to the neediest families in the city. An effort is also being made by some of the members of the committee to encourage the farmers to go back to their farms and the gardeners to go back to their gardens and to get spring crops in and thus prevent a possible famine later on. Even the most uneducated country women have a favorable attitude toward it, and if a project is sponsored by this committee they at once have confidence in it. On Thursday, March 17, there was a very simple reception down at the headquarters when after some very sincere speeches, banners expressing appreciation were presented to the members of the committee. Rev. Hubert Sone [actually, Plumer Mills] has taken Mr. Rabe's place as the chairman of the committee. The former left Nanking about February 24th, after numerous receptions and teas and tiffin parties. All were genuinely sorry to have him leave for he had been a tower of strength during the trying months since November and he had greatly endeared himself to his co-workers both western and Chinese. The twenty-five refugee camps were gradually reduced to four, and in these remaining ones are mostly the young women who still feel that it is impossible to go back to their homes and also those who have been left without homes. Milk and cod liver oil is distributed in these camps regularly and an effort is being made to provide bedding for those who still come in having been robbed of every possession.

We no longer feel that we live in "the heart of a drum." As you remember, our first contact with the outside world was firmly established when three members of the staff returned to the American Embassy. Their coming made it possible for us to send radiograms to our families and to our organizations and also to send and receive letters by means of the gunboats. Soon followed the return of members to the British and German Embassies. At this time of writing, we are connected by train, bus and merchant boat with Shanghai and it is said that 600 Japanese civilians including women and children are now here. However no American, excepting Dr. Brady, has been permitted to come to Nanking to reside and to carry on business and missionary work, [and] the reason given is that it is not yet safe for them to do so. A very real and persistent effort has been made to secure permission for the return of doctors and nurses, but so far this effort has not been successful. Within the last few days permission has been granted for the return of Mr. Gale from Wuhu. There is great need for the return of the regular evangelistic workers and for the heads of the various missions and it is hoped that by repeated requests permission may be granted. The post office was supposed to be formally opened on March 25th and within a few days after that time it began to function. I understand that there are seven branch offices now open in various parts of the city. I received my first letter from America on Saturday March 26, it having left there on February 28. Newspapers have just started coming through by train—we have not had them regularly since November 12, if I remember correctly. On February 21, I had my first ride in a ricksha, which was in the fourth ricksha which I had seen on the streets since about December 12th. There are a few carriages left in the city but many were demolished. Trucks and cars are at a great premium, the Embassies and the International Refugee Committee possessing the only ones excepting those used for military purposes. Two days ago I saw one of our former buses. Where all the others have disappeared we do not know. Mary Twinem still has hope that she will be able to secure the return of her little Austin, but I fear it is a vain hope. Recently some have seen a little Austin painted a khaki color and rather suspect that it may be her car.

Police service which has been at a minimum has been gradually increased but it is not yet sufficient or courageous enough to prevent much lawlessness in the city. Looting by the military still continues but in a different form somewhat. The poorer people are still being deprived of bedding and money, even coppers being taken now, and houses of the former well-to-do people, which were fairly safe in the Safety Zone, are now being deprived of rugs and radios and furniture. We do not see the wholesale burning of houses which took place from about December 17th to January 17th—it was on that date that I saw the last fire. The most distressing thing that now exists is the continued looting by the "lao beh sing," the common people. With no law and order in the city the poor and the lawless felt perfectly free to go into any house and take from it anything they wished. Outside of the former Safety Zone, many houses have been robbed of everything, even including doors and windows and floors. Within the last few days I have seen very good doors and windows for sale and that means that the demolishing process is still going on. Naturally our Chinese friends are distressed by this but there is nothing they can do about it. From the middle of January to the middle of February, Shanghai Road underwent an evolution. It developed rapidly into a busy mart and literally scores and scores of little make-shift shops were hastily constructed along both sides of it. There were not only shops which sold every kind of loot, but also tea houses and restaurants. I remember passing one called "The Happy People" tea house. The street became so busy and crowded that one had difficulty in getting through it when walking. Then the order came that these shops must be taken down at once or they would be torn down, and just as quickly as the street had flourished, so it receded into its former state. This development extended down into our neighborhood too. How I wish that I had some pictures of that mushroom development for you to see. During these days and weeks of free looting we longed to go to the homes of friends and salvage some of their possessions for them, but alas we had no truck or car, even if we had had the time and strength.

During this period of lawlessness in the city our campus has been fairly peaceful. At no time have "the people" come to loot or steal. Our soldier guard left us on January 14 and never returned. For many days we were fearful lest something should happen, but nothing beyond our control did happen to us. Three times soldiers came on mischief bent [bent on mischief] but were persuaded to go on their way. My calendar shows that military callers ranking from high official to soldiers numbered seventeen groups. Most of them came to see the campus and the camp. We usually show them one or two buildings occupied by refugees first and then take them to the Administration-Library Building which now looks quite normal and is open for inspection. They are always pleased to see it and we are glad to show them a clean building.

February 4 was set as the date when all refugees must leave the Safety Zone and go back to their homes. This proclamation was issued by the local autonomous government and was posted quite widely in the city. It brought consternation to the hearts of the young women on our campus and during the week preceding the date I could not go out on the campus without being besieged by a large group asking if we were going to send them away at that time. Invariably we would answer that it was not our order and that our camp was open as long as their homes were unsafe for them. One day Mr. Mills called and his car was so surrounded by kneeling, weeping young women that he finally had to walk to his home and let his driver follow when he could extricate the car. Several weeks later this terrible fear and anxiety had not left the younger women, for when we gave a tea party for Mr. Rabe down at the Practice School, some of them heard about his presence and his plan to go home and they asked Mrs. Tsen to arrange for them to see him just before he got into his car. None of us expected what really did happen. Literally hundreds and hundreds surrounded him in front of the Science building and implored him not to leave the city but to remain on in charge of the International Committee. His assurance reached only a few ears and the crowd grew instead of decreasing. Mary Twinem took him out the back way and I tried to get the crowd of weeping women to go in another direction so that we could also extricate Dr. Rosen and Mr. Ritchie, who were also guests at the same tea. It took more than an hour to bring conditions back to normal and in the meantime all three men had to walk to their homes and their cars followed later—much later. On February 4th no force was used to expel people from the Zone or the camps and the day of tension and terror passed uneventfully.

China New Year came on Monday, January 31. Even the long weeks of terror and sadness did not prevent a certain amount of celebration and feasting. Some people were bold enough to use firecrackers in their celebration, although it had not been many weeks since the sound of a big cracker would have made us start with fear and say "another civilian killed." In the afternoon Lao Shao, the old gardener, and I went out to look for some "lah mei," twelfth month plum. We wanted to go to the little farm house west of the Guling temple where we bought such lovely branches last year, but when we reached the street just east of the temple and saw that the hills and valleys beyond were a veritable "No Man's Land" we were not courageous enough to make the journey. We had passed five unburied bodies on our journey thus far and we knew that at the temple there would be many more. I also knew but did not tell Lao Shao that over in the little valley to the south of the temple beside two ponds were 143 bodies of civilians and unarmed soldiers—men who more than a month before had been cruelly burned and shot there. We came back home without the "lah mei" glad to get back in a crowd again. Few of us used freely the old greetings that are an innate part of the New Year celebration, somehow those happy carefree greetings would not come to our lips this year. The following evening, Mrs. Tsen prepared a "big meal" for us out of the wonderful basket which our friends and coworkers had sent us from Shanghai. How good it was to have pork once more and the other good dishes of food that accompanied it. I for one was glad to leave our steady diet of beans even for one meal.

On February 2nd I made my first visit into the southern part of the city. Mr. McCallum and Mr. Forster took me down to see the property of the Christian Mission first and then over to see the Episcopal compounds. The city was still lifeless save for the groups of soldiers that could be seen on many of the streets. Such terrible destruction had been meted out on our busy city! I cannot give the exact number, but of the best shops it seemed to me that almost 80% had been looted and then burned. More of the little shops were standing, but all had been looted clean of all goods. At our property, two of our school buildings had been burned and at the Episcopal compound the parish house had been destroyed. We passed a group of army trucks hauling loot, evidently from the northern part of the city for there was nothing left to loot in the section through which we passed. Just two days ago when I was again down in this part of the city older members of the community had returned and some of them were rebuilding little shops out of the remains of the big stores. The development that had taken place on Shanghai Road in January and February had been transferred to the "Street of No Sorrows," excepting that not so many temporary shops had been built—the displays were on tables and on the sides of the street. Patiently people are beginning to rebuild. Loot is still being bought and sold—it is the only way that people have of making a living for nothing is being created in the city as far as I know.

Conditions in the surrounding country are not as peaceful as in the city. Beginning late in January women began to steal their way in from the country villages, disguised in every possible way. To get past the soldier guard at the city gates was the dreaded ordeal. Older women came in first, having heard of the refugee camps, they came in first to find out if they were really existing. They begged us to accept their daughters and daughters-in-law if they could get them into the city saying that for weeks and weeks they had been hiding them in carefully concealed holes in the ground or between double walls in their homes, but even in these places they were not always safe. During the past two weeks we have received more than five hundred into our camp from the country places and the University has received an equal number. In addition to the scourge of soldiers there has been the scourge of bandits, and often when people try to come in they are robbed of everything they possess—money first, then bedding and even part of their clothing. Some of our Chinese friends who evacuated to the country places last autumn are now returning. The men come first to make sure that they can get in, they register with the local government, and then go back to bring in their families. During the last two weeks, Mr. Handel Lee, Mr. Shao Deh-hsing and others have come. Just yesterday Wang Bao-ling's brother came from Sanho south of Luchowfu. They all look as if the past months have been months of strain and deep anxiety for themselves, and we realize that most of it has been worry for the women folk in their families.

B. *Conditions in the G. C. [Ginling College] Refugee Camp:*

Our camp was one of the four selected to continue its existence by the NIRC [Nanking International Relief Committee]. According to the recommendation of the Committee, we have organized into four departments or sections, namely, business, supervision, education and health. Having been granted a small allowance by the Committee for 2 assistants, and 4 servants for each one thousand refugees, we have felt justified in taking on extra staff. These have been mostly from our "invited" refugees such as Miss Rachel Wang. Mr. Wang and Mr. Djao, personal teachers of Chinese of members of the regular faculty, Mr. Chan, the assistant registrar, and a Mr. Swen, who is a neighbor who has been living down at East Court. A new office has been started in the former guest room in the Arts Building and it is a busy place from morning to night. Mrs. Tsen has also invited three refugee women to assist her in distributing milk and cod liver oil. Keeping statistics up to date in a shifting refugee camp is no light task. During the first week in February we had a formal registration of all our refugees when the head of each family group was given a white cloth tag bearing her name and the number in her family group. These tags were sewed on by our workers with a special color of thread so that they could not be transferred to others when they wished to leave. According to that registration we numbered 3,200. By the middle of March our new staff felt that it was necessary to reregister all, and they prepared a lavender cloth tag which has been given to each member of the refugee group excepting babies in arms. According to this registration our number now is 3,310. Mr. Chen, who is head of the business department, is now with his staff working on the very difficult problem of the free rice group. Naturally many people want free rice who can afford to pay for it, and so to separate this group from those who have absolutely nothing with which to pay is a most difficult task. The free rice group were first given red tags; a month later they were rechecked and given yellow tags, and now a third system is being worked out and will be put into operation this coming week. If people were always sincere, our work would be infinitely lighter and incidentally our dispositions would be better.

After our refugees had been with us about three months we decided that we simply must work out some system whereby they could have baths. We had been playing with the idea before but were not able to get coal. We made our plan and presented it to the International Refugee [Relief] Committee and they agreed to furnish us with coal and the funds for one fireman and two women to look after each house. For two weeks now, under Mrs. Tsen's supervision we have been operating two bath houses where 168 women and children can take baths each day. The price is four coppers for adults, two for babies and children, and nothing for those who are too poor to afford even this small amount. In addition to the joy this privilege gives to the women, it also gives a livelihood to five persons.

Our Camp has also been granted a fund for cash relief and another to loan to individuals. Women who are very poor, whose homes have been burned and whose husbands have been taken are given a sum in cash when they are ready to go back to their homes. This helps them to start again and has been deeply appreciated by all who have received it. The loan fund has given loans to a number of women whose husbands are in other parts of China and are earning a salary. A good many women of this type have been left stranded in Nanking and as yet have had no means of getting funds from their husbands.

Mrs. Tsen who is head of the Health Department of our Camp has carried on very successfully the distribution of milk and cod liver oil for babies and children. Children who are undernourished are given this extra food each day, [and] the three women who have been taken on as assistants in this department distribute the milk and also attend to the mixing of it. Both of these foods are furnished us by the International Relief Committee. Mrs. Twinem and Mrs. Tsen have also been responsible for the distribution in the other refugee camps and have spent many mornings visiting these other camps and getting the distribution organized. Under our Health Department we also have had three vaccination clinics when almost two thousand were vaccinated by Dr. Brady of the Christmas Hospital staff. During these long weeks of simple living we have had more than 30 deaths and 40 births on our campus. The disposal of the night soil is still one of our major problems, but we are gradually getting the problem solved. Fortunately we have a large campus so that we have room for the huge trenches which we have dug for this purpose. Dai, the regular college bell ringer, sounds a gong about eight in the morning and again at five in the afternoon and this is the time for the women to empty the toilet buckets and clean them.

C. A Project in Religious Education:

For the six weeks from January 17 to February 26 we limited our religious work to two meetings each day, one for the adults and one for the children. As I reported in my previous letter, five pastors from the American Church Mission very generously and faithfully came each afternoon during the week, excepting Saturday, and spoke. In addition the women learned some simple songs. On February 27 we started another project, this time in the life of Christ, which is to culminate in an early service on Easter morning and in a pageant that afternoon or evening, also in special services being held throughout Holy Week. Miss Rachel Wang is dean of our Educational Department and as such she has organized 23 classes according to educational ability [for] all of those studying the life of Christ in one form or another. You will be interested in the classes so I will give you the details——

2 classes or sections of Junior-Senior Middle School ability
2 of 6th grade elementary school ability
2 of 5th grade elementary school ability
4 of 3rd and 4th grade elementary school ability
6 sections of those who have studied in private school a few years. These are
   divided according to age, some are children, some adults.
3 sections of adults who have never studied. They are being taught a Gospel
   Primer.

2 sections of illiterates from 18 to 19 years of age.
2 sections of illiterates from 12 to 27 years of age.

These last two sections meet five times each week and are taught by Mr. Wang and Mr. Djao. Our enrollment is something over a thousand and our attendance each week is perhaps between seven and eight hundred. The older women try to attend regularly but if a baby is ill they have to miss, and often they have to go back to their homes during the day or on some other errand. All the classes but the two I mentioned meet three times each week. In addition to lessons in the life of Christ all are learning certain selected Psalms and hymns and other passages from the Bible. Miss Wang has selected the 23rd Psalm, the 121st, the Beatitudes, the Lord's Prayer. How they love to sing "What a Friend We Have in Jesus" and "Jesus Lover of My Soul." Just now they are learning Easter hymns, the one for this week being "The Day of Resurrection." The teachers have wanted to share with their students those hymns and scripture passages that have been of greatest comfort to them during these days of suffering. All of our teachers, excepting Miss Hsuch, the day school teacher and myself, are refugees, some of them were invited to come, to be sure, and yet they know what it means to be refugees. Our afternoon preaching service continues, but now it is held in the big chapel. The attendance varies from 150 to almost 400 and is usually largest on Sundays. The topics for these meetings have been carefully selected by the five men who come to us from the Episcopal Church and they all are centering on the life of Christ also. You should hear a group of three hundred refugee women sing "What a Friend We Have in Jesus." They love it and how they do sing. We take turns in leading the singing and also in inviting people to the meetings so that the work does not fall too heavily on any one person. One of the difficulties connected with the class work was our lack of classrooms for as you may realize, every room in the Arts Building where our classrooms are, is occupied by refugees. We have converted the North Studio into a very good classroom, the Grecian statues in that room which were stored there by Central University when they moved last fall, being gracefully draped with a big curtain. The stage of the big auditorium is also used as a classroom and makes a very good one indeed with space for more than forty chairs. Another class meets in the chemistry laboratory, which we never used for refugees and many classes meet in the science lecture hall. After Easter we shall have a week's holiday and then begin work again. At that time we shall hope to add different types of classes such as poultry raising; personal, home and community hygiene; child training; and perhaps Japanese. We shall also try to teach some industrial work, but that will need more of a staff than we have available now. Yesterday several of us went on an expedition to the South City to see if we could find some looms and stocking knitting machines. To our disappointment we found that they all had been looted. But where there is a will there is a way.

D. Another Project:

Early in January we became conscious that many of our refugee women—especially wives and mothers were in deep distress because their husbands or sons who had been taken soon after the entry [of the Japanese] on December 13, have not returned. Many of these women were left with little children and often one or two old people and they had literally no means of support—nothing they could do but beg and even that is impossible now in a community so poor as ours. Again and again they would come to us asking if there was anything that could be done to secure the return of these men—all of them civilians as far as we were able to ascertain. We finally went to the Japanese Embassy and talked it over with one of the more thoughtful officials there and he suggested that we furnish him with the facts and he would see if he could do anything with the military about it. From January 24 to February 8 we were able to secure 738 civilian records. These we handed in not only to the official with whom we had the first conference but also to a higher official who had come up from Shanghai. As far as we know, nothing has happened for we have not heard of any men returning. In the meantime rumors began to reach us that there was a large group of civilian men imprisoned in the Model Prison over near the Central University. A trip over in that direction confirmed the rumor. The exact number of men we could not determine but we learned that men were there and in a pitiful condition. Soon the older women began to come to our campus saying that they had gone to the front of the prison and had seen the men being taken out each morning in trucks to work. A number of the women have told us that they have actually seen their husbands or sons and some of them have been permitted to talk to them. Again the pleas began to come to aid them in securing the release of these men. Chinese men in local government administration suggested that we have our women prepare a petition to be handed in not only to the head of the local government but also to the Japanese military. From March 18 to 22nd 1,245 women came in to sign this petition—most of them were very poor women and could only make a finger print underneath the name which was written in their behalf. Such a pitiful group of women I have never seen before. Most of them were poor—farmers, gardeners, coolies, little merchants; and most of them had had their only means of support taken from them. One woman had lost four of her sons; another had had five members of her family taken; another had lost three sons. There were a goodly number of young women who had been left with three or four little children and they could not possibly make a living for the children. It seems that the petition has born[e] some fruit for now the women are asked to make another giving more data with regard to the time the men were taken, their occupations, etc. Tonight Mr. Wang is making the announcement in the dormitories and tomorrow six people will begin work on this new petition. It will take from three to five days to complete it as the women will come from miles out in the country. Such news spreads like wild-fire and the poor women come trudging in even if there is but a very faint hope. One of the greatest problems facing the people interested in rehabilitation work for this district, is that of the women who have been left with no support and whose husbands will never return. I long for Ginling to help in the solution of this perhaps more than anything else.

E. *Ginling losses.*

Since the last report sent to you, we have had time to secure facts with regard to the college and faculty losses. The loss to the college property from the looting of Chinese soldiers was nil; from the looting of Japanese soldiers does not exceed $300.00. About fourteen faculty and two servants lost a certain amount through the looting of the Japanese soldiers and this we estimate at about $1,200. 00. By far the greatest loss has come from the use of the academic buildings as a refugee camp, for the housing of 10, 000 women and children even for a short time means much wear and tear on woodwork and floors. The best estimate that we have been able to secure sets the loss at about seven to eight thousand dollars, and it will probably be higher than that if our refugees continue with us through the coming months. I feel sure that somehow we can raise the money needed to put the buildings back in good repair, but even if we cannot raise the funds it is better for us to face the future with marred and soiled walls than not to have done this humanitarian service for the women and children who have come to us. We could not have closed our doors against them.

This letter is brought to a close with greetings to you from the members of the staff. You must not feel sorry for us thinking that we lack food or social life. We can get the kind of foods now that we need to keep us well. Some of us have even been to two feasts during the past months, one at the Japanese Embassy and another at the Hwei Wen Girl's School. Tomorrow, Mrs. Tsen, Mrs. Twinem, Blanche Wu and myself are giving a simple Chinese meal to a group of friends whom we are inviting to the South Hill Faculty Residence. This afternoon we went up and folded up the garments scattered in the living room—since the looting we had never taken the time to do that. The big dining room we shall not disturb, but keep it for the enjoyment and amusement of our friends. Conditions in the city are such that more and more we are able to leave the campus and not feel that our three thousand three hundred will be in danger when we are away. This past week I have had my bicycle brought down from the attic and oiled and I have ridden it when going on an errand down to the South Gate. Mary and I are planning to ride out to the National Park very soon for the thought of the blossoms there is enticing us and it is difficult to resist. We have had some illness among our staff members but all are well now. Blanche was ill with a very severe case of bronchitis and was in the hospital for three weeks. The day she returned Mary went over with the same malady and was also there for three weeks. Mrs. Tsen has had several very severe colds and has been confined to her bed for a number of days at a time. I have had a few days off but otherwise have been feeling very well.

Puh, the shrub man is busy at his work and the campus is beginning to look neat and clean once more. The Practice School campus is at its loveliest now and is a constant delight to those of us who live here. The little children who live at East Court and Mrs. Tsen's grandchildren are having great fun tending to the student flower garden at the Practice School. Every day they spend many hours there watering the flowers. Life would be so lovely if this terrible war and destruction would cease, and if families could be re-united, and the nation go forward on its plan of reconstruction which has been so bravely started. The scores of heavy bombers which fly over us to the northwest each morning make us realize that the end is not yet near and that destruction and terror and suffering continue.

Not many letters have come through from friends, but those that have come have been deeply appreciated. If when you write you prefer to send my mail to our Shanghai office at Room 512A, 133 Yuen Ming Yuen Road, I will receive it in good time. I fear that this general report must be accepted in lieu of more personal letters.

Very sincerely yours
Minnie Vautrin

NOTES

Introduction

1. For a brief account of Japan's invasion of Manchuria in 1931, please see Kung Chin-ku et al., *Jungkuo kan ri zhan zheng shi kao* [The Draft History of China's Resistance War against Japan] (Hupei: Hupei People's Publishing, 1983–84), 19–28; Frank Dorn, *The Sino-Japanese War, 1931–1941: From Marco Polo Bridge to Pearl Harbor* (New York: Macmillan, 1974), 28–29; Akira Iriye, *After Imperialism: The Search for a New Order in the Far East, 1921–1931* (Cambridge, Mass.: Harvard University Press, 1965), 285–99.

2. George Fitch's circular letter of Christmas Eve 1937 from Nanking, in Martha Lund Smalley, ed., *American Missionary Eyewitnesses to the Nanking Massacre, 1937–1938* (New Haven: Yale Divinity School Library, 1997) 1; H. J. Timperley, *What War Means: The Japanese Terror in China—A Documentary Record* (London: Victor Gollancz, 1938), 20.

3. Minnie Vautrin, diary entries for December 16, 17, and 21, 1937, in Wilhelmina [Minnie] Vautrin, Diary and Misc., 1937–40, Archives of the United Board for Christian Higher Education in Asia, Special Collection, Yale Divinity School Library (hereafter cited as Vautrin's Diary; for details, please see "A Note on the Two Diaries" in this book); John Rabe, diary entries for December 16 and 17, 1937, in *La bei ri ji* [Rabe's Diary; in Chinese], trans. Liu Hai-ning et al. (Nanjing: Jiangsu Historical Books, 1997), 185, 187–91, 197–99 (all citations to Rabe's Diary are to this edition); family letters of Dr. Robert Wilson, December 15 and 18, 1937, in Timothy Brook, ed., The *Documents on the Rape of Nanking* (Ann Arbor: University of Michigan Press, 2000), 212–17.

4. John R. Pritchard and Sonia M. Zaide, eds., *The Tokyo War Crimes Trial: The Complete Transcripts of the Proceedings of the International Military Tribunal for the Far East* (London: Garland, 1981–87), 20:49608.

5. Brook, *Documents on the Rape of Nanking*, 14–16; Daqing Yang, "Documentary Evidence and Studies of Japanese War Crimes: An Interim Assessment," *Researching Japanese War Crimes* (Washington, D.C.: National Archives and Records Administration, 2006), 29–30; Sun Zhai-wei, *Chen qi li shi: Nanjing da tu sha yan jyou yu shi kau* [To verify history: Research and deliberation on the Nanjing massacre] (Nanjing: Jiangsu People's Publishing, 2005), 273–76.

6. Chinese historians En-han Lee of the Academia Sinica of Taiwan and Sun Zhai-wei of the Historical Research Center of Jiangsu Social Sciences Academy in Nanjing,

after years of studies, conclude that the total deaths estimates of "350,000" and over "300,000" respectively, are reliable. See En-han Lee, *Ribenjun zhan zheng baoxing zhi yanju* [A Study of wartime atrocities by the Japanese military] (Taipei: Commerce Publishing, 1993), 30–33, 35–41; and Sun Zhai-wei, *Chen qi li shi*, 255–65. Japanese historians Fujiwara Akiro and Tomio Hora agree that the number of Chinese victims was between 200,000 and 300,000. See Tomio Hora, *Nanjing da tu sha: Ting ban* [The Nanking massacre: Definitive edition), trans. Mao Liang-hung et al. (Shanghai: Shanghai Translation Publishing, 1988), 3; and Fujiwara Akira, *Nankin daigyakusatsu sengen* [The Nanking massacre: New edition] (Tokyo: Iwanami Shoten Publishing, 1988), 20. See also Kaga Mitsuyoki and Himeta Mitsuyoshi, eds. and trans., *Shogen Nankin daigyakusatsu* [Testimonies on the great Nanking massacre] (Tokyo: Aoki Shoten Publishing, 1987), 53; Iris Chang, *The Rape of Nanking: The Forgotten Holocaust of World War II* (New York: Basic Books, 1997), 4–6, 211; and Hua-ling Hu, *American Goddess at the Rape of Nanking: The Courage of Minnie Vautrin* (Carbondale: Southern Illinois University Press, 2000), 80–87.

7. Please see, for example, Akira Suzuki, *Shin: "Nankin daigyakusatsu" no maboroshi* [New edition: The illusion of the "Nanking massacre"] (Tokyo: Asuka Shinsha, 1999); and Masaaki Tanaka, *"Nankin gyakusatsu" no kyoko* [The illusion of "the Rape of Nanking"] (Tokyo: Nihon Kyobunsha, 1984).

8. Chang, *Rape of Nanking*, 4, 6. However, on the jacket of the book, it simply states: "The Japanese army . . . murdered more than 300,000 Chinese civilians."

9. Please see, for example, Masahiro Yamamoto, *Nanking: Anatomy of an Atrocity* (Westport, Conn.: Praeger, 2000); Takashi Yoshida, *The Making of the Rape of Nanking* (New York: Oxford University Press, 2006); as well as Joshua Fogel, ed., *The Nanjing Massacre in History and Historiography* (Berkeley: University of California Press, 2000), and Review of *The Rape of Nanking: The Forgotten Holocaust of World War II*, by Iris Chang, *Journal of Asian Studies* 57, no. 3 (August 1998), 818–20.

10. Hu, *American Goddess at the Rape of Nanking*, 71–72; Vautrin's Diary, December 8, 1937; Rabe's Diary, December 7, 1937, 145–49. See also Hsu Shu-hsi, ed., *Documents of the Nanking Safety Zone* (Shanghai: Kelly and Walsh, 1939). The documents are reprinted in Brook, *Documents on the Rape of Nanking*.

11. John Rabe was the German chairman of the International Committee for the Nanking Safety Zone. His Nanking diary (September 7, 1937–February 28, 1938) was originally penned in German during the Rape of Nanking and translated into Chinese as *La bei ri ji* (Rabe's Diary). Selections from Rabe's Nanking diary and his Berlin diary were published in English as *The Good Man of Nanking: The Diaries of John Rabe*, trans. John E. Woods, ed. Erwin Wickert (New York: Vintage Books, 1998).

12. Please see Azuma Shiro, *Waga Nankin puraton: Ichi shoshuhei no taiken shita Nankin daigyakusatsu* [My platoon in Nanking: A conscript soldier's experience in the Nanking massacre] (Tokyo: Aki Haruo, 1987). Also see Ono Kenji, Fujiwara Akira, Honda Katsuichi, et al., eds., *Nankin daigyakusatsu o kirokushita kogun heishi tachi* [The imperial Japanese soldiers who recorded the Nanking massacre] (Tokyo: Otsuski Shoten, 1996); Matsuoka Kan, *Nan jing zhan—Xun zhao bei feng bi de ji yi: Qiu hua ri jun yuan shi bing 102 ren de zheng yan* [The battle of Nanjing—Searching for the blocked memories: Testimonies of the 102 Japanese soldiers in the aggression against China; in Chinese], trans. Xin Nei-ru et al. (Shanghai: Shanghai Books, 2002).

Biographical Sketches

1. Emma Lyon (Vautrin's niece), interview by Hua-ling Hu, May 26, 1995. According to Lyon, the tombstone was erected and dedicated by her aunt's Ginling friends after her death on May 14, 1941.
2. *Secor Centennial Book, 1857–1957* (Secor, Ill.: Secor Centennial Committee, 1957), 63.
3. Paul A. Varg, *Missionaries, Chinese, and Diplomats: The American Protestant Missionary Movement in China* (New York: Russell and Russell, 1920), 58–62, 67; Hu, *American Goddess at the Rape of Nanking*, 3–4.
4. Iris Chang mistakenly states in her book, *The Rape of Nanking*, that Vautrin joined the United Christian Missionary Association by the time she graduated from the University of Illinois in 1912 (130). In fact, the organization Vautrin first joined was the Foreign Christian Missionary Society, which sent her to China in 1912. See Hu, *American Goddess at the Rape of Nanking*, 14, 154n. 11; and R. A. Doan of the Foreign Christian Missionary Society to Elizabeth Bender, July 1, 1919, in Wilhelmina [Minnie] Vautrin, Correspondence, 1919–41, Archives of the United Board for Christian Higher Education in Asia, Record Group No. 11, Special Collections, Yale Divinity School Library (hereafter cited as Vautrin's Correspondence). Both Zhang Kai-yuan in *Eyewitness to Massacre* (329) and Smalley in *American Missionary Eyewitnesses* (10) state that Vautrin was commissioned by the United Christian Missionary Society in 1912. As a matter of fact, the Foreign Christian Missionary Society did not merge with other similar agencies to form the United Christian Missionary Society until the 1920s. According to McGarvey Ice of the Disciples of Christ Historical Society, "Legal incorporation of the UCMS took place on June 22, 1920" (Ice e-mail to Hua-ling Hu, December 23, 2008).
5. Zhang Kai-yuan states in the introduction to excerpts from Vautrin's diary in *Eyewitness to Massacre* that Vautrin "became chairman of the education department of Ginling College when it was founded in 1916" (329). This statement is repeated in Smalley, *American Missionary Eyewitnesses* (10). In fact, Ginling College was founded in 1915 and Vautrin did not join the college until fall of 1919. See Hu, *American Goddess at the Rape of Nanking*, 19–22; Mrs. Lawrence Thurston and Ruth M. Chester, *Ginling College* (New York: United Board for Christian Colleges in China, 1955), 6–10, 12, 30.
6. Vautrin's Diary, November 21, 1937.
7. Dr. Wu Yi-fang was one of the first five students graduated from Ginling College in 1919. They were the first five women ever to receive bachelor of arts degrees on China's soil. In 1928, after completing her studies for a doctorate in entomology at the University of Michigan, she was appointed the first Chinese president of Ginling, which she served with distinction until 1951. See Hu, *American Goddess at the Rape of Nanking*, 20, 44; Thurston and Chester, *Ginling College*, 13, 64, 146–147; and *Ji nien Wu Yi-fang* [Commemorating Wu Yi-fang] (Nanjing: Jiangsu Education Publishing, 1987).
8. The figure 2,750 for the number of refugees was derived from the total square footage of the eight buildings divided by sixteen square feet per person. Hu, *American Goddess at the Rape of Nanking*, 72–73; Vautrin's Diary, December 7, 1937.
9. Minnie Vautrin, "A Review of the First Month: December 13, 1937–January 13, 1938," in Vautrin's Correspondence; Vautrin's Diary, December 1 and 17, 1937. Iris

Chang mistakenly states in *The Rape of Nanking* that "the [American] embassy lent her [Vautrin] a new nine-foot American flag to lay flat on the center of the grassy quadrangle to protect the campus against Japanese pilots" and that "Vautrin . . . commissioned the sewing of a second American flag, this one twenty-seven feet long" (131).

10. Rev. James McCallum earned a master's degree from Chicago Divinity School and did doctoral studies at the Union Theological Seminary. He worked for the United Christian Missionary Society for thirty-plus years. During the Rape of Nanking, he served as the administrator of the University of Nanking hospital and was a member of the International Committee for the Nanking Safety Zone. His diary and letters to his family during the Rape were submitted to the Tokyo War Crimes Trial as evidence. Zhang Kai-yuan, *Eyewitness to Massacre*, 228; Department of Missionary Education, *They Went to China: Biographies of Missionaries of the Disciples of Christ* (Indianapolis: United Christian Missionary Society, 1948), 70.

11. Entries for December 17, 18, and 19, 1937, Rabe's Diary, 197, 201–2, 217–26. For McCallum's diary entry, see Pritchard and Zaide, *Tokyo War Crimes Trial*, 2:4467–68.

12. Vautrin's Diary, February 15 and 19, 1937.

13. Tsen Shui-fang's written statement submitted to the Tokyo War Crimes Trial, in Pritchard and Zaide, *Tokyo War Crimes Trial*, 16:40137; Hu, *American Goddess at the Rape of Nanking*, 90.

14. Vautrin's Diary, December 17, 1937.

15. Tsen Shui-fang's written statement, in Pritchard and Zaide, *Tokyo War Crimes Trial*, 2:4464, 16:40137; "Ginling College Refugee Camp," in Rabe's Diary, January 16, 1938, 366–67.

16. Vautrin's Diary, February 21, 1938; Vautrin, "As a Refugee Camp. The Period from January 14–March 31, 1938," Vautrin's Correspondence.

17. Hu, *American Goddess at the Rape of Nanking*, 117–19, 121–22.

18. Alexander Paul to Rebecca Griest, May 27, 1940, Vautrin's Correspondence.

19. Vautrin's Diary, May 1, 1938; Tsen Shui-fang, diary entries, December 26, 1937, and February 20, 1938, "Tsen Shui-fang ri ji" [Diary of Tsen Shui-fang], *Min kuo dan an* [Archives of the Republic], no. 3 (2004): 33 (hereafter cited as Tsen's Diary).

20. Hu, *American Goddess at the Rape of Nanking*, 124; Edmund Clubb, American vice consul in Nanking, to Vautrin, January 23, 1939, in Vautrin's Correspondence.

21. Hu, *American Goddess at the Rape of Nanking*, 135–36; Matilda Thurston to Mr. T. D. Macmillan, May 10, 1940, and Katherine Schutze to Griest, June 20, 1940, Vautrin's Correspondence.

22. Iris Chang inaccurately stated in her book *The Rape of Nanking* that "On May 14. 1941 . . . Vautrin sealed the windows and doors of her home with tape, turned on the gas and committed suicide" (187). In fact, Vautrin ended her life by opening the gas jet of the kitchen stove while she was alone in the apartment of Genevieve Brown, a secretary of the United Christian Missionary Society. Please see the telegram and letter of C. M. Yocum of the United Christian Missionary Society to Rebecca Griest and to "Dear Friends of Minnie Vautrin," respectively, on May 15, 1941, Vautrin's Correspondence; and Hu, *American Goddess at the Rape of Nanking*, 144.

23. C. M. Yocum to "Dear Friends of Minnie Vautrin," May 15, 1941; Rebecca Griest to the Former Members of the Staff of Ginling College in America and to the Ginling Alumnae in America, May 16, 1941, in Vautrin's Correspondence.

24. In her interview with Hua-ling Hu on May 26, 1995, Emma Lyon said that, in terms of publicizing Vautrin's courageous story, nothing really happened during the fifty plus years between her aunt's death and the time of the interview. Vautrin's mental illness was considered a stigma in the society of the 1940s. Under the protection of her close-mouthed Ginling friends, few people knew the nature of her illness and what happened to her after she left Nanking. Vautrin died in 1941, during a chaotic wartime. Unlike her counterparts during the Rape of Nanking, such as Rev. John Magee and Dr. Miner Searle Bates, she did not live long enough to testify at the Tokyo War Crimes Trial of 1946. Her surviving brother, a farmer, had no interest in promoting her heroic story. Although Mary Bosworth Treudley published *This Stinging Exultation* (Taipei: Orient Cultural Service, 1972), the Vautrin family vigorously condemned the monograph because of its "false statements," "groundless speculations," and "distorted views" (Emma Lyon's written statement of May 26, 2001 to Hua-ling Hu). In the monograph, Treudley accused Minnie Vautrin of things such as being "rather squeamish about sex" and having no right to "blame a [Japanese] soldier [barging into Ginling] for his use of leisure" (229). She also claimed that Vautrin's administrative efficiency was "subnormal" (228) and said she was "a coward" (231) during the Rape of Nanking. But the author failed to cite any source materials to support her claims and accusations. Nor did she interview Mrs. Lyon or any of the Vautrin family members.

25. Yen Ling-yun of Shanghai, phone interview by Zhang Lian-hong, November 30, 2001.

26. Vautrin's Diary, November 29, 1937.

27. Ibid., December 6, 1937.

28. Ibid., November 29, 1937

29. Ibid., December 2, 1937.

30. At the time, the teenager, along with his mother and three younger siblings, temporarily stayed with his grandmother at Ginling. See Vautrin's Diary, December 24, 1937; and Vautrin, "A Review of the First Month: December 13, 1937–January 13, 1938," in Vautrin's Correspondence.

31. Mary Twinem and Vautrin were the only two female members of the Nanking International Red Cross. During the Rape, on December 17, 1937, Twinem moved to Ginling's campus. She helped Vautrin keep the Japanese soldiers from molesting women and care for the refugees. Vautrin, "A Review of the First Month," in Vautrin's Correspondence.

32. Tsen's Diary, February 16, 1938.

33. Ibid., December 17, 1937.

34. Ibid., January 2, 1938.

35. Thurston and Chester, *Ginling College*, 131.

36. Tsen's written statement, in Pritchard and Zaide, *Tokyo War Crimes Trial*, 12:4464, 16:40137–38.

37. Yen Ling-yun, phone interview by Zhang Lian-hong, November 30, 2001.

38. In order to find documents and reliable sources regarding the exact month and day when Tsen was born and died, Zhang Lian-hong interviewed Ginling alumni and consulted Ginling's papers. Yet, his efforts were in vain. None of the alumni remembered Tsen's birthday, nor did Tsen's eighty-plus-year-old grandson Tsen Kuo-hsiang. They only remembered the years of her birth and death.

A Note on the Two Diaries

1. Martha Smalley, e-mail to Hua-ling Hu, February 15, 2008.
2. Emma Lyon, interview with Hua-ling Hu, May 26, 1995. Only Mary Bosworth Treudley in her book *This Stinging Exultation* stated that Minnie Vautrin was christened Wilhelmina (7). Hua-ling Hu contacted the county clerk's office in Woodford County, Illinois, where Secor is situated, for a copy of Vautrin's birth certificate. Unfortunately, Vautrin's birth was not recorded and the county did not require residents to record their births until 1916 (country clerk's office, e-mail to Hua-ling Hu, September 15, 2008). Further, the Church of Christ congregation, which the Vautrin family belonged to, is no longer in Secor so there is no way to check Minnie's christening record. Meantime, Hu contacted the United Board regarding the reason for using the name "Wilhelmina" instead "Minnie" to label Vautrin's diary and papers, but she received no reply.
3. Copies of both transcripts were acquired by Hua-ling Hu, with Mrs. Emma Lyon's approval, from Illinois State University at Normal and the University of Illinois at Champaign-Urbana.
4. Sarah Harwell, phone interview with Hua-ling Hu, September 22, 2008.
5. Vautrin's Diary, April 14, 1940.
6. See the note attached at the beginning of the photocopy of Vautrin's diary archived at Yale.
7. Vautrin to Mrs. T. D. Macmillan, January 10, 1940, Vautrin's Correspondence.
8. A portion of the onionskin paper carbon copies is in Hua-ling Hu's possession.
9. See Vautrin's Diary, October 20 and 21, 1938, and March 8, 1939.
10. The Chinese version of Hu's article was published by *World Weekly*, November 13, 1994, 1, 4. The English version was published by both the *Journal of Studies of Japanese Aggression against China*, no. 20 (November 1994): 36–41 and *Chinese-American Forum* 11, no. 1 (July 1995): 20–24.
11. For instance, Lu states in the introduction of the book, "Minnie Vautrin did not separate her writings into paragraphs. As a result, it is hard to read the single-spaced originals. After I made the selection of diary entries from the period between August 13, 1937 and June 12, 1938, I separated each entry into reasonable, or logical, paragraphs." Suping Lu, *Terror in Minnie Vautrin's Nanjing: Diaries and Correspondence, 1937–38* (Urbana: University of Illinois Press, 2008), xxix. This is far from the truth. The period August 13, 1937, to June 12, 1938, in Vautrin's diary comprises 298 pages (pp. 6–304). Only the first 59 pages of the diary entries (from August 13 to November 9, 1937) are single-spaced (and with some exceptions). The other 239 pages (November 10, 1937, to June 12, 1938) are double-spaced and clearly divided into paragraphs.
12. Thurston and Chester, *Ginling College*, 94.
13. The research project on the diary was subsidized by the Center for Studies on the Nanjing Massacre of Nanjing Normal University in 2004.
14. Guan Hui and Guo Bi-qiang, "Tsen Shui-fang ri ji kao shi" [On examining and interpreting Tsen Shui-fang's diary], *Min kuo dan an* [Archives of the Republic], no. 4 (2004): 132–35.
15. At the time, during the Rape of Nanking, the teenager, his mother, and three younger siblings temporarily stayed with Mrs. Tsen at Ginling.
16. Vautrin's Diary, December 8, 1937.
17. The three installments were published in *Min kuo dan an* [Archives of the Republic], no. 3 (2004): 26–34, no. 4 (2004): 10–16, and no. 1 (2005): 21–25.

1. Receiving Refugees at Ginling College under Intensifying Bombardment

1. Lloyd E. Eastman, "Nationalist China during the Sino-Japanese War, 1937–1945," in *The Cambridge History of China*, vol. 13, *Republican China, 1912–1949*, pt. 2, edited by John K. Fairbank and Albert Feuerwerker (Cambridge: Cambridge University Press, 1986), 147–48; Dorn, *Sino-Japanese War, 1937–1941*, 69–70; Hu, *American Goddess at the Rape of Nanking*, 59, 67–68; Kung Chin-ku et al., *Jung kuo kan ri zhan zheng shi kau* [The draft history of China's resistance war against Japan] , 71–73, 76, 77–78, 80–81.

2. For the details of the battle to defend Nanking, see for example Tan Tao-ping, "Hui yi 1937 nien Tang Sheng-chi wei hsu Nanjing chi zhan" [A reminiscence of Tang Sheng-chi's battle to defend Nanking in 1937], in *The Jiangsu Collection of Selected Source Materials of Literature and History*, ed. Jiangsu Provincial Council's Research Committee of Literature and History (Nanjing: Jiangsu Historical Books, 1985), 16:18–36. The special volume also published the war reminiscences of seven other participants in the battle in December 1937. Also see Sun Zhai-wei, ed., *Nanjing da tu sha* [The Nanjing massacre] (Beijing: Beijing Publishing, 1997), 57–71.

3. "Big" Wang was a Chinese language teacher of Nanking Language School and Vautrin's personal tutor. During the Rape of Nanking, he acted as Vautrin's secretary and accompanied her to the Japanese embassy to seek help on many trying visits. See Vautrin's Diary, November 28, December 8 and 17, 1937; and Vautrin, "A Review of the First Month," Vautrin's Correspondence.

4. Francis Chen served as the assistant treasurer and business manager of Ginling College from 1934 to 1939. During the Rape of Nanking, Vautrin named him to the three-member emergency committee. See Thurston and Chester, *Ginling College*, 100, 149; and Vautrin, "A Review of the First Month," Vautrin's Correspondence.

5. One of Ginling's workers surnamed Yang. "Szi-fu" is the polite way to address a blue-collar worker in Chinese.

6. Wuhsi is a city in Kiangsu Province, situated on the Nanking–Shanghai Railway. The city is split into halves by the famous Lake Tai.

7. Miss Lo was an evangelistic worker serving the neighborhood in the vicinity of Ginling campus. See Vautrin's Diary, October 5, 1937.

8. The Practice School was established by Vautrin in the 1920s for Ginling students to practice teaching what they had learned from books as one of the measures to train high school teachers and promote Chinese women's education. Hu, *American Goddess at the Rape of Nanking*, 22.

9. Hsia Kwan is the waterfront area outside the city wall northwest of Nanking.

10. Miner Searle Bates (1897–1978) received his doctorate in history from Yale University in 1935. For some thirty years, he taught history as a missionary of the United Christian Missionary Society at the University of Nanking. On the eve of the Rape of Nanking, he helped to found the International Committee for the Nanking Safety Zone and protected thousands of Chinese refugees from the Japanese soldiers. He also investigated and authored papers on opium trade in Japanese-occupied China. After World War II, he testified as a witness at the Tokyo War Crimes Trial. See Zhang Kai-yuan, *Eyewitness to Massacre*, 3–4; Gerald H. Anderson, ed., *Biographical Dictionary of Christian Missions* (Grand Rapids, Mich.: William B. Eerdmans, 1998), 48; and Pritchard and Zaide, *Tokyo War Crimes Trial*, 2:2646–57, 2665–75, 16:40133–35, 17:41247.

11. Liu Shou Hill (Cow's Head Hill, so-called because of its shape) is a famous mountain in the hilly area south of Nanking.

12. Vautrin's diary entry of December 7, 1937 stated the number was 2,750—based on the total square footage of the eight buildings assigned to house the refugees divided by 16 sq. ft. per person.

13. These were the Central Building, Arts Building, and Science Building, and all three buildings are still standing today on the campus of Ginling College of Nanjing Normal University.

14. Correspondent Yates C. McDaniel did not leave Nanking until December 16, three days after the fall of the city. He later reported that he saw "dead Chinese, dead Chinese, dead Chinese" in the ruined Chinese capital city. See Chang, *Rape of Nanking,* 146. McDaniel's report, "Nanking Horror Described in the Diary of War Reporter," was published in the *Chicago Daily Tribune,* December 18, 1937.

15. Hsin Chieh Kow was the business center of downtown Nanking.

16. The full name was Bible Teachers Training School for Women, an affiliate of the University of Nanking and Nanking Theological Seminary. It was established in 1912, under the sponsorship of the Disciples of Christ and several other American churches.

17. Tokuyasu Fukuda was the Japanese attaché in Nanking during the Rape of Nanking.

18. Da Shiao Chang was the Nanking airport.

19. A town about twenty miles east of Nanking.

20. Chen Fei-rung was Ginling business manager Francis Chen's Chinese name.

21. Chi Chao-chang was a professor at the University of Nanking. Tsen Shui-fang, "Tsen Shui-fang ri ji" [Tsen Shui-fang's diary], *Min kuo dan an* [Archives of the Republic], no. 3 (2004): 27n. 2

22. Pastor Shen Yu-shu served as the chairman of the sanitation commission of the Nanking Safety Zone. Rabe, *Good Man of Nanking,* 266.

23. Archibald Steele was the China correspondent for the *Chicago Daily News* and had reported on Japanese aggression in China since 1932. He stayed in Nanking when the city fell until December 15, 1937, and filed reports on the Japanese atrocities committed in the city. See Chang, *Rape of Nanking,* 144–45; and *Chicago Daily News,* December 15, 1937.

24. Rev. John Magee (1884–1953) was a minister of American Church Mission, one of the founding members of the Nanking International Committee for the Nanking Safety Zone. He also served as the chairman of the Nanking International Red Cross and played a key role in saving thousands of Chinese civilians from being murdered by the Japanese soldiers during the Rape of Nanking. The film he took during the Rape with his 16mm movie camera is regarded as one of the vital sources on the tragedy. After the war, he testified at the Tokyo War Crimes Trial. See Pritchard and Zaide, *Tokyo War Crimes Trial,* 2:3904–20; 16:40136–37, 17:41248; Smalley, *American Missionary Eyewitnesses,* 3; Rabe, *Good Man of Nanking,* 272; Zhang Kai-yuan, *Eyewitness to Massacre,* 166, 201–2; Anderson, *Biographical Dictionary of Christian Missions,* 427.

25. Tsen Kuo-hsiang was Tsen Shui-fang's teenage grandson.

26. Hsueh Yu-ling was a homecraft schoolteacher at Ginling College. A few days before the Japanese entered Nanking, she closed the little school and then helped Vautrin in the refugee camp with the investigation work and organizing the meetings. Vautrin, "A Review of the First Month," in Vautrin's Correspondence.

27. One of the hotels in downtown Nanking.

28. South Hill Residence was Ginling's campus residence hall for foreign faculty and staff members.

29. Catherine Sutherland taught music at Ginling from 1926 to 1945. During the Rape, she was teaching at Ginling's Wuhan branch. Thurston and Chester, *Ginling College*, 94, 163.

30. Refers to the Nanking Incident of 1927. When the Chinese Nationalist troops of the Northern Expedition entered Nanking in March of 1927, they went on a rampage of attacking foreigners in the city. For details of the incident, see Dorothy Borg, *American Policy and the Chinese Revolution, 1925–1928* (New York: American Institute of Pacific Relations/Macmillan, 1947), 291–95.

31. Miss Rachel Wang was a student of Nanking Theological Seminary. On November 30, 1937, she moved to Ginling for protection and was asked to be in charge of teaching Bible classes for the refugees. Vautrin's Diary, November 30, 1937.

32. General Tang Shen-chi was a warlord and later became a general of the Chinese Nationalist army. He was appointed by Chiang Kai-shek as the commanding general for the defense of Nanking in 1937. Hu, *American Goddess at the Rape of Nanking*, 41, 71–72, 75–76; Sun, *Nanjing da tu sha*, 52–55.

33. The New Life Movement was initiated by the Nationalist government in 1934 to reform old Chinese habits, fight corruption, and promote new spiritual life.

34. George Fitch (1883–1979) was born in Soochow, China, to Presbyterian missionary parents. He graduated from Union Theological Seminary of New York and went to China to work with the YMCA in Shanghai. During the Rape of Nanking, he was the head of the Nanking YMCA and secretary of the International Committee for the Nanking Safety Zone. His Nanking diary was reprinted in Hsu Shu-hsi, ed., *Documents of the Nanking Safety Zone* (Shanghai: Kelly and Walsh, 1939). Part of the diary was published in *Reader's Digest*, July 1938. His autobiography is titled *My Eighty Years in China* (Taipei: American-Asian Publishing, 1963). See Zhang Kai-yuan, *Eyewitness to Massacre*, 4; and Anderson, *Biographical Dictionary of Christian Missions*, 213–14.

35. Refers to the Sian Incident of December 12, 1936, when two top military generals arrested Generalissimo Chiang Kai-shek at Sian. They wanted to convince Chiang to change his appeasement policy towards the Japanese aggressors and cease all military campaigns against the Chinese Communists. Shortly, Chiang was released and a united front between the Nationalists and the Communists was formed to fight the Japanese. For details of the incident, please see Tien-wei Wu, *The Sian Incident* (Ann Arbor: University of Michigan, Center for Chinese Studies, 1976).

36. W. Plumer Mills (1883–1959) was the minister of the Presbyterian Foreign Mission Board in Nanking. On the eve of the Rape of Nanking, he was appointed vice chairman of the International Committee for the Nanking Safety Zone and then became its chairman after Chairman John Rabe left the city on February 23, 1937. See Smalley, *American Missionary Eyewitnesses*, 6; and Anderson, *Biographical Dictionary of Christian Missions*, 460.

37. Shao was Ginling's gatekeeper.

38. Hwa was Minnie Vautrin's Chinese surname.

2. Japanese Occupation of Nanking—Soldiers' Rampage, Residents' Terror

1. Miao Ting-ling was a faculty member teaching Chinese at Ginling, 1931–38. See Thurston and Chester, *Ginling College*, 157.

2. John Rabe was born in Hamburg, Germany, on November 23, 1882. After working in Hamburg and parts of Africa for a few years, he moved to China and was employed

by the Siemens Company there. In 1931, he was transferred to Nanking, where he served as the manager of Siemens and was very active in the German community. He started his own German school for elementary and junior high school students and was a leader of the Nazi Party in Nanking. On the eve of the Japanese attack on Nanking, when most of his friends left the city, he chose to remain to protect his office and employees as well as help the Chinese refugees. When the International Committee for the Nanking Safety Zone was established, Rabe was elected its chairman. He courageously led a group of twenty some Americans and Europeans to protect Chinese refugees from the Japanese soldiers. He even opened his own home to shelter some 600 innocent men and women during the Rape of Nanking. Later he was transferred to Berlin and left Nanking on February 28, 1938. His Nanking diary, covering September 21, 1937, to February 28, 1938, is the equal of Vautrin's diary as a primary source on the Rape of Nanking. On his diary and life after Nanking, please see note 11 in the introduction and note 15 in chapter 7. See Chang, *Rape of Nanking,* 109–10; and Hu, *American Goddess at the Rape of Nanking,* 159n. 22.

3. Lewis. S. C. Smythe, who received his doctorate in sociology from the University of Chicago, was a professor at the University of Nanking and a founding member of the International Committee for the Nanking Safety Zone. In the spring of 1938, he led a team of students to conduct a survey of damages in Nanking and its surrounding area and published *War Damage in the Nanking Area, December 1937 to March 1938: Urban and Rural Surveys.* See Smalley, *American Missionary Eyewitnesses,* 5; and Department of Missionary Education, *They Went to China,* 80–81.

4. Hillcrest was an American school in Nanking.

5. Hubert L. Sone taught at Nanking Theological Seminary. He was a member of the International Committee for the Nanking Safety Zone succeeded George Fitch as the committee's administrative director. Zhang Kai-yuan, *Eyewitness to Massacre,* 451–52.

6. Tillman Durdin was a correspondent with the *New York Times.* He did not leave Nanking until December 15, 1937, two days after the fall of the city, and witnessed Japanese soldiers gun down some two hundred Chinese within minutes. His report "Butchery Marked Capture of Nanking" was carried in the *New York Times,* December 18, 1937.

7. Wei was a messenger at Ginling, as mentioned in Vautrin's diary entry of the same day.

8. Charles Riggs was an American professor of the University of Nanking and a member of the International Committee for the Nanking Safety Zone when it was first established. See Zhang Kai-yuan, *Eyewitness to Massacre,* 450; and Rabe, *Good Man of Nanking,* 272.

9. The four were Frank Tillman Durdin of the *New York Times,* Archibald Steele of the *Chicago Daily News,* Arthur Menke, a Paramount newsreel cameraman who wrote for AP, and Leslie Smith of Reuters. Yates McDaniel of AP did not leave Nanking until the next day. Chang, *Rape of Nanking,* 144–47; Yamamoto, *Nanking,* 171; Suping Lu, *Terror in Minnie Vautrin's Nanjing,* xvi.

10. It was the Arts Building, according to Tsen's diary of the same day.

11. The National Women's Relief Association was established by Madame Chiang Kai-shek on August 1, 1937, to organize Chinese women to participate in the resistance war against Japan and to volunteer their services, such as helping in the hospitals, tending to the wounded soldiers, and sewing uniforms. See Zhang Xian-wen et al.,

eds., *Jung hua min kwo li shr da tsz dien* [Dictionary of the history of the Republic of China] (Nanjing: Jiangsu Historical Books, 2001), 359.

12. Tung was Ginling's gardener.

13. Mr. Li was the assistant business manager of Ginling.

14. Neither side could speak the other's language, but there are many Chinese characters used in the Japanese written language. So they tried to communicate with each other by writing Chinese characters.

15. A blue-collar worker surnamed Li serving at the South Hill Residence.

16. Blanche Wu, a Ginling graduate who held a master's degree in biology from the University of Michigan, taught biology at Ginling (1937–38, 1946–48). During the Rape of Nanking, she helped Vautrin in the Ginling camp and worked on a project to improve poultry production. Her autobiography is titled *East Meets West* (Baltimore: R. C. Hwang., 1985). See Thurston and Chester, *Ginling College*, 100, 159.

17. Mr. Yang was a staff member of the South Hill Residence.

18. Refers to Chang Yung-kwang, a Chinese-language interpreter at the Japanese embassy who later served as the vice chairman of the puppet Nanking Self-ruling Council. "Tsen Shui-fang ri ji," *Min kuo dan an* [Archives of the Republic], no. 3 (2004): 29n. 5.

19. Same as "Du," the gatekeeper, in Vautrin's diary entry of the same day.

20. Refers to Smythe, Mills, and Fitch.

21. Hsieh Wen-chou was a Ginling graduate who served as chair of the physical education department of Ginling. "Tsen Shui-fang ri ji," *Min kuo dan an* [Archives of the Republic], no. 3 (2004): 30n. 4.

22. Vautrin is transliterating a Japanese phrase meaning "Christian college."

23. Tanaka was vice consul at the Japanese embassy in Nanking.

24. Chung Hwa was a girls school founded by the United Christian Missionary Society in Nanking in the 1890s.

25. Refers to one of Ginling's blue-collar workers and dormitory keepers surnamed Chang.

26. George Atcheson was a second secretary of the American embassy during the Rape of Nanking. On the eve of the fall of Nanking, Atcheson evacuated from the city and boarded the USS *Panay*. When the *Panay* was sunk by the Japanese on December 12, he and others were rescued and taken to Shanghai.

27. James Jenkins was a third secretary of the American embassy and evacuated from Nanking to Shanghai before Japanese occupied the city on December 13, 1937.

28. San Pai Lou was a neighborhood in north Nanking.

29. In fact, according to the "List of Foreign Nationals in Nanking on 21 December 1937," there were five Germans in Nanking at the time: John Rabe, Eduard Sperling, Christian Kroger, R. Hempel, and Zaudig. The first three served as chairman, inspector-general, and treasurer of the International Committee for the Nanking Safety Zone, respectively. Rabe, *Good Man of Nanking*, 266, 272.

30. Hwei Wen was a girls school established by the American Methodist Episcopal Church in Nanking in the 1880s.

31. Ernest H. Forster, a graduate of Princeton University, went to China as an Episcopal missionary and served at St. Paul's Episcopal Church in Nanking. He was a member of the International Committee for the Nanking Safety Zone and protected thousands of Chinese refugees during the Rape of Nanking. His papers and photographs are archived

at the Yale Divinity School Library. See Zhang Kai-yuan, *Eyewitness to Massacre*, 107; and Smalley, *American Missionary Eyewitnesses*, 8.

32. General Chi Hsieh-yuan was a warlord and the military governor of Kiangsu Province in the 1920s. When the second Sino-Japanese war broke out in July 1937, he collaborated with the Japanese and served in the puppet North China provisional government. See O. Edmund Clubb, *Twentieth-Century China* (New York: Columbia University Press, 1964), 125; and Zhang Xian-wen, *Jung hua min kuo li shr da tsz dien*, 777.

33. Hu Chu Kwan was a street west of Ginling.

3. Observing Holidays in a Time of Horror and the Refugees' "Goddess of Mercy"

1. Hsuchow is a city in north Kiangsu Province.
2. Lossing J. Buck was a professor at the University of Nanking and husband of Pearl S. Buck, a Nobel Prize laureate in literature. They were divorced in 1935.
3. Grace Bauer was a medical missionary from Christian Temple of Baltimore who went to China in 1919, where she served as a technician at the University of Nanking hospital laboratory. On the eve of the Rape, because a large number of medical personnel had left the city, Bauer doubled as the dietitian and treasurer of the hospital. See Rabe, *Good Man of Nanking*, 272; Vautrin's Diary, December 5, 1937; and William S. Ryan and Narka Ryan, "Life's Interconnectedness," http://www.globalministries.org/index.pyh.
4. Refers to Miner Searle Bates.
5. Ginling's Science Hall janitor; same as Djang Szi-fu, in Vautrin's diary entry of December 16, 1937.
6. Domei was a Japanese government-controlled news agency.
7. Harriet E. Whitmer taught biology at Ginling from 1924 to 1948. During the Rape, she was at Wuhan and returned to Nanking in 1942. See Thurston and Chester, *Ginling College*, 102, 163.
8. Y. H. Chen was a architecture professor at the Central University and owned a construction company in Nanking.
9. Chen Chung-fan was a professor in the Chinese Department at Ginling from 1935 to 1951. See Thurston and Chester, *Ginling College*, 94, 152.
10. Elmion was one of the buildings on the campus of the American Ming Deh Girls School in Nanking.
11. Djao was Eva Spicer's Chinese language teacher. During the Rape, he and his family sought shelter in Ginling. Eva was the daughter of Sir Albert and Lady Spicer. After graduating from Oxford, she joined the London Missionary Society. In 1923, as a representative of the society, she went to China and taught history and religion at Ginling until 1951. She was Vautrin's best friend at Ginling. See Thurston and Chester, *Ginling College*, 46, 47, 54.
12. Hsia Lingwei was a small town about two miles from Nanking's east gate.
13. Refers to Bible Teachers Training School for Women.
14. Same as Mr. Chang in Tsen's diary entry of December 17, 1937. See chapter 2, note 18.
15. Wuhu is a city in southeast Anhui Province along the south bank of the Yangtze River, about forty miles from Nanking.
16. Kuling is a resort town in Kiangsi Province.

17. Vautrin wanted to indicate that the young Russian had been down to the Hwa Pai Lou section of the long, busy Tai Ping Road.
18. Refers to Bible Teachers Training School
19. Refers to John Rabe

4. Registration of Women and the Return of American and European Diplomats

1. Lilliath Robbins Bates was the wife of Miner Searle Bates. She taught English at Ginling from 1920 to 1923. During the Rape of Nanking, she and her two sons temporarily stayed in Japan. Thurston and Chester, *Ginling College*, 162.
2. Refers to Vautrin and Twinem.
3. Twinem was a naturalized Chinese citizen.
4. Refers to the popular business district around the Confucius Temple in south Nanking.
5. Dr. P. T. Yuen taught education classes at Ginling from 1936 to 1939. See Thurston and Chester, *Ginling College*, 83, 160.
6. Yen Tzu Chi is a breathtaking scenic spot with cliffs along the Yangtze River, about seven miles from the city of Nanking.
7. Dr. Ruth Chester received her M.A. from Smith College and her doctorate from Columbia University. She taught chemistry at Ginling (1917–51) and served as its dean of studies from 1939 to 1949. She was in Shanghai during the Rape of Nanking. Thurston and Chester, *Ginling College*, vi, 16, 37, 111, 143.
8. On the eve of the Japanese occupation of Nanking, American and European diplomats were order to leave Nanking by their respective governments.
9. Tsai was Dr. Ruth Chester's Chinese surname. Mrs. Lawrence (Matilda) Thurston, a graduate of Mount Holyoke College, married Rev. Lawrence Thurston in 1902 and went to Peking with him to study Chinese language. After her husband passed away in 1904 in the United States, she served as secretary of the student Volunteer Movement for Foreign Missions. In 1913, she was appointed to Nanking by the American Presbyterian Board of Foreign Missions and elected the first president of Ginling College (two years before the college was formally founded in 1915). She served in that position until 1928, when she resigned in favor of Dr. Wu Yi-fang, and continued her service at Ginling as an adviser, supervisor of building construction, and treasurer until 1942. See Thurston and Chester, *Ginling College*, vi, 5–6.
10. The three American diplomats were James Espey, vice consul of Shanghai, John Allison, third secretary, and Archibald McFadyen Jr., code clerk. They were ordered to proceed to Nanking on the USS *Oahu* to reopen the American embassy in the city in late December of 1937 but did not land there until January 6, 1938. They first arrived at Nanking on December 31 but were denied landing by the Japanese military, so they proceeded to Wuhu and then went back to Nanking again. See Rabe's Diary, January 6, 1938, 361; Rabe, *Good Man of Nanking*, 113; Suping Lu, *Terror in Minnie Vautrin's Nanjing*, 245n. 22.
11. Ping Tsang Hsiang was a lane (*hsiang*) near the University of Nanking.
12. Takatama was an employee at the Japanese embassy in Nanking.
13. Rebecca Griest taught English and history at Ginling from 1919 to 1927. Later, she became a member of Ginling's executive committee in New York. She and Vautrin were good friends. Hu, *American Goddess at the Rape of Nanking*, 61, 137–40, 146. Also see Thurston and Chester, *Ginling College*, 37, 162.

14. Florence A. Kirk taught English at Ginling from 1932 to 1950. During the Rape, she was in Shanghai. See Thurston and Chester, *Ginling College*, 82, 93, 95, 138, 162.

15. Alice Morris served as Ginling's librarian in 1936–37. Ibid., 83, 93, 95, 162.

16. *North China Daily News*.

17. *Sheng Pao* was a widely circulated Chinese newspaper in Nanking.

18. A Chinese *li* equals one-third of a mile.

19. *Hsi-fan* is the Chinese transliteration for rice porridge.

20. Hankow is the capital city of Hupei Province. Hankow and two other cities, Hanyang and Wuchang, form a triangle where the Han River joins the Yangtze River. The three cities are grouped together as Wuhan.

21. Hangchow is the capital city of Chekiang Province.

22. *Lao-ban* was a polite way to address a craftsman or businessman in Chinese. Tung was the man's surname.

23. Elsie Priest served as Ginling's treasurer from 1928 to 1951. See Thurston and Chester, *Ginling College*, 111, 162.

24. Miss Gray was an American evangelical worker in Nanking. Before the Rape of Nanking, Gray evacuated from the city and went to Szechwan Province in southwest China. She was a naturalized Chinese citizen. See Tsen's diary entry of the same day.

25. Pi was Elsie Priest's Chinese surname.

26. James Espey, the American vice consul in Shanghai, was one of the three American diplomats ordered to open the American embassy in Nanking in late December of 1937 (see note 10 above). He stayed in the city until June 6, 1938, and filed many reports on Japanese soldiers' crimes committed in the city. See Rabe, *Good Man of Nanking*, 113; and Suping Lu, *Terror in Minnie Vautrin's Nanjing*, 246n. 31.

27. The three were Dr. George Rosen, Alfred Hurter, and Paul Scharffenberg of the German embassy in Nanking. On January 9, 1938, they arrived at Nanking on the British gunboat *Cricket*, which also brought British Consul Prideaux-Brune, and two military attachés, Colonel Lovat-Fraser, and Walser. However, Walser was not allowed to land by the Japanese authorities on the pretext that they had not been informed of his arrival beforehand. See Rabe's Diary, January 6 and 9, 1938, 361, 386; and Rabe, *Good Man of Nanking*, 114, 118.

28. Dr. T. C. Trimmer was an American physician working at the University of Nanking hospital. He served as an associate on the food commission for the Safety Zone administration. Rabe, *Good Man of Nanking*, 266, 272.

29. Ming Deh Girls School was founded by American North Presbyterian Church in Nanking during the nineteenth century.

30. The Americans were Espey, Allison, and McFadyen (see note 10 above). The three British were Prideaux-Brune, Lovat-Fraser, and Walser, and the Germans were Rosen, Scharffenberg, and Hurter (see note 27 above).

5. Life and Problems inside the Ginling Camp

1. Mrs. Way Sung New was one of the first five graduates of Ginling in 1919. She later served as the chairwoman of the board of directors of Ginling College. See Thurston and Chester, *Ginling College*, 66, 97.

2. The Metropolitan Hotel in Nanking

3. The expressions *beh sing* and *lao beh sing*, meaning "civilians," are used interchangeably. The word *lao* means "old." When it is used with *beh sing*, it doesn't mean "aged," but more like "good-old" civilians.

4. Hsuchow, in north Kiangsu Province, was located where two major railroads, the Tsin-Pu line and the Lung-Hai line, meet.

5. Chiukiang is a city in northern Kiangsi Province.

6. Changsha is the capital city of Hunan Province.

7. Chen Yueh-mei was a graduate of Ginling who received her master's degree from Wellesley College and returned to teach physical education at Ginling (1935–38, 1943). Chen was married to Dr. Han Li-wu, who served as the chairman of the board of directors of the University of Nanking. He was one of the initiators of the idea of establishing a safety zone in Nanking on the eve of the Japanese attack in 1937. But before the safety zone was formally established, Han was ordered by the Nationalist government to escort the national treasures of the Palace Museum to a safer place and left the city. Thurston and Chester, *Ginling College,* 154; Hu, *American Goddess at the Rape of Nanking,* 71.

8. Christian Kroeger, a German employee of Carlowitz and Company, was not a member of the International Committee but served as its treasurer at the request of Chairman Rabe. See Zhang Kai-yuan, *Eyewitness to Massacre,* 452.

9. Fiyoshi Fukuei was the acting Japanese consul general in the city during the Rape of Nanking.

10. Refers to the National Christian Council. Vautrin liked to listen to the council's broadcast from Shanghai on the work of the NCC and other local churches across China. Vautrin's diary, September 19 and October 1, 1937.

11. Blanche Wu.

12. Refers to Vautrin and Twinem.

13. Paul Tang taught at Central Theological Seminary in Nanking. Suping Lu, *Terror in Minnie Vautrin's Nanjing,* 250n. 13.

14. Ginling's Board of Founders in New York. The report is reprinted in the appendix of this book.

15. The ministry of foreign affairs of the Nationalist Chinese government.

16. *Hsin Shen Pao* was a Japanese military-controlled Chinese newspaper published in Shanghai.

17. Edna Whipple Gish was an evangelical worker for women in south Nanking. In August 1937, when the Japanese began to bomb Nanking, she went to Kuling and taught Bible study classes there until Christmas. Then she went to Hankow and Hong Kong. In 1945, Gish flew back to Nanking. Department of Missionary Education, *They Went to China,* 42–43.

18. Ibid., 20–21. Mary Frances Kelly was an evangelical worker in Nanking, one of the best-known missionaries to China. She opened two day schools for girls and the Bible Teachers Training School for Women in Nanking and served as one of the trustees of Ginling College and the Bible Training School. Later, she authored *Some Chinese Friends of Mine* and co-edited *Macklin of Nanking.*

19. All four ladies were Ginling faculty members. Yen En-wen taught Chinese from 1934 to 1941. Hwang Chun-mei taught chemistry from 1935 to 1939. Liu En-lan taught practice school and geography from 1925 to 1951. Wang Ming-jen taught mathematics and physics from 1932 to 1938 and from 1939 to 1940. On the eve of the fall of Nanking in 1937, they first taught at Ginling's Wuhan branch and then joined its Shanghai branch. See Thurston and Chester, *Ginling College,* 48, 87, 94, 103, 155, 156, 160.

20. Changhsin is a town in north Chekiang Province.

21. A military officer, especially a battalion leader.
22. Ihsing is a town about a hundred miles east of Nanking.
23. Kwangde is a town in Anhui Province.
24. Li Shui and Li Yang are small towns east of Nanking.
25. Miss Hyde was an American Presbyterian missionary and evangelical worker in Nanking.
26. Mah jong is a popular Chinese gambling game, which requires four players to play at the same time.
27. Sir Kuat Hugeson was the British ambassador to China from 1936 to 1937. On August 26, 1937, on his way from Nanking to Shanghai by car, he was injured by the bombs of two Japanese military planes. See Han Qin-fu, ed., *Jung hua min kuo da shr ji* [Records of major events of the Republic of China] (Beijing: Literature and History Publishing, 1997), 4:143.
28. Chungking is a city of Szechwan Province in southwest China. It served as the wartime capital of the Nationalist government after the fall of Nanking in the winter of 1937.
29. Mrs. Grace Zia Chu taught physical education at Ginling. During the Rape of Nanking, she was one of the five Chinese faculty members teaching at Ginling's branch in Shanghai. Thurston and Chester, *Ginling College,* 82, 96.

6. The Japanese Demand to Close Refugee Camps and Vautrin's Defiance

1. Vautrin might refer to Kung Hsieh's old home in Ching Liang Hill near the Hu Chu Kwan area. Kung was a famous painter of the early Ching Dynasty (1644–1911). The home could not have been bestowed to Kung by the first emperor of the Ming dynasty (1368–1644), as Vautrin stated. See Minnie Vautrin, *Wei te lin ri ji* [Vautrin's Diary; in Chinese], trans. Center for Studies on the Nanjing Massacre of Nanjing Normal University (Nanjing: Jiangsu People's Publishing, 2000), 256n. 1.
2. The Swastika Society was a private Chinese charitable organization in Nanking, similar to the Red Cross. It mercifully buried many dead bodies in and around the city in the winter of 1938.
3. Lu Chowfu (or Luchowfu) refers to Hofei, the capital city of Anhui Province.
4. Ginling's old campus in Nanking from 1915 to1922 was located at a rented mansion of "a hundred rooms." The mansion belonged to the fifth son of the famous Li Hung-chang, the powerful minister of the late Ching dynasty. The college moved to its newly built campus on Ninghai Road in July 1922. See Thurston and Chester, *Ginling College,* 7–8; and Hu, *American Goddess at the Rape of Nanking,* 22–23.
5. Dr. George Rosen was the secretary of political affairs of the German embassy in Nanking who returned to the city to reopen the embassy on January 9, 1938.
6. Chang Nan-Wu served as the head of the Red Swastika Society after its first chairman, Tao Bao-gin, became the head of the Self-ruling Committee in Nanking. After only a month on the job, Chang was succeeded by Chen Kwang-lin. See Sun Zhai-wei, *Cheng qi li shi,* 188.
7. Vautrin mistook "Book of Earth" for the title of Pearl S. Buck's famous novel *The Good Earth.*
8. Pukow, or Pukou, is a town on the north bank of the Yangtze River across from Nanking. It served as the transportation hub for the city and was the south end of the Tientsin-Pukou Railroad.

9. Kuo-hsiang was Mrs. Tsen's second grandson.
10. Mr. Hidaka was the counselor of the Japanese embassy in Nanking during the Rape of Nanking.
11. Refers to the International Committee for the Nanking Safety Zone.
12. At the time, many Chinese in Nanking wore armbands with the Japanese rising sun emblem, distributed by the puppet Chinese government, to protect themselves and ensure their safety on the streets. Hu, *American Goddess at the Rape of Nanking*, 100.
13. Eva Spicer's Chinese surname.
14. Dr. George Rosen.

7. Slowly Restoring Law and Order but Soldiers Keep Searching for *hwa gu-niang*

1. Charles Gee (Chi), an architect of the University of Nanking, was a member of the Housing Commission of the Nanking Safety Zone administration. Rabe, *Good Man of Nanking*, 266.
2. Helen Boughton was an American missionary in Anhui Province.
3. Refers to Paul Tang of Central Theological Seminary in Nanking.
4. Pengpu and Hwai Yuen were two towns in Anhui Province.
5. Swatow is a city in southeast Kwangtung Province.
6. Refers to the USS *Oahu* anchored at Hsia Kwan. See Vautrin diary entry of the same day.
7. Refers to Dr. Wu Yi-fang.
8. Vautrin's Chinese transliteration of a phrase meaning "civilians should (or want to) report [incidents]."
9. Refers to a business street with the name of the long torn-down building "Chang Chin Lou."
10. *Shiao-bing* is a favorite Chinese baked pastry with sesame seeds.
11. One Chinese catty equals one-and-a-third pounds.
12. Ritchey was a British subject. In 1937, he served as the commissioner of the Postal District of Kiangsu Province.
13. Stella Marie Graves taught music at Ginling from 1934 to 1948. See Thurston and Chester, *Ginling College*, 93, 161.
14. The second report, titled "As a Refugee Camp: January 14–March 31, 1938," is reprinted in the appendix of this book.
15. Rabe was transferred back to Germany by his company, Siemens, and left Nanking on February 23, 1938. After returning to Germany, at first he made efforts to publicize the Nanking massacre by lecturing and showing the films made by Rev. John Magee. Before long, he was arrested by the Gestapo. Although he was released shortly, he was prohibited from giving lectures on the massacre. During his later years, he and his wife lived in poverty. When Rabe's financial plight reached Nanking, the city government and people enthusiastically rendered helping hands with food and money. Rabe started his Berlin diary on April 24, 1945, a continuation of his Nanking diary. On January 5, 1949, Rabe suffered a stroke and passed away. For Rabe's last years, see Chang, *Rape of Nanking*, 190, 193; and Rabe, *Good Man of Nanking*, 254–57.
16. Esther Tappert taught English at Ginling from 1929 to 1937. In August of 1937, she was in western China when the Japanese attacked Shanghai, and she thought there

would be no chance for her to return to Nanking so she accepted a teaching job at the English department of the National Chungking University. See Thurston and Chester, *Ginling College,* 93, 163.

17. For the farewell party in his honor at Ginling, Rabe wrote in his diary of February 17, 1938, that the tea party was very nice but "saying goodbye was dreadful." He continued, "The refugees . . . besieged the door and demanded that I promise not to leave them in the lurch, that is, not to leave Nanking. They all went down on their knees, weeping and wailing and literally hanging on my coattails . . . when I tried to depart." Rabe, *Good Man of Nanking,* 199.

18. This is the same Miss Rachel Wang mentioned in Vautrin's Diary, December 11, 1937. See chapter 1, note 31.

19. Miss Wu—not to be confused with Blanche Wu—was a graduate of Ming Deh Girls School. She sought protection in Ginling during the Rape of Nanking and later taught one of the Bible classes on the campus.

20. Under the pressure of the Japanese authority to close all the refugee camps and eliminate the Safety Zone, on February 19, 1938, the International Committee for the Nanking Safety Zone formally changed its name to the Nanking International Relief Committee in order to be more consistent with the nature of its task thereafter. The Safety Zone no longer existed. See John Rabe's letters to the embassies of the United States, Great Britain, and Germany in Nanking as well as his letter to the Chinese Self-ruling government, February 19, 1938, in *Qin hua ri jun Nan Jing da tu sha shi liao* [Source materials relating to the horrible massacre committed by the Japanese troops in Nanjing] (Nanjing: Jiangsu Historical Books, 1985), 257; Rabe's Diary, February 19, 1938, 673–74.

21. Refers to No. 3 Ping Tsang Lane.

22. Dr. Richard Brady received his medical training at Western Reserve School of Medicine and interned at the University Hospital of Oklahoma City. He, along with his wife, went to Nanking as a medical missionary and served at the University Hospital. On the eve of the Japanese occupation of Nanking, Dr. Brady was called to Kuling, where his wife and children were vacationing, to attend his seriously sick daughter. Then, from Kuling, he took his family to Hankow, Hong Kong, and Shanghai. In Shanghai, he got permission from the Japanese military for himself to return to Nanking to treat the sick and the injured. He was one of the first few foreigners permitted to return to the city in early 1938. Department of Missionary Education, *They Went to China,* 83–84.

23. From the context, it should be "husbands," instead of "doctors."

24. Because most of the women were illiterate, they were not able to sign their names. Stamping their thumb prints with red ink was used in lieu of the signatures.

25. It should be "Nanking International Relief Committee." See note 20 above.

26. Hwang Li-ming taught physical education at Ginling (1927–38, 1941–42, and 1946–47). During the Rape, she taught at Ginling's Shanghai branch. See Thurston and Chester, *Ginling College,* 82, 96, 125, 155.

Aftermath

1. "April 2 [1938]: Letter of John Magee to Rev. J. C. McKim," in Smalley, *American Missionary Eyewitnesses,* 63; "The Report of Dr. George Rosen of the German Embassy in Nanking to the Foreign Affairs Ministry at Berlin on March 4, 1938," *Journal of*

Studies of Japanese Aggression against China, no. 6 (May 1991): 51–52; *People's Daily* (overseas edition), February 18, 1991.

2. Vautrin's Diary, March 15, May 13, 1938, January 3, 1939.

3. Ibid., April 26, May 3, May 23, 1938.

4. Ibid., May 11, 1939.

5. Vautrin's Diary, April 14 and 20, June 2 and 4, 1938; Hu, *American Goddess at the Rape of Nanking*, 115–16.

6. Hu, *American Goddess at the Rape of Nanking*, 117–19; Minnie Vautrin, "A Homecraft Industrial Course," reprint from *Chinese Recorder*, February 1939. The reprint was given to Hua-ling Hu by Mrs. Emma Lyon on May 26, 1995. It is also included in Vautrin's Correspondence. See Vautrin's Diary, January 23, 1939; "Miss Vautrin Shares Her Thoughts on Ginling's Task in Nanking," March 23, 1939, in Vautrin's Correspondence.

7. Minnie Vautrin, "An Experiment in the Field of Secondary Education," reprint from the *Chinese Recorder,* February 1939; also given to Hua-ling Hu by Mrs. Lyon in 1995 and included in Vautrin's Correspondence; Vautrin, "Tentative Budget—Project in Secondary Education, 1938–39," in Vautrin's Correspondence.

8. Hu, *American Goddess at the Rape of Nanking*, 123, 131.

9. Ibid., 112–15; Vautrin's Diary, May 18 and June 3, 1939.

10. Hu, *American Goddess at the Rape of Nanking*, 130, 132.

11. Matilda Thurston to Helen [?], May 12, 1940; Thurston to Mrs. T. D. Macmillan, May 10, 1940, in Vautrin's Correspondence.

12. Thurston and Chester, *Ginling College*, 102.

SELECTED BIBLIOGRAPHY

Anderson, Gerald, ed. *Biographical Dictionary of Christian Missions.* Grand Rapids, Mich.: Eerdmans, 1998.

Azuma Shiro. *Waga Nankin puraton: Ichi shoshuhei no taiken shita Nankin daigyakusatsu* [Our infantry platoon in Nanking: A conscript soldier's personal experience in the Nanking massacre]. Tokyo: Aoki Shoten, 1987.

Bergamini, David. *Japan's Imperial Conspiracy.* New York: William Morrow., 1971.

Boorman, Howard L., ed. *Biographical Dictionary of Republican China.* New York: Columbia University Press, 1968.

Boyle, John Hunter. *China and Japan at War, 1937–1945: The Politics of Collaboration.* Stanford: Stanford University Press, 1972.

Brackman, Arnold C. *The Other Nuremberg: The Untold Story of the Tokyo War Crimes Trials.* New York: William Morrow, 1987.

Brook, Timothy, ed. *Documents on the Rape of Nanking.* Ann Arbor: University of Michigan Press, 2000.

Center for Studies on the Nanjing Massacre of Nanjing Normal University. *Wei te lin zhuan* [Biography of Vautrin]. Nanjing: Nanjing Publishing, 2000.

Chang, Iris. *Nanjin da tu sha: Er tz shr jye da zhan bei yi wangde hao qie* [*The Rape of Nanking: The Forgotten Holocaust of World War II*; in Chinese]. Translated by Hsiao Fuyuan. Taipei: Commonwealth, 1997.

———. *The Rape of Nanking: The Forgotten Holocaust of World War II.* New York: Basic Books, 1997.

Cheng Cheng-sun, ed. *Ri ben qui hua shi liao tu bian ji* [A collection of pictorial source materials of Japanese aggression against China]. Beijing: New China, 1984.

Chiang Kung-ku. *Hsan du san yueh chi* [Three months' records of the fallen capital]. Taipei: Central Library, 1981.

Chow Tse-tsung. *The May Fourth Movement: Intellectual Revolution in Modern China.* Cambridge, Mass.: Harvard University Press, 1960.

Clubb, O. Edmund. *Twentieth-Century China.* New York: Columbia University Press, 1964.

Cohen, Warren I. *America's Response to China: An Interpretative History of Sino-American Relations.* New York: John Wiley and Sons, 1971.

Crowley, James B. *Japan's Quest for Autonomy: National Security and Foreign Policy, 1930–1938.* Princeton: Princeton University Press, 1966.

Department of Missionary Education. *They Went to China: Biographies of Missionaries of the Disciples of Christ*. Indianapolis: United Christian Missionary Society, 1948.

Dorn, Frank. *The Sino-Japanese War, 1931–1941: From Marco Polo Bridge to Pearl Harbor*. New York: Macmillan, 1974.

Durdin, Tillman. "Butchery Marked Capture of Nanking." *New York Times*, December 18, 1937.

Dwan Yueh-ping: "La bei ri ji de zi liao jia zhi ji qi li shi ju xian xing" [The value of Rabe's diary as a source material and its historical limitations]. *Journal of Studies of Japanese Aggression against China* 27 (April 1998): 118–22.

Eastman, Lloyd E. "Nationalist China during the Nanking Decade, 1927–1937." In *The Cambridge History of China*. Vol. 13, *Republican China, 1912–1949*, pt. 2, edited by John K. Fairbank and Albert Feuerwerker. Cambridge: Cambridge University Press, 1986.

———. "Nationalist China during the Sino-Japanese War, 1937–1945." In *The Cambridge History of China*. Vol. 13, *Republican China, 1912–1949*, pt. 2, edited by John K. Fairbank and Albert Feuerwerker. Cambridge: Cambridge University Press, 1986.

Fairbank, John K. *China: A New History*. Cambridge, Mass.: Belknap Press of Harvard University Press, 1992.

———, ed. *The Missionary Enterprise in China and America*. Cambridge, Mass.: Harvard University Press, 1974.

———. *The United States and China*. Cambridge, Mass.: Harvard University Press, 1983.

Fenn, William Purviance. *Christian Higher Education in Changing China, 1880–1950*. Grand Rapids, Mich.: William B. Eerdmans, 1976.

Fitch, George. *My Eighty Years in China*. Taipei: American-Asian Publishing, 1963.

Fogel, Joshua, ed. *The Nanjing Massacre in History and Historiography*. Berkeley: University of California Press, 2000.

———. Review of *The Rape of Nanking: The Forgotten Holocaust of World War II*, by Iris Chang. *Journal of Asian Studies* 57, no. 3 (August 1998): 818–20.

Fujiwara, Akira. *Nankin daigyakusatsu sengen* [The Nanking massacre: New edition]. Tokyo: Iwanami Shoten, 1988.

Gao Xingzu. "*Nan Jin da tsa an*" [On the great Nanking tragedy]. *Journal of Nanking University* 3 (1985). Reprinted in *Journal of Studies of Japanese Aggression against China* 4 (November 1990): 7–17.

———. *Ri jun qin hua bao xing—Nan Jing da tu sha* [Atrocities of the Japanese invasion army—The Nanjing massacre]. Shanghai: People's Publishing, 1985.

Guan Hui and Guo Bi-qiang. "Tsen Shui-fang ri ji kao shi" [On examining and interpreting Tsen Shui-fang's diary]. *Min kuo dan an* [Archives of the Republic], no. 4 (2004): 132–35.

Han Qin-fu, ed. *Jung hua min kuo da shr ji* [Records of major events of the Republic of China]. Vol. 4. Beijing: Literature and History Publishing, 1997.

Harrison, John A. *China since 1800*. New York: Harcourt, Brace and World, 1967.

Hata Ikuhiko. *Nan Jing da tu sha jen xing* [The true picture of the Nanking massacre; in Chinese]. Translated by Yang Wen-hsin. Hong Kong: Commerce, 1995.

Hicks, George. *Japan's War Memories: Amnesia or Concealment?* Brookfield, Eng.: Ashgate, 1997.

Ho Chi-fang et al. "Lu kou jiao shi pein ji shr" [Factual account of the Marco Polo Bridge incident]. *Journal of Studies of Japanese Aggression against China* 2 (August 1992): 6–10.

Ho Ying-chin. *Pa nien kan chan chi chin kuo* [History of eight years of China's resistance war against Japanese aggression]. Taipei: Bureau of History and Policy Compilation and Translation of the Defense Department, 1985.

Honda Katsuishi. *The Nanjing Massacre: A Japanese Journalist Confronts Japan's National Shame.* Edited by Frank Gibney, translated by Karen Sandness. Armonk, N.Y.: M. E. Sharpe, 1999.

―――. *Sabakareta Nankin daigyakusatsu* [The Nanking massacre on trial]. Tokyo: Asahi Shinbunsha, 1987.

Hora Tomio. *Ketteiban: Nankin daigyakusatsu* [Nanking massacre: Definitive edition]. Tokyo: Gendaishi Shuppan-kai, 1982.

―――. *Nanjin da tu sha: Ting ban* [The Nanking massacre: Definitive edition; in Chinese]. Translated by Mao Liang-hung et aı. Shanghai: Shanghai Translation Publishing, 1988.

―――. *Nankin daigyakusatsu:"Maboroshi" ka kosaku hiban* [The Nanking massacre: Criticism of the making of an illusion]. Tokyo: Gendaishi Shuppankai, 1975.

―――. *Nankin daigyakusatsu no kenkyu* [Studies of the Nanking massacre]. Tokyo: Banseisha, 1992.

―――. *Nankin daigyakusatsu no shomei* [The proof of the Nanking massacre]. Tokyo: Asahi Shinbunsha, 1986.

Hsu Chi-ken. *Nan Jing da tu sha: Mu ji dzan tsan yan* [The great Nanking massacre: Testimonies of the eyewitnesses]. Taipei: China's News Cultural Publishing, 1993.

―――, ed. *Xue ji: Qiu hua ri jun Nan Jing da tu sha shr lu* [Bloody sacrifice: Factual records of the great Nanking massacre committed by the invading Japanese military]. Beijing: Chinese People's Affairs, 1994.

Hsu Shu-hsi, ed. *Documents of the Nanking Safety Zone.* Shanghai: Kelly and Walsh, 1939.

Hu, Hua-ling. *American Goddess at the Rape of Nanking: The Courage of Minnie Vautrin.* Carbondale: Southern Illinois University Press, 2000.

―――. *Ginling yun shen: Wei teh lin nyu shr chuan* [Ginling forever: A biographical account of Minnie Vautrin]. Taipei: Chiu Ko Publishing, 1997. Revised edition, Beijing: People's Literature Publishing House, 2000.

―――. "Nan Jing da tu sha hsia de chung hua fu nyu" [Chinese women under the Nanking massacre]. *Journal of Studies of Japanese Aggression against China* 8 (November 1991):15–19. Reprinted (in English) in *Chinese American Forum* 7, no. 4 (April 1992): 20–23; and in *United Daily,* November 16, 1991.

―――. "Wei teh lin nyu shr: Ku nan chung kuo ren de hwo pu sha" [Miss Minnie Vautrin: The living goddess of the suffering Chinese people]. *World Weekly,* November 13, 1994, 1, 4. Reprinted in English in *Chinese American Forum* 11, no. 1 (July 1995): 20–24; and in Chinese and English in *Journal of Studies of Japanese Aggression against China* 20 (November 1994): 36–41.

―――. "Wu wan lu k'uo chiao shr pien" [Don't forget the Marco Polo Bridge incident]. *World Weekly,* July 4, 1993, 1.

Hung Kwei-chi, ed. *Ri ben chin hua bao hsin lu, 1928–1945* [Records of Japanese atrocities in China, 1928–1945]. Taipei: National Historical Bureau, 1985.

Hunter, Jane. *The Gospel of Gentility: American Women Missionaries in Turn of-the-Century China.* New Haven: Yale University Press, 1984.

Inoue Hisashi. "Kaisetsu" [Foreword]. *Nankin jiken shiryoshi* [A collection of historical materials on the Nanjing incident]. Edited by the Research Committee on the Nanjing Incident. Vol. 2. Tokyo: Aoki Shoten, 1992.

Iriye, Akira. "Japanese Aggression and China's International Position, 1931–1949." In *The Cambridge History of China.* Vol. 13, *Republican China, 1912–1949,* pt. 2, edited by John K. Fairbank and Albert Feuerwerker. Cambridge: Cambridge University Press, 1986.

Iriye, Akira, and Warren Cohen, eds. *American, Chinese, and Japanese Perspectives on Wartime Asia. 1931–1949.* Wilmington, Del.: Scholarly Resources, 1990.

Jones, F. C. *Japan's New Order in East Asia: Its Rise and Fall, 1937–1945.* London: Oxford University Press, 1954.

Kaga, Mitsuyoki, and Himeta Mitsuyoshi, eds. and trans. *Shogen Nankin daigyakusatsu* [Testimonies on the great Nanking massacre; in Japanese]. Tokyo: Aoki Shoten, 1987.

Ko Chi. *Nan Jing da tu sha* [The great Nanking massacre]. Taipei: Chinese and West Magazine, 1978.

———. *Xian du xue lei lu* [Blood and tears: Records of the fallen capital]. In *Qui haw ri jun Nan Jing da sha tu sha shi liao* [Source materials relating to the horrible massacre committed by the Japanese troops in Nanjing in December 1937]. Compiled by the Historical Source Material Compilation Committee of the Nanjing Massacre and the Nanjing Library. Nanjing: Jiangsu Historical Books, 1997.

Kung Chin-ku et al. *Jung kuo kan ri zhan zheng shi kao* [The draft history of China's resistance war against Japan]. Hupei: Hupei People's Publishing, 1983–84.

Latourette, Kenneth Scott. *A History of Christian Missions in China.* New York: Russell and Russell, 1929.

Lee, Dun J. *The Ageless Chinese: A History.* New York: Charles Scribner's Sons, 1978.

Lee En-han. *Ribenjun zhan zheng baoxing zhi yanju* [A study of wartime atrocities by the Japanese military]. Taipei: Commerce, 1994.

Liu, F. F. *A Military History of Modern China, 1924–1949.* Princeton: Princeton University Press, 1956.

Lu, David J. *From the Marco Polo Bridge to Pearl Harbor: Japan's Entry into World War II.* Washington, D.C.: Public Affairs, 1961.

Lu, Suping. *Terror in Minnie Vautrin's Nanjing: Diaries and Correspondence, 1937–38.* Urbana: University of Illinois Press, 2008.

Lutz, Jessie Gregory. *China and the Christian Colleges, 1850–1950.* Ithaca, N.Y.: Cornell University Press, 1971.

Magee's Testament. Produced by the Alliance in Memory of Victims of the Nanjing Massacre. Peter Wang Films, 1991 (videocassette).

Matsuoka Kan. *Nan Jing zhan—Xun zhao bei fen bi de ji yi: Qiu hua ri jun yuan shi bing 102 ren de zheng yan* [The battle of Nanking—Searching for the blocked memories: Testimonies of 102 Japanese soldiers in the aggression against China; in Chinese]. Translated by Xin Nei-ru and Chuan Mei-ying. Shanghai: Shanghai Books, 2002.

McAleavy, Henry. *The Modern History of China.* New York: Praeger, 1973.

McDaniel, Yates C. "Nanking Horror Described in Diary of War Reporter." *Chicago Daily Tribune,* December 18, 1937.

Modern China Association, ed. *Tien tsen ru shan* [Ironclad proof]. Taipei: Modern China Magazine, 1982.

Morley, James W., ed. *The China Quagmire: Japan's Expansion on the Asian Continent, 1933–1941.* New York: Columbia University Press, 1983.

Omata Yukio. *Chin luo* [Invasion and pillages; in Chinese]. Translated by Chiang Lang. Taipei: Central Daily News, 1984.

Ono Kenji, Fujiwara Akira, Honda Katsuichi, et al. *Nankin daigyakusatsu wo kirokushita kogun heishi tachi* [Imperial soldiers who recorded the Nanjing massacre]. Tokyo: Otsuki Shoten, 1994.

Peters, Scott J. *The Promise of Association: A History of the Mission and Work of the YMCA at the University of Illinois, 1873–1997.* Champaign, Ill.: University YMCA, 1997.

Phillips, Clifton J. "The Student Volunteer Movement and Its Role in China Missions." In *The Missionary Enterprise in China and America,* edited by John K. Fairbank. Cambridge, Mass.: Harvard University Press, 1974.

Pritchard, R. John, and Sonia M. Zaide, eds. *The Tokyo War Crimes Trial: The Complete Transcripts of the Proceedings of the International Military Tribunal for the Far East.* 27 vols. London: Garland, 1981–87.

Qin hua ri jun Nan Jing da tu sha dan an [Archival documents relating to the horrible massacre committed by the Japanese troops in Nanjing in December 1937] .Compiled by China's Second Historical Archives et al. Nanjing: Jiangsu Historical Books, 1997.

Qin hua ri jun Nan Jing da tu sha shi gao [Draft manuscript of the horrible massacre committed by the Japanese troops in Nanjing in December 1937]. Compiled by the Historical Source Material Compilation Committee of the Nanjing Massacre. Nanjing: Jiangsu Historical Books, 1997.

Qin hua ri jun Nan Jing da tu sha shi liao [Source materials relating to the horrible massacre committed by the Japanese troops in Nanjing in December 1937].Compiled by the Committee of the Horrible Massacre Committed by the Japanese Troops and the Nanjing Library. Nanjing: Jiangsu Historical Books, 1985.

Qin hua ri jun Nan Jing da tu sha tu ji [Picture Collection of Japanese Aggression Troops' Massacre in Nanjing]. Compiled by China's Second Historical Archives et al. Nanjing: Jiangsu Historical Books, 1997.

Rabe, John. *The Good Man of Nanking: The Diaries of John Rabe.* Translated by John R. Woods, edited by Erwin Wickert. New York: Vintage Books, 1998.

———. *La bei ri ji* [Rabe's diary; in Chinese]. Translated by Liu Hai-ning et al. Nanjing: Jiangsu People's Publishing and Jiangsu Educational Publishing, 1997.

Ryan, William S., and Narka Ryan. "Life's Interconnectedness." *Global Ministries of the Christian Church (Disciples of Christ) and United Church of Christ,* May 2007. http://www.globalministries.org.

Schlesinger, Arthur, Jr. "The Missionary Enterprise and the Theories of Imperialism." In *The Missionary Enterprise in China and America,* edited by John K. Fairbank. Cambridge, Mass.: Harvard University Press, 1974.

Secor Centennial Book, 1857–1957. Secor, Ill: Secor Centennial Committee, 1957.

Smalley, Martha Lund, ed. *American Missionary Eyewitnesses to the Nanking Massacre, 1937–1938.* Occasional Publication No. 9. New Haven, Conn.: Yale Divinity School Library, 1997.

Smythe, Lewis S. C. *War Damage in the Nanking Area, December 1937 to March 1938: Urban and Rural Surveys.* Shanghai: Mercury Press, 1938.

Sun Zhai-wei. *Chen qui li shr: Nan Jing da tu sha yan jyou yu shi kau* [To verify history: Research and deliberation on the Nanjing massacre]. Nanjing: Jiangsu People's Publishing, 2005.

———, ed. *Nanjing da tu sha* [Nanjing massacre]. Beijing: Beijing Publishing, 1997.

Sung Hsi-lian. *Yin zhuan jiang jun* [Generals of hawks and dogs]. Beijing: Chinese Literature and History Publishing, 1986.

Suzuki, Akira. *Shin: "Nankin daigyakusatsu" no maboroshi* [New edition: The illusion of the "Nanking massacre"]. Tokyo: Asuka Shinsha, 1999.

Tan Tao-ping. "*Hui yi 1937 nien Tang Sheng-chi wei hsu Nanjing chi zhan*" [A reminiscence of Tang Sheng-chi's battle of defending Nanjing in 1937]. In *The Jiangsu Collection of Selected Source Materials of Literature and History*, vol. 16, edited by Jiangsu Provincial Council's Research Committee of Literature and History. Nanjing: Jiangsu Historical Books, 1985.

Tanaka Masaaki. "*Nankin gyakusatsu*" *no kyoko* [The illusion of the "Rape of Nanking"]. Tokyo: Nihon Kyobunsha, 1984.

———. *Nankin jiken no sokatsu: Gyakusatsu hitei 15 no ronkyo* [An outline of the Nanking incident: Fifteen grounds for the denial of the rape]. Tokyo: Kenkosha, 1987.

Teaching Committee of the Modern Chinese History. *Chung kuo chin ta shi* [The modern Chinese history]. Taipei: Youshi Books, 1972.

Thurston, Mrs. Lawrence, and Ruth M. Chester. *Ginling College*. New York: United Board for Christian College in China, 1955.

Timperley, H. J. *What War Means: The Japanese Terror in China—A Documentary Record*. London: Victor Gollancz, 1938.

Tong, Nancy, ed. *Nan Jing: Yi jyou san chi nien shryi yueh tsz yi jyou san pa nien wu yueh* [Nanking: November 1937 to May 1938; in Chinese]. Translated by Zhang Kai-yuan. Hong Kong: San Lian Publishing, 1995.

Tsen Shui-fang. "Tsen Shui-fang ri ji" [Diary of Tsen Shui-fang]. *Min kuo dan an* [Archives of the Republic], no. 3 (2004): 26–34; no. 4 (2004): 10–16; no. 1 (2005): 21–25.

U.S. State Department. *Papers relating to Foreign Relations of the United States: The Far East*, pt. 4. Washington, D.C., 1937.

Vautrin, Wilhelmina [Minnie]. Correspondence, 1919–1941. Archives of the United Board for Christian Higher Education in Asia. Record Group No. 11. Special Collections. Yale Divinity School Library.

———. Diary and Misc., 1937–1940. Archives of the United Board for Christian Higher Education in Asia. Record Group No. 11. Special Collections. Yale Divinity School Library.

———. "An Experiment in the Field of Secondary Education." Reprinted from *Chinese Recorder* (February 1939).

———. "A Homecraft Industrial Course." Reprinted from *Chinese Recorder* (February 1939).

———. *Nankin jiken no hibi: Minibotorin no nikki* [Every day of the Nanking incident: Minnie Vautrin's diary; in Japanese]. Translated by Okada Ryonosuke and Ihva Yoko, annotated by Kasahara Tokushi. Tokyo: Ostsuki Shoten, 1999.

———. *Wei te lin ri ji* [Vautrin's diary; in Chinese]. Translated by the Center for Studies on the Nanjing Massacre of Nanjing Normal University. Nanjing: Jiangsu People's Publishing, 2000.

Wilson, Dick. *When Tigers Fight: The Story of the Sino-Japanese War, 1937–1945*. New York: Viking, 1982.

Wu, Blanche. *East Meets West*. Baltimore: R. C. Hwang, 1985.

Wu Hsiang-hsiang. *Di er chung ri chan tsen shi* [History of second Sino-Japanese War]. Taipei: Cosmopolitan Monthly Publishing, 1973.

Wu, Tien-wei. "Commemorating the 56th Anniversary of 'The Great Nanking Massacre': Unmask the Japanese Army's Creating the Massacre." *Journal of Studies of Japanese Aggression against China* 17 (February 1994): 10–11.

————. *Let the Whole World Know the Nanking Massacre*. San Francisco: Society for Studies of Japanese Aggression against China, 1996.

————. *The Sian Incident: A Pivotal Point in Modern China*. Ann Arbor: University of Michigan, Center for Chinese Studies, 1976.

Yamamoto, Masahiro. *Nanking: Anatomy of an Atrocity*. Westport, Conn.: Praeger, 2001.

Yang, Daqing. "Documentary Evidence and the Studies of Japanese War Crimes: An Interim Assessment." In *Researching Japanese War Crimes*, edited by Edward Drea et al. Nazi War Crimes and Japanese Imperial Government Records Interagency Working Group. Washington, D.C.: National Archives and Records Administration, 2006.

Yin, James, and Shi Young. *The Rape of Nanking: An Undeniable History in Photographs*. Chicago: Innovative Publishing, 1996.

Yoshida, Takashi. *The Making of the "Rape of Nanking": History and Memory in Japan, China, and the United States*. New York, Oxford University Press, 2006.

Yoshida, Yutaka. *Tenno no guntai to Nankin jiken* [The Emperor's Imperial Army and the Nanking Incident]. Tokyo: Aoki Shoten, 1986.

Zhang Kai-yuan. "Bei deh shr yanzhang de Nan Jin da tu sha" [The Nanking massacre in the eyes of Miner Searle Bates]. *Journal of Studies of Japanese Aggression against China* 25 (November 1996): 77–84.

————, ed. *Eyewitness to Massacre: American Missionaries Bear Witness to Japanese Atrocities in Nanjing*. New York: M. E. Sharpe, 2001.

————. "Miner Searle Bates: Records of a Historian in Nanking." Translated by Nancy Chapman. *Yale-China Review* 4, no. 2 (Fall 1996): 5–6.

————. *Tian li nan rong: Meiguo chuan jiao shi yanzhang de Nan Jin da tu sha (1937–1938)* [Unforgivable: The Nanjing massacre in the eyes of American missionaries (1937–1938)]. Nanjing: University of Nanjing Press, 1999.

Zhang Lian-hong, ed. *Jin ling nyu zi da xue shi* [History of Ginling College]. Nanjing: Jiangsu People's Publishing, 2005.

Zhang Xian-wen et al., eds. *Jung hua min kwo li shi da tsz dien* [Dictionary of the history of the Republic of China]. Nanjing: Jiangsu Historical Books, 2001.

————, eds. *Nan Jing da tu sha shi liao ji* [Collections of historical source materials on the great Nanjing massacre]. 55 vols. Nanjing: Jiangsu People's Publishing, 2005–7.

INDEX

—•—◄◆►—•—

Allison, John, 141, 150, 151, 213n10, 214n30;
American rights and, 113; at Japanese Embassy dinner, 117
American Church Mission, 130, 131
American consuls, 87, 89, 96; complaint filings
and, 91; return of, 88, 213n10
American diplomats, 213n8
American Embassy, 2, 24, 29, 48, 96, 117, 124;
coal and, 144; gifts from, 104; military
police and, 67
American North Presbyterian Church, 214n29
American proclamations, 131
American rights, 113
Americans, 2, 89, 90, 109, 140; in Nanking,
68; travel permits for, 154–155; as witnesses
to Japanese atrocities, 79
Anhui burial ground. *See* Anhwei burial ground
Anhwei (Anhui) burial ground, 160–161
armbands, Japanese, 137, 188
Atcheson, George, 55, 56, 74, 211n26
Autonomous Government, 102, 119

babies: chicken pox inoculations for, 160; food
for, 132, 136, 143, 148, 157 (*see also* cod liver
oil; milk powder). *See also* children
Bates, Lilliath Robbins, 81
Bates, Miner Searle, 25, 29, 33, 38, 41, 49, 76, 81,
91, 93, 143, 151; biographic information on,
207n10; Christmas article by, 65; Christmas Day and, 60, 66; farewell reception
for Rabe and, 156–157; Japanese Embassy
dinner and, 105
Bauer, Grace, 65, 105, 212n3
Baughton, Helen. *See* Boughton, Helen
bedding, 118, 121, 159

Beh men chiao (Pei Men Chiao), 69
Belimen chiao (North Gate Bridge), 78
Bible classes, 150–151, 152, 156, 160
Bible Teachers' Training School for Women,
26, 74, 78, 133, 208n16, 212n13, 213n18
Big Wang, 24, 45, 49, 54, 65, 147; work of, 207n3
birth(s), 30, 34, 51, 60, 65, 70, 87, 95, 96, 114,
120, 126, 135, 144, 164; midwives and, 99;
procedure for giving, 128
Bishopric, Mr., 132
blimp, 129, 154
Board of Founders: Vautrin's first report to,
111, 121, 123, 173–188, 215n14; Vautrin's second report to, 150, 188–191
bonfires, 60, 85, 91, 95
books, 157
Boughton (Baughton), Helen, 141, 144, 217n2
boycotts, 143, 169
Brady, Richard, 155, 160, 195, 218n22
British Embassy, 26, 95, 214n27, 214n30
Buck, Lossing J., 65, 212n2
Buck, Pearl S., 212n2
buildings: burning of, 54, 93, 130–131; looting of, 93 (*see also* houses, looting of). *See
also* houses, burning of; private property,
destruction of
burning, 25, 103; of buildings, 54, 93, 130–131; of
Chinese military uniforms, 37; by Chinese
soldiers, 25, 30, 73; of dead bodies, 61, 74,
108, 113, 122; of houses, 30, 91, 93, 99, 121–122,
130, 146, 164, 190; of Hsia Lingwei, 73; lessening of, 102; in Nanking, 69; near Belimen
chiao, 78; of papers, 175–176; of school buildings, 130; of shops, 64, 68, 92, 93. *See also* fires
butter, 101

229

camp heads: meetings of, 98–99, 104, 108, 119; registration by, 129, 131, 132. *See also individual camp heads*
carbon monoxide poisoning, 118–119
cars, 28, 190; with flags, 57; theft of, 36, 50, 51, 160. *See also* trucks
cash relief fund, 194
census taking, 99
certificate of passes, 86
Chan, Mr., 186
Change Szi-fu. *See* Djang Szi-fu
Chang Ging Lou, 147, 217n9
Changhsin, 116, 215n20
Chang Kai-shek (Chiang Kai-shek), 32
Chang Nan-Wu, 126, 216n6
Changsha. *See* Chengsha
Chang Szi-fu (janitor), 54, 66, 163, 211n25
Chang Yung-kwang (Jan Yung-gwan; Jan Yung-kuon), 46, 74, 75, 76, 78, 104, 211n18
charcoal, 61, 64, 73
Chemistry Institute, 153
Chen, Francis (Chen Fei-rung), 7, 24, 30, 33, 38, 44–45, 47, 55, 66, 69, 78, 86–87, 101, 158, 173, 208n20; birth of son and, 145; Christmas Day and, 65; looting from, 48, 61; registration and, 129; slapping of, 46; work of, 185, 207n4
Chen, Mary, 130
Chen, Mr., 32, 61, 67, 81, 88, 142; gun and, discarding of, 37, 40
Chen, Y. H., 70, 212n8
Chen Ben-li, 94
Chen Chung-fan, 70, 212n9
Chen Chun-liang, 30
Chen Djung-fan (Chung-fan), 71, 85
Chen Fei-rung. *See* Chen, Francis
Chengsha (Changsha), 104, 119, 215n6
Chengtu, 103
Chen Kwang-lin, 216n6
Chen Ming-chi, 68
Chen Szi-fu, 36
Chen Yueh-mei, 104, 215n7
Chester, Ruth (Tsai), 84, 87, 88, 89, 90, 95, 96, 213n7, 213n9
Chi, Charles. *See* Gee, Charles
Chi, Mr., 51
Chiang Kai-shek, Madame, 210n11
Chiang Kai-shek. *See* Chang Kai-shek
Chiang Kai-shek (Chiang Kai-shek), 77, 209n32, 209n35

Chi Chao-chang. *See* Chi Chao-kao
Chi Chao-kao (Chi Chao-chang), 27, 208n21
chicken pox inoculations, 155, 160, 161, 162, 163, 195
chickens, 33, 34, 42, 178; from American Embassy, 104; from Japanese Embassy, 109; price of, 81; saving of, 53; scarcity of, 61; taking of, 109; from Wu, Blanche, 53, 109, 144–145
Chi Hsia Hill. *See* Chi Hsia Shan
Chi Hsia Shan (Chi Hsia Hill), 154
Chi Hsieh-yuan, 59, 78, 212n32
Chi Hsueh-yuen (Hsieh-yuan), 88
children: cod liver oil for, 11–12, 119, 132, 136, 144, 148, 152, 159, 160, 165, 189, 194, 195; death of, 164; health issues of, 65, 96, 99, 118; milk powder for, 11–12, 132, 136, 143, 148, 152, 157, 159, 160, 165, 189, 194. *See also* babies
children's meetings, 108, 110, 111, 113, 184–185
Chin, Mrs., 155
Chinese characters, 86–87, 211n14
Chinese collaborators, 68
Chinese language, 42, 211n14
Chinese military uniforms: burning of, 37; discarding of, 42, 57; removal of, by Chinese soldiers, 32–33
Chinese New Year, 81, 124–125; church service, 127; firecrackers, 127, 128, 192
Chinese New Year's Eve dinner, 126
Chinese police, 101, 106. *See also* police
Chinese Self-ruling Committee, 78
Chinese soldiers: burning by, 25, 30, 73; civilian clothes for, 32; identification of, 64; killing of, 38, 40, 82, 83, 112, 148–149; looting by, 131, 165; military uniforms and, removal of, 32–33; search for, 40, 41–42, 44, 68, 70, 72, 73–74, 180
Christian Mission Compounds, 130, 131
Christian workers meeting, 160
Christmas Day, 60, 65–66, 168; decorations, 63; dinner, 66; services, 185
Christmas Eve, 63–64, 168
Chu, Grace Zia, 119, 216n29
Chung-fan. *See* Chen Djung-fan
Chung Haia (Hwa) School, 123
Chung Hwa, 51, 211n24
Chung Hwa Street, 130–131
Chungking, 23, 119, 216n28
Chung Shan Road, 93

Hua-ling Hu taught at several Chinese and American universities, including the University of Colorado–Boulder, where she received a doctorate in history. In addition to having written over eighty published papers and short stories, Hu is the author of five books, among them *American Goddess at the Rape of Nanking: The Courage of Minnie Vautrin*. She was awarded the Chinese Literature and Arts Medal of Honor for the Chinese-language edition of her biography of Vautrin.

Zhang Lian-hong received his doctorate in history from Nanjing University. He is a professor of history and chairman of the Center for Studies on the Nanjing Massacre of Nanjing Normal University, as well as associate chairman of the Modern Chinese Historical Society of Kiangsu Province and Nanjing Historical Society. He has coauthored and coedited many works in Chinese, including *Heartstring Memory: The Nanjing Massacre and the Chinese Society*, *A History of Ginling College*, and *Collections of Historical Source Materials on the Nanjing Massacre: Oral History by the Survivors*.

Hu and Zhang were featured in a documentary, *Minnie Vautrin*, produced by Shantung Television and Motion Pictures and broadcast on Central China Television (CCTV) and Phoenix Television of Hong Kong in October 2002.